DIPLOMATIC SAVAGERY

*DARK SECRETS BEHIND THE
JAMAL KHASHOGGI
MURDER*

FERHAT ÜNLÜ
ABDURRAHMAN ŞIMŞEK
NAZİF KARAMAN

THE ISHMAEL TREE
NEW YORK

www.ishmaeltreebooks.com
rightsandpermissions@ishmaeltreebooks.com

Originally published in the Turkish language under the title *Diplomatik Vahşet: Cemal Kaşıkçı Cinayetinin Karanlık Sırları* by Turkuvaz Publishing.

ISBN: 978-1-945959-36-3

Ferhat Ünlü was born in Adana, Turkey on 5 October 1975. He graduated from Istanbul University's School of Communication in 1997. Ünlü is the author of the novels *The Frozen Tear* (2002), *The Revenge of the Shadow* (2003), The Organization for the *Elimination of the Impertinent* (2006), *The Bad Novel* (2011) and *The Sacred Crypto* (2017), and three investigative works – The Susurluk Customs (2000), Eymür's Mirror (2001) and Sadettin Tantan (2001). He started his journalism career at Yeni Şafak and worked for the Weekly magazine under the Vatan newspaper in 2005-2007 before moving to Sabah newspaper in January 2007. In 2009, he took became the editor of the newly-established Special Intelligence Unit. Ünlü hosted the television shows Intelligence and News Analysis on TVNet in 2012-2016 and The Red Bulletin on TRT Haber in 2018. He currently produces and hosts The Cosmic Table on TGRT Haber, works for the Sabah newspaper, and appears on A Haber and Habertürk as a commentator.

Abdurrahman Şimşek started his journalism career in 1993 at ATV Haber, where he contributed to popular shows including The Courthouse Aisles, The Emergency Service and Police Emergency. He worked with ATV's News Department as a reported for two years. Şimşek joined the Sabah newspaper as a Special News Correspondent in 2002 and became the Director of the Special Intelligence Unit when it was established in 2009. He was awarded the Çetin Emeç Special Prize by the Turkish Journalists Association in 2009 for a story that identified airport security loopholes at Istanbul's Sabiha Gökçen International Airport.

Nazif Karaman was born in Istanbul, Turkey in 1977. He graduated from Marmara University's School of Economic and Administrative Sciences in 2001. Karaman started his journalism career at the *Akit* newspaper in 1997 and moved to Sabah's Special Intelligence Unit in 2010. On the night of the July 15, 2016 coup attempt in Turkey, he broke the news that the authorities had launched a formal investigation into the coup plotters. Karaman became Chief of the Special Intelligence Unit in 2016. An award-winning journalist, Karaman continues to work with the Sabah newspaper and appears on A Haber as a staff commentator.

In Memoriam *Jamal Khashoggi*

PREFACE TO THE TURKISH EDITION

If one were asked to identify one of the most curious –or, per-haps, the most curious– murder of all time, it wouldn't be inaccu-rate to pick the murder of Jamal Khashoggi. Since the Saudi journal-ist died inside his country's consulate general in Istanbul on October 2, 2018, the Turkish people and global audiences witnessed a series of developments which supported that seemingly unrealistic claim. The Special Intelligence Unit at the daily newspaper *Sabah* broke many news regarding the Khashoggi murder by obtaining informa-tion, documents, photographs and footage.

This book isn't just an extensive collection of the Unit's findings to date. It aims to make public documents and information, which reveal the dark secrets behind the Khashoggi murder, and augment them with previously unseen evidence that shed light on what ex-actly happened. In this regard, this book promises to bring the inci-dent back to the public's attention.

The Khashoggi murder became the top item[1] on the Turkish and global media's agenda for several reasons. It is necessary to grasp those reasons to develop a complete understanding of that incident's background. Let us try to find the answers by subjecting the Khashoggi murder to the six fundamental questions of journal-ism – the 5W1H.

Even when one asks the questions what, where, when, why, who and how regarding the Khashoggi murder, some of the extraor-dinary aspects of the case begin to reveal themselves.

---

1   According to the media monitor MTM, the media covered the murder of Jamal Khashoggi more extensively than any other topic in October 2018. During the same period, the Khashoggi murder was among the most closely followed stories globally.

iii

The story relates to the killing of a journalist, a member of a prominent Saudi family, who was not a hardcore dissident but a strong critic of the government of Saudi Arabia.

The event took place inside a consular building, which was unprecedented in diplomatic history. No other person had ever lost their lives in this particular way. To be clear, certain individuals were killed by assailants who opened fire from consular buildings. Yet none of those cases are the same as, or even remotely similar to, the Khashoggi affair. Here's the most memorable of those incidents:

On April 5, 1991, a group of Turkmens marched to the Iraqi consulate general in Istanbul's Beyoglu district to protest the killing of 102 of their kinsmen near Altun Kopru, a small town to the north of Kirkuk, along the Kirkuk-Erbil highway. When some protestors threw stones at the building, a consular officer responded by opening fire on the crowd with an automatic rifle, killing Nejdet Bakkaloglu and Yilmaz Haci Sait, and injuring many others.

The Turkish police detained the consular officer, Ayad Faik Taha, and dragged him out of the consulate after seizing the murder weapon – an AK-47. On 10 March 1992, a Turkish court sentenced Faik Taha to death. His sentence was reduced to 30 years in prison on grounds of 'incitement'. After spending eight months in a Turkish prison, he was extradited to Iraq under a special agreement. [2]

As mentioned above, however, the Khashoggi affair was completely different. Khashoggi was the victim of a gruesome, premeditated murder. His body was dismembered. The post mortem torture, to which the killers subjected him, make the answer to the question how even more dramatic.

Likewise, it is significant that Khashoggi was killed shortly after entering the Saudi consulate at 1.14 p.m. on October 2 and his body was moved out of the consular building by a vehicle with diplomatic plates at 3.08 p.m., because those facts demonstrate that the death squad was racing against the clock.

This book consists of six chapters based on the golden rule of

---

2   İtiraf gelirse Kaşıkçı'nın faillerini kim yargılayacak [Who will hold Khashoggi's killers accountable in case of a confession], Yeni Şafak Online, 16 October 2018.

journalism – the 5W1H principle.

The first chapter, which focuses on the what, tells the story of Khashoggi's murder with references to some previously unavailable details. The second chapter, which relates to the where, reflects on the unprecedented nature of the crime –that it was committed at a diplomatic mission— to analyze its diplomatic causes and outcomes. This chapter contains information about the audio recordings, for which the whole world has been looking.

In Chapter III, we provide a chronology of events and answer the question when to understand and explain whether Jamal Khashoggi's murder, which took place at a time when the strategic balance of power was shifting, various countries engaged in asymmetrical conflicts and formed asymmetrical alliances, carried any particular significance.

Chapters V and VI, in turn, concentrate on the why and the who.

To be clear, even the most comprehensive answer to the question why –which is the most important part of 5W1H and therefore the question that many journalists are still trying to answer— fails to account for the targeting, murder and disappearance of a journalist in such a barbaric manner. Of course, we did our best to explain why the killers decided to kill Khashoggi in Turkey based on the information and findings at our disposal. We built on the exclusive information and contents that we acquired from trusted government sources and open source material to answer that question to the best of our ability.

In addition to Turkish media outlets, the open sources that we indexed included leading U.S. newspapers and TV stations, including *The Washington Post*, where Khashoggi served as a columnist, *The New York Times*, CNN and ABC, British news organizations such as *The Guardian*, *The Times* and BBC, the world-renowned Qatari television channel *Al Jazeera* and other international media outlets.

During our research for this book, we indexed 899 stories and opinion pieces from the Washington Post, 567 stories and opinion essays from the New York Times, 212 news stories and essays from *The Guardian*, 237 stories and opeds from *The Wall Street Journal*, 213 stories and articles from USA Today, 101 news stories and opinion pieces from *The New York Daily News*, 78 stories and essays from the Independent and 90 stories from BBC. We have included the 1000+ sources that we analyzed in footnotes.

The final part of the 5W1H principle, the who, was what made the Jamal Khashoggi murder 'popular' and interesting. The victim's personal background, including his career as an experienced and prominent journalist, and his family's origins –the Khashoggis are a prominent Saudi family with roots in Kayseri, Turkey— made the story more interesting for the media.[3]

At the same time, the Khashoggi murder isn't just a crime story but an incident with complex diplomatic and intelligence connections – which fuels media attention even more. The fact that the whereabouts of the victim's body remains unknown – which means that the criminal aspects of what happened are yet to be fully discovered— accounts for its continued significance to law enforcement.

That the murder took place inside a consulate and the incident has the potential to impact relations between the United States, Turkey and Saudi Arabia hints at the diplomatic repercussions of Khashoggi's death – which is becoming more and more complex. Since the incident occurred at a diplomatic mission, it has diplomatic consequences at the global level – which we have witnessed over the past two months.

Hence our decision to pick an oxymoron, *Diplomatic Savagery,* as the name of this book. It should go without saying that the words *diplomacy* and *savagery/violence* cannot go hand-in- hand due to their very nature. As Henry Kissinger wrote in his namesake book, *diplomacy is an art born our of the experiences and efforts reflecting the balance of power between the forces of war and peace in the twentieth century.* In that volume, Kissinger talks about diplomacy with references to specific incidents that

3   Murat Bardakçı, 'Kaşıkçı, daha doğrusu Hâşukcî ailesi' [The Khashoggi, or Hashukchi, family], Habertürk, 15 October 2018.

took place after World War I and World War II. *Diplomacy* is the art of fighting without waging war. In other words, it is the art of getting results without exercising violence.

In this sense, violence and savagery are inherently opposed to diplomacy. Yet the Saudis wrote a story, whose likes have never been encountered in history, that gave us ample reasons to use the words diplomacy and savagery together. That is why we landed on this name for our book.

Finally, the fact that the 15+3-strong death squad consisted of public officials with specialized skills and the murder was committed as a covert operation hints at the intelligence-related aspects of what happened. The Khashoggi affair was such an extraordinary intelligence story, in which Turkey's National Intelligence Organization, the Saudi domestic and external intelligence services, the Central Intelligence Agency, the British Secret Intelligence Service, the Canadian Security Intelligence Service, the Russian Foreign Intelligence Service, the German Federal Intelligence Service, the French Directorate-General for External Security and even Mossad became involved one way or another. Those intelligence agencies occasionally competed against each other to uncover the secrets of the Khashoggi murder and, at different times, joined forces under Turkish leadership.

Turkey managed the diplomatic process regarding the Khashoggi murder in a calm, collected and careful manner – like a poker player with a strong hand. During this period, Turkey exercised cautious discretion to offer previews of the information at its disposal to persuade all sides that it was not bluffing. It was no coincidence that U.S. Secretary of State Mike Pompeo and CIA Director Gina Haspel visited Turkey in the aftermath of the murder. For the record, nor did Saud al-Mujib, the Saudi attorney general, come to Turkey by mistake.

Turkey shared its intelligence and police reports on the dark secrets behind the Khashoggi murder with various countries including Saudi Arabia, the United States, the United Kingdom, France, Canada and Germany – again, in a measured way.

In addition to the intelligence connections, the fact that Khashoggi went to the Saudi consulate general in order to obtain official proof of his singledom means that the murder story has everything, including romance, necessary to mystery fiction.

For those reasons, it wasn't surprising that the Khashoggi murder became a trending topic, to borrow from Twitter, among conventional media outlets in Turkey and around the world. Likewise, the incident was closely followed on social media for an extended period of time. It remains one of the major topics of online conversation to this day.

Sabah was the most cited Turkish news organization by the U.S. and European media in Khashoggi-related stories. Various outlets, including *The New York Times*, *The Guardian*, BBC and CNN, cited exclusive stories from Sabah and shared their details with their audiences.

The news of the 15-member Saudi death squad, which *Sabah* broke, was featured prominently in the stories of those news organizations. CNN reported that, "*Sabah* published footage of a mysterious 15-member intelligence team, which was involved in the disappearance of Jamal Khashoggi, entering Turkey at Atatürk Airport." The New York Times announced that *Sabah* had revealed the names of individuals believed to have played some role in the incident.

Those developments compelled us, the special intelligence department at Sabah, to dig deeper into what happened, publish additional stories to shed light on what happened, and, in the end, write this book. We used our time, which was limited due to the vast interest shown in the Khashoggi story, most effectively to finish this book. It provides answers to the following ten questions:

1-   Who ordered the hit on Jamal Khashoggi? Why was he killed?

2-   How was the murder planned? What happened in the Saudi consulate within the 7.5 minutes, in which Khashoggi lost his life?

3-   Who carried out the operation on the ground?

4-   How was Khashoggi's body dismembered and disappeared?

5-   What type of tools were used to commit the murder and dismember the body? What were the 'crypto weapons' used in the assassination?

6-   What was in the audio recordings that proved that the Saudi death squad committed the murder? What was discussed among the directors of secret services at the National Intelligence Organization headquarters?

7-   How did the Saudi intelligence operatives destroy evidence of murder?

8-   What are the professional skills of the Saudi death squad's 15 members?

9-   Who are the three unknown individuals, who played some role in the murder, and what are their specialties?

10- Where could Khashoggi's remains be?

As we search for the answers to those questions and analyzed and narrated this most curious story in journalism history, which is located at the intersection of diplomacy, intelligence and criminology, we were careful to remain within the limits of objective journalism. Obviously, we did analyze the political repercussions of what happened on occasion. Yet our main goal was to present concrete evidence, which is independent of the political debate.

With the exception of open sources, which have been cited where necessary, all information that this book contains was exclusively obtained in meetings with trusted government sources. Those details had not been made public until now. In other words, they are contained in this book alone.

We hope that the book you hold in your hands will help you understand the most complex murder story of all time in its totality.

We are indebted to senior government officials, who have supported our team with new information, during our preparations for this book. The unsung heroes that cracked the Khashoggi case, whose names will remain in our custody forever, have not only foiled a conspiracy against our country but also made it possible for the world to witness this 'diplomatic savagery'.

We would like to thank Damla Kaya, Serkan Bayraktar and Sema Dalgıç from the Sabah Special Intelligence Department, who worked on online indices at the preparatory stages, and our young colleagues Mustafa Batuhan Gür and Beyza Kartal, two successful students of Koç University who contributed to the indexing of foreign sources.

20 November-10 December 2018
Istanbul

CHAPTER I

What?

*"Good-bye," says the dying man to
the mirror they hold in front of him.*

*"We won't be seeing each other any
more."* – Paul Valery

1

JAMAL KHASHOGGI
THE FINAL 24 HOURS

The Victim's Eternal Journey

The vibrant voice of Imam Ali Tos, who was leading a funeral prayer in absentia perhaps for the first time in his life, echoed around the DCA[1] mosque in the U.S. state of Maryland:

"Do you give your blessings to the deceased?"
"We do."
"Do you give your blessings?"
"We do."
"Do you give your blessings?"
"We do."

The congregation's answer to the question, which the imam asked three times in line with ritual, was going to be heard not just in Maryland but also Istanbul, Mecca, London, Paris, Islamabad and many other places.

The funeral prayer, as part of which Muslims do not bow nor prostrate and wrap up with the qiyam and the takbeer, was a ritual intended to bid farewell to those who transitioned to the hereafter – a act of worship before one's final journey.

[1]   The Diyanet Center of America

The man, for whom the congregation held an absentee funeral service, was Jamal Khashoggi, the Washington Post columnist who was killed inside the Consulate General of Saudi Arabia on October 2, 2018 in complete violation of the Islamic faith, the principles of Abrahamic religions and all human values.

Thousands of people, who performed the absentee funeral prayer, would have greeted the angels upon hearing the fourth takbeer and carried the coffin, which would have contained even the smallest part of the remains had any piece been located, on their shoulders to the burial site. In this particular case, however, there was no coffin on the altar. As such, there was no burial site either.

On Friday, November 16, another absentee funeral prayer was performed at the Fatih Mosque in Istanbul – Khashoggi's place of death. The participants included the deceased/victim's close friend Yasin Aktay, an advisor to the chairman of the Justice and Development Party, parliamentarian Ahmet Hamdi Çamlı, Sultanbeyli Mayor Cahit Altunay and the president of the Turkish-Arab Media Association, Turan Kışlakçı, along with Jamal Khashoggi's friends and others, who did not know him and probably had never heard his name before his murder. Those that did not know him gave Khashoggi their blessings – again, in line with ritual.

Jamal Ahmed Hamza Khashoggi, who died eleven days before his 60th birthday, was a Libra man born on October 13, 1958.[2] Obviously, he was unaware that he was going to die in the same month that he was born. Yet he wished to be buried in his birthplace of Mecca. Given the nature of his gruesome slaying, it remains highly unlikely that his wish will ever come true. Still, everyone, starting with his friends and loved ones who attended his absentee funeral service, agrees that Khashoggi's wish as a human and a Muslim must be granted at the very least.

---

2   According to his passport, Jamal Khashoggi's official date of birth was 22 January 1958. His fiancée, however, told the authors of this book that Khashoggi was actually born on 13 October 1958.

AT ATATÜRK AIRPORT ON HIS DAY OF DEATH

Before departing on his eternal journey, Saudi journalist Jamal Khashoggi made his final trip in this life from London to Istanbul.

It was a beautiful early October morning in Istanbul. Upon getting off a commercial airliner that departed from London and reached Atatürk Airport at 3.50 a.m., Khashoggi headed to the passport control counter reserved for foreign nationals.

He was engaged to Hatice Cengiz, a Turkish citizen born on 18 July 1982 and registered in Davutkadı near the Yıldırım county in Bursa. Provided that they weren't formally married yet, Khashoggi did not carry a Turkish passport.

Khashoggi cleared passport control at 4.06 a.m. sharp.[3] Two minutes later, he walked towards customs control with a single piece of luggage. By 4.09 a.m., he left the arrival hall. Another two minutes later, he took a yellow cab to his apartment in Topkapı.

Khashoggi had purchased that apartment on September 25, just a week prior to his killing. Located inside the Kale, a gated community inside the Avrupa Konutları, or Europe Residences, that apartment was the home that he hoped to share with Hatice Cengiz after their marriage. Yet that plan was never going to come to fruition. The apartment that they expected to enter as a married couple after picking up an official proof of Khashoggi's marital status from the Saudi consulate in Istanbul would become the workplace of an police discovery team after the murder.[4]

Khashoggi was home by 4.40 a.m. At 4.56, he was joined by his fiancée, Hatice Cengiz, who arrived with a shopping bag.[5] At the apartment, they talked for a while. They went over the marriage procedures and, naturally, talked about their dreams.

---

3   The authors provided a detailed account of Khashoggi's movements at the airport based on CCTV footage that they obtained.

4   The police entered the apartment with the help of a locksmith and looked for evidence for three hours. They found Khashoggi's DNA. Khashoggi had left his traces on some items at the apartment, where he arrived hours before his murder.

5   According to CCTV footage from the gated community, Hatice Cengiz entered the apartment at 4.56 a.m.

THE MYSTERY TEAM AT GENERAL AVIATION

Around the same time, just 23 minutes after Jamal Khashoggi left Atatürk Airport, there was movement at the same airport's General Aviation Terminal. A nine-member team entered the arrival hall after getting off a private jet with the tail number HZ-SK2, which had left Riyadh some 3.5 hours earlier. The aircraft was registered to Sky Prime Aviation, a company owned by the Saudi government.

At 4.29 a.m., the group of men led by Maher Abdulaziz Mutreb, a major general in the Saudi intelligence, entered the arrival hall. Members of that team would be seen in various parts of Istanbul between their arrival on October 2 and their departure the same day: Atatürk Airport, the lobbies of their hotels in the Levent district and around the Saudi consulate and the residence of the consul general.

At the time, the Saudi operatives were unaware that the Turkish intelligence and police would subject them in some kind of retroactive electronic surveillance.[6] That surveillance, however, did not take place in real time – it wasn't, as law enforcement jargon goes, suitable for catching the criminals in the act. Why they travelled to Istanbul and what they did there wasn't clear until after the incident. The National Intelligence Organization and the Turkish police rolled back the tape when everything was said and done, and cracked the codes of what happened – with the exception of the body's whereabouts.

The most prominent members of the death squad that was dispatched to Turkey on that fateful morning were Maher Abdulaziz Mutreb and Salah Muhammed al-Tubaigy. Tubaigy, 47, was the head of Saudi Arabia's Forensic Medicine Institution. His job was to get rid of the body and remove all evidence from the Saudi consulate.

Mutreb, also 47, was known for accompanying Saudi Crown Prince Mohammed bin Salman, also known as MBS, on his international trips. A general who had previously served at the Saudi Embassy in the United Kingdom, he was the most important mem-

6   The authors agreed to describe the process as 'electronic surveillance'.

ber of the team.

When Mutreb arrived at Istanbul along with his team, he had booked a room at a hotel just several hundred meters away from the Saudi consulate in the Levent district until 5 October. Yet he left that hotel on the same day.

CCTV footage has established that all members of the team were in various parts of Istanbul on October 2. We suspect that the Saudi intelligence team knew when Jamal Khashoggi was going to travel from London to Istanbul before they left Riyadh aboard a private jet – although there is no footage or other evidence supporting this claim.

The Saudis were aware that Khashoggi was among the speakers at an event in London –Oslo at 25: A Legacy of Broken Promises— alongside former cabinet ministers, ambassadors and parliamentarians. They also knew that he had criticized Saudi Arabia's approach to the Palestinian Question.

The Saudi intelligence had planned in advance what would happen when and everything else to the finest detail. Yet there was one very crucial detail that they had forgotten to consider: The Turkish intelligence and police was going to track their footsteps back in time and find out why exactly the Saudis had come to Istanbul – and what exactly they had done.

A SAUDI CRIME THRILLER

The Saudi team made their carefully-thought-out plan, which turned into a scandal thanks to Turkey's vigilance, on September 28. The chain of events that led to Jamal Khashoggi's murder on 2 October started with an unscheduled visit by the Saudi journalist to Saudi Arabia's consulate in Istanbul after leaving the Marriage Office in Fatih, holding his fiancée's hand, on 28 September. On his first visit to the consulate, Khashoggi had asked for an official document stating that he could proceed with his marriage in Turkey.

The Saudi consulate told him to come back on October 2. Khashoggi spent the next four days in London. The men, who had arrived at Atatürk Airport's General Aviation Terminal earlier the same day, were members of a death squad that would murder Khashoggi in cold blood.

As the Saudi death squad set foot in Turkey, Khashoggi was still at Atatürk Airport. In other words, he was in the same place at the same time as his executioners – the members of the team that proceeded to kill him inside the consulate of Saudi Arabia just nine hours later.

The team had planned in advance how exactly they were going to execute Khashoggi and how they would get rid of their victim's body. They were determined to stick to that plan. A number of CCTV cameras at the airport recorded their emotionless, robot-like stares like everything else. Their gazes were devoid of expression, as if they were robots getting ready to carry out their orders. It was like they were guided by remote control. They were like soldiers from hell, hitmen turned into mutants by some deadly virus unknown to the world until then. Had they not been in that state, they would not have been able to perpetrate one of the most gruesome murders in history.

Journalists like to use a certain phrase to explain how to determine the 'value' of a news story: "It's news if a man bites a dog – not the other way around."

That phrase encapsulates why the murder of Jamal Khashoggi, which everyone has been talking about for over two months, received such attention from the public. The Khashoggi murder amounts to the figurative man biting the figurative dog in terms of diplomacy, intelligence and law enforcement. After all, no such incident had ever been recorded in the history of diplomacy, intelligence or law enforcement until that day.

Have you ever heard of any other instance where members of a 15-strong death squad travelled to another country aboard private jets registered to a government-controlled aviation company over two days –with their real-life ID papers, no less—, went to their country's consulate there and returned home after murdering and dismembering someone within two hours? Have you even heard of a consulate being turned into a crime scene?

The Khashoggi murder is a kind of event untold since the day Edgar Allan Poe invented mystery literature – neither in the works of John Le Carré, Frederick Forsyth and other grandmasters of spy thrillers nor in Henry Kissinger's Diplomacy, which tells the story of diplomacy in the twentieth century.

The Khashoggi murder represents a kind of idiosyncratic brutality unmatched by detective novels. The only known link between detective fiction and real-life crime is believed to be *Murder on the Orient Express*, which the British author Agatha Christie, a mystery literature legend, wrote at the Pera Palace Hotel in Istanbul in 1933. Many believe that the real-life murderer, who inspired the book, was never caught.[7]

Had Khashoggi not become the victim of a crime too gruesome even for novels and instead taken alive to some other place, the Saudis would have bowed to the vast international pressure and compelled to bring him back secretly – even if they had taken him to Riyadh.

As a matter of fact, they could have brought him back publicly as well. After all, the news that Sabah broke and a number of international media outlets, including *The New York Times* and *The Washington Post*, cited, demonstrates that all members of the Saudi death squad have been publicly identified.

No other murder in history was so remarkable in criminal terms, so dismissive of the rules of the game of intelligence and so devoid of diplomatic ethics. In that sense, the Khashoggi affair was indeed a poor Saudi crime thriller.

---

7   *125 Unknown Facts About Agatha Christie*, CNN Türk Online, 21 October 2015.

2

LOVE AT FIRST SIGHT

Holding Hands At The Marriage Office

Jamal Khashoggi went to the Saudi consulate in Istanbul, located at 6 Camlik Street in the 4 Levent district, on September 28 – four days prior to his death on October 2. Earlier that day, he had gone to the Marriage Office in the Fatih district holding his fiancée's hand, only to be told that he needed a document indicating that he was indeed single. In other words, Khashoggi had to visit his eventual place of death to obtain 'proof of singledom'.

Fully aware of what he needed, the Saudis told him to come back at 1 p.m. on October 2. Over the following four days, they planned the Khashoggi murder. Where the 18 members of the team, who were involved in the murder directly or indirectly, were during those days and how they trained for their mission will be discussed below. Let us first go over where Khashoggi was and what he was doing.

The four days between Khashoggi's first visit to the Saudi consulate and his murder are crucial.[1] Yet we must go back to the beginning of the love at first sight, which resulted in Khashoggi

---

[1]   The main point of reference for the authors' reconstruction of the four-day period between September 28 and October 2 was the information that Khashoggi's fiancée, Hatice Cengiz, shared with the authors and various news organizations. Moreover, the information that Khashoggi's friend and the president of the Turkish-Arab Media Association, Turan Kışlakçı, was crucial to our understanding of that time period. After all, Kışlakçı was one of Khashoggi's closest friends.

going to the consulate to obtain marriage documents – the day he met Hatice Cengiz, his fiancée and a graduate of the Imam Hatip High School in Bursa.

Hatice Cengiz describes herself as a scholar of Gulf states who wanted to familiarize herself with that part of the world. She attended a conference on 4-6 May 2018, which Khashoggi attended as a speaker, for that purpose. On October 26, Cengiz recalled how she met Khashoggi in an interview with the Turkish television channel *Habertürk*:

> *I followed Mr. Jamal very closely. Although the Gulf region doesn't attract a lot of attention, I believed that it was crucial to get to know that part of the world. My work takes me to many conferences – especially related to the Gulf region. That's how I met Mr. Jamal. I wanted to meet him. There were many questions in my mind about Saudi Arabia. Our conversation evolved into what it was supposed to become. Mr. Jamal was well known in Europe and elsewhere, but not in [Turkey].*

> *After our initial meeting, I told him that I wanted to publish my interview with him and hoped to expand on it. He proposed to meet next time he would be in Istanbul. He subsequently came to Turkey and we met. It was a quick meeting, as our schedules were quite busy that day. That's when our relationship began. Most of the questions, perhaps 70 percent of them, were private. The follow-up showed that it was indeed a private meeting. Upon returning to the United States, he told me that he wanted to see me. Hence our relationship began.[2]*

THE JOURNALIST WHO ASKED FOR THE FAMILY'S BLESSING

Turan Kışlakçı, one of Khashoggi's closest friends and the president of the Turkish-Arab Journalists Association, was the

---

2   Transcript of a 26 October 2018 interview with Hatice Cengiz on Habertürk

---

person who asked Hatice Cengiz's father to give his blessing to his daughter's marriage with Jamal Khashoggi. When Khashoggi crossed his legs during the meeting with Hatice's family, it was Kışlakçı who warned him in Arabic and made Khashoggi uncross his legs.

Originally from the Eastern Turkish province of Erzurum, the Cengiz family resided in Fatih, Istanbul. Hatice's father managed a café in the Fatih district. In an interview with the authors of this book, Kışlakçı described Khashoggi's introduction to Hatice Cengiz as follows:

> After their meeting at the conference in May, Hatice Cengiz attended a musical event that Khashoggi attended on Fridays. That's how they got close in the first place. The event involved performances of religious music. I believe that it was on August 3.
>
> Khashoggi called me in late August or early September. "Turan, I want to tell you something," he said. "I am going to marry a Turkish girl." I told him that I was surprised and asked who it was. "You know her already. Remember Hatice, whom I brought to the musical event that one night? It's her."
>
> I asked him how it happened. "I will tell you all about it when I'm there," he said. "But I have a favor to ask: Could you ask for her father's blessing on my behalf?" I told him that I would happily visit Hatice's father if she was on board. He rejoiced: "Come on, Turan!" I proceeded to tell Hatice Cengiz that I wanted to speak with her father. She gave me her father's phone number, but warned me that her father was, "an Anatolian man, so speak with him accordingly."
>
> Her father asked me what I thought. I said told him not to worry about the age difference: "I am against such things. If a woman and a man love each other, the parents have no right to intervene. The only thing you'd have to consider is what you can do to protect her. Your girl is a reasonable person and that man is quite mature."

He told me that he did not demand anything for him-self, but wanted the best for his daughter. I do not wish to go into the details. Those things happened in mid-September – roughly one week before he visited the consulate for the first time on September 28.

Finally, I told Hatice's father that I wanted to take a step back and recommended that he let his daughter and Jamal take care of the rest. "Let us not meddle in their af-fairs," I said. Jamal proceeded to buy the apartment at the Europe Residences in Topkapi.

Kışlakçı proceeded to tell us that he spoke with Jamal Khashoggi by phone once between September 28 and October 2:

He was in London to attend a conference. I was quite busy and we could not speak in detail. We spoke by phone once during his stay in London. I called him and asked where he was. He told me that was with some Turkish friends at the Sharq Forum and invited me there. I told him I couldn't go. I did not know that he had travelled to London twice

FROM THE MARRIAGE OFFICE TO THE CONSULATE

On September 28, Khashoggi had arrived at Istanbul from London early in the morning – just as he did on the day of his murder. A CCTV camera captured his image at the passport con-trol counter at 4.07 a.m. Khashoggi was wearing a yellow sweater.

The fact that he cleared passport control around the same time as he did on October 2 indicates that he took the same commercial flight from London twice. On September 28, Khashoggi took a yellow cab from Atatürk Airport to his apartment in Topkapi.

He met his fiancée, Hatice Cengiz, in the morning. They went to the City Hall in the Fatih district for marriage formalities. Ac-cording to video footage obtained by the authors, Khashoggi and

Cengiz entered the building, holding hands, at 9.20 a.m.

The couple sat down across an official at the Marriage Office. They obtained information for the next five minutes and received a list of official documents necessary to finalize their application. Hatice Cengiz picked up the list and got up from her chair. Khashoggi and his fiancée went over the piece of paper that they had received from the official. Cengiz proceeded to take another piece of paper from her wallet and show it to the municipal official. They proceeded to talk among themselves. At 9.28 a.m., the couple left the Marriage Office and talked briefly outside building. They decided to go directly to the Saudi consulate, where Khashoggi was supposed to obtain proof of marital status. The couple hailed a taxi at 9.32 a.m. from Fatih and drove to Saudi Arabia's consulate in the 4 Levent district.

Traffic was light and they arrived at their destination in 30 minutes. Jamal Khashoggi handed over his cell phones to Hatice Cengiz, as he did on the day of his murder, and proceeded to enter the building. According to his fiancée, the Saudi journalist was somewhat concerned at the time. Yet he left the consulate with a smile on his face some 90 minutes later. Upon coming back, he told Hatice Cengiz that the consular staff had been surprisingly friendly and added: "They told me that the document will be ready in a few days and they will give me a call."

The reasons for his concern prior to his visit to the Saudi consulate on September 28 will be discussed in greater detail in the relevant sections of this book. Here's the short version: Khashoggi was a columnist for *The Washington Post,* where he had criticized the government of Saudi Arabia. Specifically, he targeted not King Salman himself but Crown Prince Muhammed bin Salman, who seemed like a reformist but actually used totalitarian methods, including murder, to crack down on dissent. Khashoggi also criticized the Saudi administration at public events. Although he was not a dissident *per se*, Khashoggi, a journalist who used to be close to the Saudi establishment, used an unmistakably critical language in his statements about Saudi Arabia.

Although the Saudi officials had told him that they would need a few days to prepare the official papers, they planned Khashoggi's eventual murder in line with Riyadh's orders. Khashoggi would spend the next four days in London, where he was attending a conference.

Khashoggi's flight back to London was due to depart in three hours. As such, he took another taxi to Atatürk Airport. He was accompanied by his fiancée, Hatice Cengiz.

KHASHOGGI'S LAST BREAKFAST

Four days later, when Jamal Khashoggi returned from London, he and his fiancée met in their apartment in the Topkapi district early in the morning. They went out for breakfast and picked a nearby café. At breakfast, Hatice Cengiz told her fiancée that she wanted to go with him to the Saudi consulate. Khashoggi called the consulate to check if his papers were ready. A consular official told him to wait for their call.

Upon receiving Khashoggi's call, the Saudis probably checked whether the death squad was ready to go – rather than the status of the *Washington Post* columnist's paperwork. Having confirmed that the killers had completed their preparations, the officer called Khashoggi to tell him that his papers would be ready for pick-up at 1 p.m. According to CCTV footage, the couple returned to their apartment at the Europe Residences at 12.27 p.m. and left 15 minutes later. The police received that footage from the building administration when the discovery team went to the apartment to look for evidence. At 12.43 p.m., Khashoggi and Cengiz left their apartment for the last time.

By 1 p.m., they had covered the 11-kilometer distance from the gated community to the Saudi consulate. Khashoggi handed over both his iPhones to Hatice Cengiz.

They spoke briefly by the police barricade surrounding the Saudi consulate. One last time, Khashoggi looked his fiancée in the eye and told her to wait for him there. That was going to be the last thing he'd ever say to her.

In an interview with the *Sabah* newspaper's Special Intelligence Unit, Hatice Cengiz described Khashoggi's contacts with the Saudi authorities between September 28 and October 2 as follows:

On September 28, Mr. Jamal and I met at the Marriage Office in Fatih. We learned that we had to visit the consulate to obtain necessary documents. Jamal was concerned. He was wondering whether anything would go wrong.

Quite the contrary, the consular staff were apparently hospitable and friendly. As a matter of fact, some officials approached him to inquire about his well-being. [Jamal] was pleasantly surprised. When he told me about his experience, he was very happy. As such, there were no questions in his mind when he showed up for his second appointment on October 2. Had I thought that he was seriously worried, I would have absolutely prevented him from going there.

In the morning of October 2, Mr. Jamal and I had breakfast. He wanted to go to the consulate and pick up the documents that he had requested in advance. When we went to the consulate, Mr. Jamal gave me his phones, as he had done the first time, and walked right in.

On the ride to the consulate, we talked about our plans after picking up his papers. We were going to browse some stores to purchase some items for our apartment. Later that day, we were going to meet our friends and loved ones for dinner to announce the intended date of our wedding ceremony.

I waited for him patiently and hopefully until 4 p.m. As a matter of fact, I went to a supermarket near the consulate, bought a newspaper and read it. I purchased some chocolate and water to give to Jamal when he came out. When he failed to leave the consulate, I called my closest friend to ask them to join me immediately. I proceeded to call Yasin Aktay, one of Jamal's old friends, and Turan Kışlakçı. Finally, I called some of Jamal's Arab friends that I knew were close to him.

At 4 p.m., my curious wait gave way to serious concern and fear. I approached the consulate. First, I tried to get some information from the security guards. When I failed, I called the consulate and told the consular official that Mr. Jamal had entered the building and failed to come out. The officer hung up the phone, approached me and told me that there was nobody left inside the building. Everyone was gone, he said. At that moment, I felt my world turning dark. My head started spinning to such an extent that I could barely stand.

It's been eleven days since Mr. Jamal went missing. [October 13] was his birthday. There are few things that are worse than having to make public statements about the last time I saw a man, whose birthday I had been planning. Sorrow, disappointment, anger, uncertainty and fear have killed me a thousand times over the past eleven days. Initially, I want back there, thinking that they subjected Jamal to a simple interrogation and could release him at any moment. I waited outside the consulate until the dead of night. Then the sense that something hidden was happening became stronger and stronger.

It is unacceptable for myself and my government that this incident took place in our country and some people tried to send a message on our country's behalf. As part of an official investigation, the prosecutor's office has been looking into all evidence and all details that could explain what happened. Our country hasn't issued a formal statement because the investigation is still underway. Although I say that I have been waiting patiently, I aged ten years over the last fourteen days. Even though I have little hope left, I am still eagerly awaiting Jamal's return.[3]

In an October 26 interview with *Habertürk's* Mehmet Akif Ersoy, Hatice Cengiz shared significant details about the developments between September 28 and October 2:

_____ *We wanted to split our time between the United States*

3   Damla Kaya, *'Cemal Kaşıkçı'nın nişanlısı Hatice Cengiz: Birilerinin zalim planlarına kurban oldum'* [Khashoggi's fiancée, Hatice Cengiz: I became the victim of some people's cruel plans], Sabah, 14 October 2018.

*and Istanbul. He used to say that beginnings were import-
ant, so he'd purchased an apartment in Istanbul. He visited
Turkey frequently and loved it here. He was a close friend
of the president. He attended three events, even though he'd
come [to Turkey] for the wedding. My father also demanded us to live in Istanbul.*

*In the time period between September 10 and October
2, we began to make preparations for the wedding. At the
same time, he had plans there. As soon as my family gave
their blessing, we started the preparations. He bought an
apartment and we began placing orders for furniture, as the
official procedure tends to take some time. We thought we'd
make some progress and throw a wedding party afterwards.
That's what we did until October 2. We went to the munici-
pality to formally apply for a marriage license.*

*The reason for our visit to the consulate was that [Ja-
mal] needed an official document stating that he was not
currently married, so that he could marry a Turkish citizen.
Mr. Jamal and I went to the City Hall in Fatih to see how
we could obtain that document.*

*I had told [Jamal] that he'd have to visit the consulate
to obtain marriage papers. He thought that there could be
a problem at the consulate, but decided to inquire once he
got [to Turkey]. There are rumors that he went to the Saudi
consulate in the United States to request that document, but
was turned down and directed to [the consulate in] Turkey.
He would have told me if that were the case.*

THE INEVITABLE NERVOUSNESS OF THE FIRST DATE

Later in the same interview, Hatice Cengiz explains that Jamal Khashoggi was concerned that he had to visit the consulate
to obtain a 'proof of singledom'. "He did not want his writings to

cause tensions at the consulate. He was worried that they'd turn him down," she adds. "He hoped that they wouldn't ask him to go back [to Saudi Arabia] or perhaps subject him to something like an interrogation." Let us recall that Khashoggi was visibly nervous before showing up for his first appointment at the Saudi consulate on September 28. Cengiz continues:

[Jamal] believed that Turkey was a safe country and [the authorities] would shed light on the incident with relative ease if something were to happen to him. He thought that Turkey was a powerful player in the international arena and Saudi Arabia would not risk fueling tensions with Turkey.

When we realized at the Marriage Office that there was nothing we could do, we asked each other whether we should go [to the consulate] and give it a try. I told him that I could go with him, as we were together and did everything together during the wedding preparations. His flight was at 2 p.m. that day. We hailed a nearby taxi and headed to the consulate.

An hour passed after he walked in, and I thought to myself that I'd have to walk up [to the consulate] and ask for him if were to stay there for another ten to fifteen minutes, since he was going to miss his flight. Jamal walked out just then. He had left his cell phones with me. To the best of my knowledge, he was supposed to leave them [at the entrance of] the consulate, but he may have thought it was safer to leave them with me. He was rejoiced. That made me very happy. He had set foot in his native country's soil for the first time in 18 months. He told me that the consulate's employees were very caring, approached him to greet him, and treated him very well.

The consular staff told him that the paperwork would be ready in a few days. [Jamal] told them that he had travel plans and would like to leave. It is my understanding that they asked him when he'd be back. He told them that he was coming back on Tuesday. They said that they'd have the papers ready by then. We left the consulate joyfully and he flew to London.

Hatice Cengiz recalls that October 2, by contrast, was a very difficult day because her fiancée entered the Saudi consulate and never came out. She notes that the consular staff's warm reception on September 28 boosted their confidence and they did not suspect anything would go wrong during the second appointment:

October 2 was a very, very difficult day. I still do not understand what happened and I can't explain it either. When I think back to that day, I ask myself whether we missed something or I failed to pick up on some detail. He came back from London. We made plans for the rest of the day. I wasn't aware that he was going to visit the Saudi consulate as soon as he arrived on Tuesday. I had to go to class that day, but I asked him if I should accompany him to the consulate. He told me he'd go with a friend.

At that moment, I felt that I had to go with him – that I shouldn't leave him alone. He immediately called the consular staff and I believe that the [Saudi] official told him they'd get back to him as soon as possible. They called later to say that he could come in at 1 p.m. We hailed a taxi and drove to the consulate. Judging by his body language, he was not concerned about his second visit.

Keeping in mind that we were going to settle on a wedding date, we agreed to have dinner together. I requested to walk into the consulate alongside him, but [the Saudis] did not accept. We were familiar with the entry procedure from the first appointment, so [Jamal] handed me his cell phones. That was followed by a long wait.

During an earlier event, Mr. Jamal caught the flu and he got sick. He had invited me to that event, and we spent a long time at the hospital that day. After leaving the hospital, I asked him what I was supposed to do if something were to happen to him [in Turkey], as his friends and family weren't here. I wondered if there was someone he could recommend me to contact in that case. That was a few days before the incident at the consulate. He told me that I could call Yasin [Aktay], whom he called an old friend: "This is Turkey and what happens here would be related to the Turks, so Yasin would be the right person to contact."

To be clear, Jamal did not tell me to call Yasin Aktay if something went wrong at the consulate. If he had instructed me to take specific action, then it would mean that he was worried and I took too long to place the call – that I was extremely negligent. He did not have any second thoughts [about walking into the consulate] the second time around.

I assumed that Jamal was having a conversation with [the consular staff] because they were possibly wondering what he'd done after leaving his country. I thought that there was a friendly atmosphere. His attitude led me to believe that. Had I felt that the Saudi consulate was conspiring against [Jamal], I would have rushed into the building. I waited there for a long time. I thought: "Let them chat for however long they please, as long as they give him his papers." I absolutely did not think that something was wrong.[4]

Jamal Khashoggi, whose fiancée was not worried and "eagerly awaited" his return, was never going to come back. For he had become the victim of an unprecedented crime. A death squad, many of whose members had travelled to Turkey aboard a private jet, was responsible for that murder.

---

[4] Transcript of the 26 October 2018 interview with Hatice Cengiz on Habertürk

3

THE DARK SECRETS
BEHIND THE MURDER

Murderers Aboard A Private Jet

Six days after the murder, on October 8, it was already clear that the killers had dismembered Jamal Khashoggi's body and moved his remains out of the Saudi consulate in a van with tinted windows.[1]

On October 10, however, *Sabah* broke the news that Saudi government officials were responsible for Khashoggi's death. The story offered important insights into the 15-member death squad's arrival to kill the *Washington Post* columnist. Written by the authors of this book, the story was as follows:

Sabah reveals when and aboard which aircraft the mysterious individuals, whom the authorities believe to have been involved in the disappearance and death of Saudi journalist Jamal Khashoggi inside Saudi Arabia's consulate in Istanbul on Tuesday, October 2, came to Turkey.

On October 2, two Gulfstream IV business jets took off from the Saudi capital Riyadh and arrived at Atatürk Airport – one before and the other after Khashoggi entered the

---

1   Nazif Karaman, Emir Somer and Kenan Kıran, 'Sır perdesini camı film kaplı siyah minibüs aralayacak' [The black van with tinted windows will unveil the mystery], Sabah, 8 October 2018.

consulate general. The authorities established that the two jets belonged to Sky Prime Aviation, a Riyadh-based company that has been working with the government of Saudi Arabia for long years. According to the flight manifest obtained by Sabah, the first jet carried nine passengers and the second aircraft had six persons on board. A total of seven crew members served on those flights.

According to information that *Sabah's* Special Intelligence Unit obtained from trusted sources, the aircraft with the tail number HZ SK2 landed at Atatürk Airport at 3.15 a.m., hours before Khashoggi set foot in the consulate and taxied to the General Aviation Terminal.

ONE FLEW TO CAIRO, THE OTHER TO DUBAI

Another jet with the tail number HZ SK1 arrived at Atatürk Airport at 5.15 p.m. and taxied to the General Aviation Terminal. That flight departed at 6.30 p.m. and flew to Cairo, Egypt. Keeping in mind the close relations between Egyptian coup leader [Abdel Fattah] al-Sisi's administration and Mohammad bin Salman's government, the aircraft's destination raises eyebrows.

The private jet with the tail number HZ SK2, which was first to arrive, left Atatürk Airport at 10.45 p.m. and landed at Dubai [International] at 2.48 a.m.[2] It proceeded to fly to Riyadh. That the jet flew to Dubai, from which Salman's associate, Mohammad Dahlan, manages anti-Turkey operations, raises eyebrows as well. According to sources, the jet travelled to Riyadh from Dubai. According to the special team that oversees the [Turkish] investigation, those details establish that the 15-member death squad had intended to kill [Jamal] Khashoggi in the first place.

The authorities have established that the operatives aboard the first jet –with the tail number HZ SK2— checked into a hotel near

2   The other private jet with the tail number HZ SK1 left Riyadh at 1.23 a.m. on October 2 and arrived at Istanbul Atatürk at 5.15 p.m. local time. After its departure at 6.30 p.m., it landed in Cairo at 11.31 p.m. and proceeded to fly back to Riyadh.

Saudi Arabia's consulate general on October 2 and headed to the
consulate after dropping off their luggages. Although their rooms
were booked until October 5, the team picked up their bags and
left aboard that jet on the same day. The rest of the operatives,
who arrived [at Atatürk Airport] on commercial flights, went to
the [Saudi] consulate in the morning and returned to the airport
after the murder.

The special investigative team working on the Khashoggi
case watched CCTV footage from the vicinity of said hotel. They
also inspected the vehicles that entered or left the consulate after Khashoggi went missing. Camera footage has established that
some of those vehicles with diplomatic plates entered and left the
residence of Consul General Mohammad al-Otaiba some 300 meters away on the day of the incident. Finally, the authorities established that the Turkish staff at the consular residence was abruptly
told to go on leave on October 2.

We have also learned that the two jets received ground services, parking, cleaning, passenger pick-up, fuel and catering services from B Aviation Limited. According to sources, the special
investigative team that Turkey formed to look into the Khashoggi
case continues to investigate the two mysterious airplanes and is
going over CCTV footage from the airport. In addition to the passenger manifests from the two flights, the team is reportedly in-
specting in detail video footage from the passport control counter
and elsewhere.[3]

THE DEATH SQUAD'S DOG TAGS

The following day, Sabah ran a new story on the death squad
and published the names and photographs of the 15 Saudi operatives. Written by the Special Intelligence Unit, the story shed light
on the murder and came to be widely cited by various international media outlets:

Sabah reveals the identities of the individuals who were part

3   Abdurrahman Şimşek and Nazif Karaman, 'İşte sır seyahat' [The Secret Trip],
Sabah, 9 October 2018.

of a mysterious 15-member intelligence team that were involved in the abduction of Saudi journalist Jamal Khashoggi, who went missing after entering Saudi Arabia's consulate general in Istanbul on October 2.

The up-to-date information on the death squad, whose members were identified in the above-mentioned story, is as follows:

1- Mashal Saad al-Bostani (born 1987) cleared passport control at 1.45 a.m. and stayed at the W.G. Hotel. He left Turkey aboard the private jet with the HZ SK2, which belonged to Sky Prime Aviation, at 10.45 p.m. after passing the passport control counter at 9.46 p.m.

2- Salah Mohammed al-Tubaigy (born 1971) arrived at Atatürk Airport at 3.15 a.m. on October 2 aboard the private jet with the tail number HZ SK2, passed passport control at 3.38 a.m. and stayed at the M Hotel. He had his passport stamped at 8.29 p.m. and left aboard HZ SK2 at 10.45 p.m.

3- Naif Hassan S. Alarifi (born 1986) took a commercial flight from Riyadh to Istanbul on October 1, the day before the Khashoggi murder, and cleared passport control at 4.12 p.m. He stayed at the W.G. Hotel, completed passport formalities at 9.45 p.m. on October 2 and departed aboard HZ SK2 at 10.45 p.m.

4- Mohammed Saad al-Zahrani (born 1988) arrived at Atatürk Airport aboard a commercial flight from Riyadh on October 1 and stayed at the W.G. Hotel. He cleared passport control at 9.44 p.m. and left with HZ SK2 at 10.45 p.m.

5- Mansour Othman Aba Hussein (born 1972) arrived at Atatürk Airport on a commercial flight from Riyadh on October 1 and stayed at the W.G. Hotel. He had his passport stamped at 9.45 p.m. and departed aboard HZ SK2 at 10.45 p.m.

6- Khaled Aiz Al-Tabi (born 1988) took a commercial flight from Cairo to Istanbul on October 1 and arrived at Ataturk Airport after midnight. He cleared passport control at 1.44 a.m. on October 2, stayed at the W.G. Hotel and left aboard the private jet with the tail number HZ SK2.

7-   Abdelaziz Mohammed al-Hussawi (born 1987) came to Turkey from Egypt on a commercial flight and cleared passport control at 1.43 a.m. on October 2. He stayed at the W.G. Hotel and went through passport control at 8.28 p.m. to leave Turkey aboard HZ SK2 at 10.45 p.m.

8-   Walid Abdullah al-Shahry (born 1980) arrived at Ataturk Airport aboard the private jet with the tail number HZ SK2 at 3.41 a.m. on October 2. He stayed at the M Hotel and took HZ SK1 on his return trip. He cleared passport control at 5.44 p.m. and his plane departed at 6.30 p.m.

9-   Turki Musharrif al-Shahry (born 1982) took HZ SK2 to Istanbul and entered the country at 3.39 a.m. He stayed at the M Hotel and cleared passport control at 5.44 p.m. before departing at 6.30 p.m. aboard HZ SK1.

10- Sair Ghalib al-Harbi (born 1979) arrived at Ataturk Airport aboard HZ SK2 and entered Turkey at 3.41 a.m. He stayed at the M Hotel and had his passport stamped at 5.44 p.m. before leaving on HZ SK1 at 6.30 p.m.

11- Maher Abdulaziz Mutreb (born 1971) arrived at Atatürk International on HZ SK2 and entered the country at 3.38 a.m. Mutreb stayed at the M Hotel and cleared passport control at 5.49 p.m. to board the private jet with the tail number HZ SK1, which departed at 6.30 p.m.

12- Fahd Shabib al-Balawi (born 1985) took HZ SK2 to Istanbul and cleared passport control at 3.41 a.m. on October 2. He had his passport stamped at 5.46 p.m. and boarded HZ SK1 to leave Istanbul at 6.30 p.m.

13- Badr Lafi al-Otaiba (born 1973) arrived at Ataturk International aboard HZ SK2 and entered the country at 3.41 a.m. He was among the operatives that stayed at the M Hotel. He cleared passport control at 5.44 p.m. to board HZ SK1.

14- Mustapha Mohammed al-Madani (born 1961) took HZ SK2 to Istanbul and entered the country at 3.41 a.m. He stayed at the M Hotel and had his passport stamped at 12.18 a.m. before boarding the Turkish Airlines flight TK144 to Riyadh at 1.25 a.m. on October 3.

15- Saif Saad al-Qahtani (born 1973) arrived at Atatürk Airport aboard HZ SK2 and cleared passport control at 3.41 a.m. After staying at the M Hotel, he had his passport stamped at 12.20 a.m. to return to Riyadh on the Turkish Airlines flight TK144 at 1.25 a.m.

THE KHASHOGGI ASSASSINATION: PLAY-BY-PLAY

We shed light on the missing pieces in our exclusive story, which was published eight days after Jamal Khashoggi's death, with additional research for this book. According to information and documents that we have obtained from trusted government sources, here's what happened before, during and after the murder:

According to CCTV footage, Jamal Khashoggi entered the Saudi consulate at 1.14 p.m.[4] His fiancée, Hatice Cengiz, waited outside the compound for three hours, as Khashoggi became the victim of a dark stain on history, whose details are featured in Chapter II. When the Saudi journalist failed to exit the consulate, Cengiz told the Turkish authorities at 5.50 p.m. that her fiancée had been either forcibly detained inside the consulate or was in trouble.

A police examination of footage from surveillance cameras directed at the various entrances and exits of the Saudi consulate, which covered the time period between 1.14 p.m. on October 2 and 11.59 p.m. on October 5, revealed that Khashoggi had not left the compound on foot.

Having received information about the incident at 5.30 p.m., the the Turkish intelligence agency's Istanbul field office began to look into all vehicles exiting the Saudi consulate. Between 1.14 p.m and 6 p.m. on October 2, they found, a total of six vehicles had left the building.

A Mercedes-Benz Vito van with the diplomatic plate 34 CC

---

4   The time setting of the CCTV camera at the police checkpoint outside the Saudi consulate in Istanbul was off by six minutes. Although footage from the area was time-stamped as 1.14 p.m., which the media reported as is, Khashoggi actually entered the building at 1.08 p.m.

1865 left the consulate at 3.05 p.m. and entered the consular residence just 300 meters away. The vehicle drove into the residence's indoor parking garage and remained there for three days before going back to the consulate at 9.40 a.m on October 5. Its next stop was the car wash.

Another Mercedes-Benz vehicle with the diplomatic plate 34 CC 2248 drove to the M Hotel at 3.05 p.m.[5] and returned to the consulate an hour later.

A third vehicle, 34 CC 2342, arrived at the consulate at 10.05 a.m. and drove to Atatürk Airport at 8.26 p.m.

Another vehicle with the plate number 34 CC 2464 left the consulate at 3.05 p.m., arrived at the consular residence three minutes later, and drove to Atatürk Airport at 4.53 p.m.

Finally, a diplomatic vehicle with the plate number 34 CC 3071 reached the consular residence at 11.06 a.m. and drove to the airport at 8.11 p.m.

According to the Turkish police and intelligence, the Mercedes-Benz Vito with the plate number 34 CC 1865 raised a lot of red flags. That was the vehicle that the Saudi operatives used to move Jamal Khashoggi's body parts from the Saudi consulate to the consul-general's residence down the road.

According to official reports that we have obtained exclusively, three members of the Saudi death squad –Mohammed Saad al-Zahrani, Mansour Othman Aba Hussein and Naif Hassan Alarifi— had arrived at Atatürk Airport on Saudia flight SV263 at 4 p.m. on October 1. Those were the first Saudi operatives to reach Turkey. They entered the Saudi consulate in Istanbul at 7.14 p.m. before driving the vehicle with the license number 34 CC 3071 to a luxury kebab joint in the Etiler district at 10.57 p.m. and checking into their hotel, the W.G. in Levent, at 11.52 p.m.

The second group of operatives, featuring Mashal Saad al-Bostani, Khaled Aiz al-Tabi and Abdulaziz Mohammed M. Al-Hussawi, arrived at Atatürk Airport on Turkish flight TK695 at 1.40 a.m. on October 2 and entered the W.G. Hotel at approximately 2.20 a.m.

5   The time setting of the CCTV camera at the police checkpoint outside the consular residence was two minutes off. As such, the vehicles actually entered the building at 3.03 p.m.

The main team, which landed in Istanbul aboard the private jet with the tail number HZ SK2 at 3.15 a.m. on October 2 and check into the M Hotel in the Levent district at 5.20 a.m., included the following operatives:

Maher Abdulaziz M. Mutreb, Sai Ghaleb Al-Harbi, Salah Mohammed Al-Tubaigy, Mustapha Mohammed M. Al-Madani, Fahd Shabib Al-Balawi, Turki Musharraf M. Al-Shahry, Badr Lafi Al-Otaiba, Walid Abdullah M. Al-Shahry and Sayf Saad Al-Qahtani.

On the day of the murder, Mutreb, Al-Harby and Al-Otaiba drove a vehicle with the license number 34 NL 1806 from the M Hotel to Saudi Arabia's consulate in Istanbul at 9.49 a.m.

At 9.52 a.m., Al-Zahrani left the W.G. Hotel and walked to the Saudi consulate.

Three minutes later, Turki Musharrad Al-Shahry, Walid Abdullah M. Al-Shahry and Fahd Shabib al-Balawi left the M Hotel with the diplomatic vehicle with the license number 34 CC 3071 and arrived at the consulate at 10.05 a.m.

Al-Hossawi, Al-Tabi, Al-Arifi and Al-Bostani arrived at the consular residence on the vehicle with the 34 CC 3071 plates at 11.06 a.m. from the W.G. Hotel. An additional member of the death squad, Mansour Othman Aba Hussein, want to the residence separately. He got there at 12.38 p.m. by walking from the W.G. Hotel.

The remaining members of the team –the forensic scientist Al-Tubaigy, the body double Al-Madani and Al-Qahtani, left the M Hotel at 10.48 a.m. and arrived at the consulate nine minutes later with the vehicle with the 34 TR 8985 plates.

At 3.05 p.m, Mutreb, Al-Tubaigy and Al-Harbi boarded the vehicle with the plate number 34 CC 1865 from the tunnel entering the consulate and drove to the residence. Those three men were the most senior members of the Saudi death squad. They were directly involved in the death of Jamal Khashoggi, his dismemberment and the disposal of his body.

Al-Madani and Al-Qahtani were the first two Saudi operatives to leave the consulate after the murder. At 2.53 p.m., they exited the compound.[6]

The first men to head to the airport, in turn, were Turki Al-Shahry, Fahr Al-Balawi, Walid Al-Shahry and Badr Al-Otaiba, who took the diplomatic vehicle with the plate number 34 CC 2248 at 3.11 p.m. from the consulate to the M Hotel, where they gathered their things and checked out before driving to Atatürk Airport at 4.05 p.m.

At 4.53 p.m., Mutreb and Al-Harbi left the consular resence with the diplomatic vehicle bearing the license number 34 CC 2464 and went to Atatürk Airport.

Those six members of the Saudi death squad –Turki Al-Shahry, Al-Balawi, Walid Al-Shahry, Al-Otaiba, Mutreb and Al-Harbi— departed Istanbul aboard the private jet with the tail number HZ SK1 at 6.30 p.m.

At 7.37 p.m., Hussein, Al-Arifi and Al-Bostani drove from the consular residence to the W.G. Hotel with the diplomatic vehicle with the 34 CC 3071 plates and, from there, headed to the airport at 7.42 p.m.

Al-Zahrani left the Saudi consulate from a rear exit alone at 3.42 p.m. He took a taxi to the M Hotel. Al-Zahrani was one of the five-member main team that had choked Jamal Khashoggi to death. Unlike all others, he seemed to be operating alone throughout the mission. (He came to the airport alone and entered and left the consulate by himself.) Wearing sunglasses and carrying a backpack, Al-Zahrani appeared to have disguised himself as an ordinary tourist. He went to Atatürk Airport at 8.56 p.m.

At 7.46 p.m., the Mercedes-Benz Vito with the diplomatic plate number 34 CC 2342 left the consular residence with Al-Hussawi, Al-Tabi and Al-Tubaigy on board and headed straight to Atatürk Airport.

Seven members of the Saudi death squad –Hussein, Al-Arifi, Al-Bostani, Al-Zahrani, Al-Hussawi, Al-Tabi and Al-Tubaigy— left Istanbul aboard the private jet with the tail number HZ SK2.

Others, Al-Madani and Al-Qahtani, boarded Turkish flight TK144 to Riyadh. At 10.26 p.m., that group of operatives took a

---

6   For more details, see the section titled *"The Fake Beard,"* in Chapter IV.

taxi to Atatürk Airport, cleared passport control at 12.18 a.m. and departed at 1.25 a.m. on October 3.

The 15 members of the Saudi death squad carried out their gruesome task, which we have described above, and return to their country. Before leaving Turkey, however, they left their finger-prints all across Istanbul – to some extent that Turkish intelligence and law enforcement agents apparently joked that the Saudis "could have left their business cards just as well."

LOOKING FOR BODY PARTS IN LUGGAGE

On the day of the Khashoggi murder, officials from the Turkish intelligence agency's Istanbul field office and the Istanbul police searched the Saudi business jet with the tail number HZ SK2 as it waited outside the General Aviation Terminal at Atatürk Airport. Upon receiving news of Khashoggi's reported disappearance, se-curity officers swept the aircraft extensively. They found no murder clues on board or in the passengers' bags before their de-parture.

There were some 'crypto weapons' in the checked luggage and carry-on bags of Saudi operatives who left Turkey aboard HZ SK1, which stayed at Atatürk Airport for 75 minutes and was not searched before taking off at 6.30 p.m., but there was no evidence of murder. The authorities detected those items upon retroactive inspection of X-ray images.

A police report that the Turkish officials filed after search-ing the Saudi business jet indicated that the authorities found out whether the operatives' personal belongings had been scanned upon entering the General Aviation Terminal:

When the x-ray machine operator was asked whether the device would pick up on chopped up body parts if there were any inside those bags, they responded that it would be possible to identify traces of body parts with the help of the screening equipment and stated that there was nothing out of the ordinary about the contents of the Saudi team's luggages. [The authorities] used the CCTV system to monitor the private jet, which departed at 10.00 p.m., in real time, identified where the aircraft was parked, and recorded footage to the fullest extent of the camera angles.

On October 2, the day of the murder, intelligence and law enforcement agents searched the private jet with the tail number HZ SK2 and inspected all relevant video recordings. Upon completing their inspection, the authorities reported that they "confirmed the possibility that Jamal Khashoggi was being abducted, which was raised by intelligence officers, immediately instructed the supervisor of Gate E to obtain information about the aircraft's passengers and crew, visually monitored seven passengers waiting in the lounge, and concluded that the person of interest was not among them. Seeing that there was nothing out of the ordinary, they permitted the aircraft to depart."[7]

Sedat Ergin, a columnist for the daily newspaper *Hürriyet,* made references to the Sabah Special Intelligence Unit's October 10 story in his column published a week later and shared additional information with the public:

That a Saudi delegation of 15 individuals, many of whom had military backgrounds, travelled to Istanbul just before Saudi journalist Jamal Khashoggi's disappearance and left the same day in a hurry is one of the strongest pieces of evidence regarding the Riyadh regime's culpability in this crisis.

By bringing together open source information about the delegation's arrival, their movements in Istanbul over the course of less than 24 hours, and their departure in groups, we arrive at a curious picture. That picture hints at a detailed plan.

My source for the arrival and departure of the Saudi [operatives] is a story that Abdurrahman Simsek and Nazif Karaman published in Sabah on October 10. That story provides concrete information about the airport's entry and departure records.

A second team, consisting of nine individuals, arrived at Atatürk Airport aboard a Gulfstream private jet with the tail num-

---

7   Abdurrahman Şimşek and Nazif Karaman, 'İşte 15 kişilik suikast timi' [Here's The 15-Member Assassination Squad], *Sabah,* 10 October 2018.

ber HZ SK2 at 3.15 a.m. on October 2. The aircraft was parked in Terminal E – also known as General Aviation. The entry of those individuals to the passport control system was completed between 3.38 and 3.41 a.m. It would appear that the two teams were intended to stay at different hotels. As such, the second group that arrived by a private jet checked into the M Hotel.

Against the backdrop of those developments, a second Gulf-stream jet with the tail number HZ SK1 arrived at Atatürk Airport from Riyadh at 5.15 p.m. with no passengers on board.

Let us stress a critical point here: The Saudi delegation, which came to Istanbul in three groups, left the city on the same day in three groups. This is how they planned their return trip:

1- Six of the nine individuals that arrived by private jet early in the morning boarded a second private jet, which landed in the evening, and left Istanbul immediately. That aircraft departed at 6.30 p.m. It would appear that the Saudi planners intended to get the majority of those operatives out of Turkey without delay. That jet flew to Cairo, where it stayed for 25 hours, and proceeded to go to Riyadh.

2- The first private jet, which arrived [at Atatürk Airport] on the morning of October 2, left a little later – at 10.45 p.m. All six operatives, who took a commercial flight to Istanbul, boarded that aircraft. Additionally, one of the nine operatives that travelled to Istanbul aboard that jet –Mohammed al-Tubaigy— flew back in that plane.

The passports of those individuals were processed between 8.28 p.m. and 9.45 p.m. The seven men aboard that aircraft flew straight to Dubai. After being delayed over Nallıhan, it landed in Dubai at 2.30 a.m. and proceeded to fly to Riyadh in the morning.

3- What happened to two out of the nine operatives that took the first private jet [to Istanbul]? Those two men left Istanbul on a commercial flight. Their passports were processed at 12.18 a.m. and 12.20 a.m. on October 3. Judging by their movements, it is clear that nothing happened by co-incidence, that [the operatives did] everything according to a plan – that everything, including which operative would take which flight to and from Turkey, where they would stay and where they would go, were strictly tied to a serious plan.[8]

TURKEY'S CRIMINAL STRATEGY

As Sedat Ergin pointed out, Turkey was aware that the Saudis carried out the Khashoggi murder according to an existing plan. As such, the Turkish authorities wanted to adopt a strategy in advance to discover criminal evidence.

The Turkish request to inspect the Saudi consulate using lumi-nol, a substance that reveals blood traces, reflected that strategy. Turkish investigators used luminol and infrared light in an attempt to find Khashoggi's DNA samples in the crime scene. Yet the inspection yielded no concrete results.

Around the same time, a Turkish official told the news website Middle East Eye that Turkey knew, "when and in which room Khashoggi was killed," and "where his body was dismembered." According to the same anonymous source, the Saudi consulate had scheduled an appointment for Khashoggi at 1 p.m. on October 2. The Turkish staff at the consulate, they said, was told to leave the premises due to a high-level diplomatic meeting.[9]

The Saudi operatives had planned the murder in great detail. As a matter of fact, Turkish investigators discovered that the van, which Khashoggi's killers used to drive his dismembered body to the consular residence down the road, had made the same trip to the residence in an apparent dress rehearsal. The security forces reached that conclusion upon close inspection of CCTV footage showing the vehicle's movements.

The Saudis wanted to establish whether the Mercedes-Benz

---

8   Sedat Ergin, 'Suudi infaz ekibinin İstanbul planı böyle işledi' [Here's how the Saudi execution team's Istanbul plan played out], Hürriyet, 17 October 2018.
9   Nazif Karaman, Suudi makamları neyi saklıyor [What Are The Saudi Authorities Hiding?], Sabah, 12 October 2018.

Vito with the tinted windows was going to fit into the consular residence's indoor parking garage. At 1.38 a.m. on October 2, just hours before the murder, a driver for the Saudi consulate, S. K., got behind the wheel for the dress rehearsal. He parked the van in front of the consular residence at 2 a.m. – before being told to take some time off.

The discovery about the van, which the Saudis used to transport Khashoggi's body to the residence, established that the intelligence operatives had repeatedly gone over their plan. Let us recall that the same van remained at the consular residence for three days after the murder.[10] During those three days, Saudi Arabia's consulate general, Al-Otaiba, did not leave his residence.

ELECTRONIC SURVEILLANCE OF THE DEATH SQUAD

Shortly after *Sabah* published photographs of Khashoggi killers, including Maher Abdulaziz Mutreb, a leading U.S. newspaper, *The New York Times*, unveiled images of Mutreb and Saudi Crown Prince Mohammed bin Salman.[11]

According to CCTV footage, Mutreb entered the Saudi consulate in Istanbul at 9.55 a.m. on October 2. At 4.53 p.m., he was detected outside the consular residence. Mutreb left his hotel in Levent, along with his men, at 5.15 p.m.

To be clear, Mutreb and the rest of his accomplices had a reservation at the hotel in Levent for four nights. After the murder, they cancelled the rest of their stay and checked out of their rooms.

At 6.30 p.m., those six members of the Saudi death squad flew to Cairo aboard the private jet with the tail number HZ SK1, which had arrived at Atatürk Airport just 75 minutes ago.

On October 19, *Sabah* published new photographs of the following killers: Al-Bostani, Al-Tubaigy, Al-Arifi, Al-Zahrani, Al-Tabi, Al-Hussawi, Walid Al-Shahry, Turki Al-Shahry and Al-

---

10   Nazif Karaman, Konsoloslukta Kaşıkçı provası [A dress rehearsal for Khashoggi at the consulate], *Sabah*, 15 October 2018.
11   David Kirkpatrick, Malachy Browne, Ben Hubbard and David Botti. The Jamal Khashoggi Case: Suspects Had Ties to Saudi Crown Prince, *The New York Times*, 16 October 2018.

Madani.

Stills from the security camera footage showed the Saudi operatives leaving the airport and standing by the passport control counter. According to CCTV footage, the Saudi death squad was seen by the passport control counter and at the General Aviation Terminal. The Turkish authorities also established that some of the killers had traveled to Turkey in the past.[12]

A POLICE CAMERA WITH SAUDI ENCRYPTION

One of the Saudi death squad's greatest mistakes was to secretly encrypt the hard drives hooked up to CCTV cameras at the police checkpoint on October 6 in an attempt to cover up the Khashoggi murder. The Saudis did not know, however, that the Turkish police had obtained that footage the day before.

On October 2, Saudi consular officers uninstalled the recorder of the compound's security system and attempted to meddle with security cameras at the police checkpoint to destroy evidence of Khashoggi and the Saudi operatives entering the building.

At 1 a.m. on October 6, Saudi officials accessed the computer at the police checkpoint, pretending to go over the footage, and encrypted the files in the process. They did not know that Turkish law enforcement agents had obtained a copy of the video recording at 7 p.m. on October 5 – six hours earlier.

It became clear that the Saudis had encrypted the digital video recorder when the Turkish police went back to obtain a second copy of the file. Nonetheless, the Turkish authorities were able to break the code and access additional footage. The Saudi operatives' goal was to cover up evidence of Jamal Khashoggi entering the compound.[13] Hence their initial claim that the consulate's security cameras weren't functioning properly at the time of Khashoggi's fatal appointment.[14]

---

12   Abdurrahman Şimşek and Nazif Karaman, İşte infaz ekibinin yeni görüntüleri [New Footage Of The Execution Team], *Sabah*, 19 October 2018.

13   Abdurrahman Şimşek and Nazif Karaman, Polis noktasındaki görüntüleri şifrelediler [They Encyrpted Footage From The Police Checkpoint], *Sabah*, 6 November 2018.

14   Toygun Atilla, Kayıp gazeteci olayında kameralı ipucu [The Camera Offers A Clue

CRYPTO WEAPONS ON X-RAY

The Saudi killers had taken with them some tools that they would use to kill Jamal Khashoggi on the flight from Riyadh. Some of those instruments were inside bags loaded on the first private jet, which took the operatives back to Saudi Arabia at 6.30 p.m. Under the ironclad rule of diplomatic immunity, the death squad brought their tools back to Riyadh.

The Turkish police inspected not just CCTV footage but also images from the X ray machine. Those images revealed that certain tools, which the police described as 'crypto weapons', were loaded on the private jet that departed at 6.30 p.m. with Khashoggi's killers on board.

Police and intelligence sources told the authors of this book that they submitted two reports on those crypto weapons. According to those reports, the Saudi operatives carried the type of tools and instruments included certain items that intelligence agencies would use for physical surveillance purposes as well as tools of the trade for assassins.

The Saudi death squad's equipment and tools, which went through the X-ray machine, included the following: 10 cell phones, five radio handsets and compatible intercom devices, two syringes used to inject chemicals, two electroshock devices, a signal blocking device to prevent surveillance, three stamp machines and some kind of scalpel.

The intelligence and security units stated in their official reports that those items and equipment were regularly used in international intelligence operations. They speculated that the cell phones and radio equipment were used for surveillance purposes, whereas the electroshock devices and syringes may have been used to sedate and kill the victim. The staplers, the report suggested, may have been used to prevent fluid leaks from plastic bags after Khashoggi's dismemberment.

A retroactive inspection of images from the X-ray machine at Atatürk Airport did not reveal any traces of Jamal Khashoggi's body parts. The second private jet, which left Istanbul after the

In The Case Of Missing Journalist], *Hürriyet*, 8 October 2018.

37

Turkish authorities became aware of Khashoggi's disappearance, was inspected by intelligence agents before departing at 10.45 p.m. Yet Turkish officials could not search the first aircraft, since it departed at 6.30 p.m. – just 40 minutes after Hatice Cengiz reported that her fiancée was missing.[15]

The Saudis had gotten rid of the bodies of their victims before the Jamal Khashoggi murder. Although their track record was clear, no assassination that they had carried out in the past matched the Khashoggi murder's gruesomeness. The Khashoggi murder was a Saudi operation in its own league.

The authors of this book studied the history of covert Saudi operations and reached that conclusion. They also went over notable intelligence operations in world history and could not find any case that was similar to what happened inside the Saudi consulate in Istanbul.

The Russian SVR and Israel's Mossad are among the most notorious secret services when it comes to covert operations of this particular sort. Although the Saudi death squad's methods were far less refined, it would appear that their actions were inspired by Mossad operations.

---

15   Abdurrahman Şimşek and Nazif Karaman, İnfaz timinin X-Ray'e takılan cinayet aletleri: Telsiz, telefon, şırınga, şok cihazı [The execution team's murder tools caught on X-Ray: Radio, phones, syringes, electroshock devices], Sabah, 13 November 2018.

4

MYSTERIOUS ASSASSINATIONS BY SECRET SERVICES

Mossad: A Source of Inspiration for the Saudis

Intelligence agencies measure the success of their actions by their accomplishments and their ability to leave behind no traces. Although the Saudi intelligence operatives conducted a reckless and unsuccessful operation in Istanbul, their role model was the Israeli secret service Mossad. In other words, it would appear that Riyadh follows in the footsteps of Tel Aviv when it comes to these types of operations.[1]

In an oped essay for the Telegraph, former British foreign minister Boris Johnson claimed that Saudi Arabia's assassination of journalist Jamal Khashoggi was possibly inspired by Russia.[2]

That claim did not catch anyone by surprise. After all, the United Kingdom accuses Moscow of using a nerve agent to target Sergey Skripal, a former Russian military intelligence officer, and his daughter in Salisbury. On March 14, British prime minister Theresa May said that Russia was responsible for the poisoning and announced that 23 Russian diplomats would have to leave the

1   In Chapter III, we discuss in detail the Saudi regime's covert operations prior to the murder of Jamal Khashoggi. Moreover, Chapter II engages the question whether Saudi Arabia was supported by any or multiple foreign intelligence services within the context of the Khashoggi assassination. Chapter VI, in turn, provides insights into the Central Intelligence Agency's take on the Khashoggi affair.
2   Boris Johnson: Suudi Arabistan Kaşıkçı cinayetinde Rusya'yı örnek almış olabilir [Boris Johnson: Saudi Arabia May Have Been Inspired By Russia In The Khashoggi Murder], BBC Turkish, 22 October 2018.

United Kingdom within seven days.

Ten days prior to May's announcement, Skripal and his daughter were found unconscious at a shopping mall in London's Salisbury district. A British investigation of the crime scana revealed that the two victims were poisoned with Novichok, a Russian-made nerve agent used in military operations.[3] The Kremlin denies that accusation.

At the time, Dmitry Peskov, the Kremlin spokesman, urged certain Western governments, which moved to expel Russian diplomats at London's request, to make sure that the evidence they received from Britain was indeed credible.

Experts at the British research facility Porton Down were unable to conclude that the nerve agent used to poison Skripal and his daughter was manufactured in Russia. The Russian ambassador to London, Alexander Yakovenko, responded by asking whether the British government stored Novichok at Porton Down, the country's largest secret military site. The research station, he added, was just 12 kilometers away from Salisbury.

Vassily Nebenzia, the Russian ambassador to the United Nations, told the UN Security Council, "You are playing with fire and you will be sorry." He warned that London was "poisoning" Moscow's relations with third countries.

According to media reports, the 66-year-old Skripal was a double agent that worked for the British intelligence in Europe. The Russian government claimed that MI6 had paid $100,000 in return for leaking information to the British intelligence since the 1990s. In 2006, a Russian court sentences Skripal to thirteen years in prison. Four years later, he was released as part of a spy swap between Moscow and London, where he proceeded to live.

However, this wasn't the first time that Britain and Russia experienced tensions over spies in the post-Cold War period. In 2006, Alexander Litvinenko, a former Russian intelligence agent who sought refuge in the United Kingdom, was poisoned with a radioactive agent in London. Litvinenko, who was arrested in 1999 and 2000 on charges of abuse of power, had sought asylum in the United Kingdom in 2000. After relocating to London, the

---

3   *Novichok* means "newcomer" in Russian.

former Russian agent remained an opponent of Vladimir Putin's government and published two books about his experiences in the Russian secret service. On 1 November 2006, Litvinenko was hospitalized and diagnosed with radioactive poisoning – Polonium 210. He died on November 23.

At the time, the British authorities accused Russia (specifically, Russian President Vladimir Putin) of killing Litvinenko. The Kremlin, in turn, repeatedly denied its alleged involvement in the assassination.

DEATH BY UMBRELLA

It is the world's worst kept secret that the Russian intelligence carried out a series of assassinations during the Cold War that screamed covert action. One of the most interesting cases in point was a 1978 operation by the SVR's notorious ancestor, KGB, in London.

Compared to not just Saudi Arabia's assassination of journalist Jamal Khashoggi but also more 'professional' secret service operations, the Russian secret service demonstrated back then that it was in another league. To appreciate the daylight between those operations, it is necessary to delve into the details of what happened in 1978.

On 7 October 1978, on a rainy and gloomy London morning, the Bulgarian dissident writer Georgi Markov parked his car by the southern foot of the Waterloo Bridge, walked up the stairs and approached a nearby bus stop to catch one of London's world famous double-decker buses. He was planning to rise the bus to the BBC headquarters, where he worked as a Bulgarian news anchor. As Markov waited, he felt a sting in his right calf. He turned around.

A man in his forties, wearing a dark coat, was picking up his umbrella from the sidewalk. He apologized, hailed a taxi and left. Markov assumed at the time that what happened was nothing more than an honest mistake. The man's umbrella, he thought, had hit his leg. Yet nothing could have been farther from the truth.

Markov was hospitalized shortly afterwards. The doctor found a tiny pellet filled with the poison risin. In a crime where the strange man's umbrella served as a firearm, that pellet was like a bullet from the murder weapon.

Georgi Markov passed away four days later. Behind this most curious secret service assassination of the Cold War years was the Bulgarian intelligence agency Durzhavna Sigurnost. Yet the KGB was pulling the organization's strings from behind the iron curtain.

Markov was a fierce critic of Todor Zhirkov, Bulgaria's communist leader. It was no coincidence that the Bulgarian dissident was killed on October 7 – Zhirkov's birthday. Years later, some sources claimed that Francesco Gullani, one of the SD's Italian agents, was the man in the dark coat. Another Bulgarian dissident writer, Vladimir Kostov, felt the same sting in his back and spotted a rash shortly after the Markov assassination. A pellet, akin to what the doctors had discovered in Markov's calf, was removed from Kostov's back. In the end, Kostov survived the assassination attempt.[4]

AN ISRAELI IN A HONEY TRAP

Georgi Markov's unparalleled assassination shows that the Bulgarian intelligence and its sponsor, KGB, carried out similar operations at the time. Yet the Saudi death squad's style resembled more closely the methods used by the Israeli intelligence agency Mossad. As a matter of fact, one of the most significant Mossad operations in history may have inspired Saudi Arabia's recent efforts to abduct members of the royal family and hunt down Saudi citizens.

On September 30, 1986, Mordechai Vanunu, who was born into a Moroccan Jewish family in 1956, travelled to Rome with his American girlfriend Cindy. He was detained and sedated upon arrival, and opened his eyes in Tel Aviv. He had been taken to Israel

---

4   For details of Operation Dagger, see: Ferhat Ünlü, Lazkiye'deki Hançer Operasyonu'nun Şifreleri [*The Codes of Operation Dagger in Latakia*], Sabah, 16 September 2018.

on a yacht. Cindy, his girlfriend, was actually a Mossad operative who had set a 'honey trap'.

At the heart of this mysterious spy thriller was a debate on Israel's nuclear secrets. As a matter of fact, various intelligence services, including the Central Intelligence Agency, were aware already in the 1960s that Israel was manufacturing nuclear weapons. Yet the Israeli government denied such claims at the time.

On October 5, 1986, *The Sunday Times* published a story that put Tel Aviv's denials to bed. Vanunu, whom the newspaper had interviewed prior to his abduction on September 30, had leaked information about Israel's nuclear weapons to the press.

Mordechai Vanunu had emigrated to Israel with his family in 1963. After serving in the military, he worked for the Dimona nuclear plant as a nuclear technician.

During his time there, Vanunu experienced an 'enlightening' and decided to air Israel's nuclear secrets. Vanunu left Dimona in 1985 after nine years and went on an 'exotic trip' with his severance package. He visited Nepal, Burma, Thailand and Australia, where he adopted Christianity at the Anglican Church.

Vanunu emerged as an activist and made a series of anti-nuclear statements. His revelations about his time in Dimona caught the eye of a local reporter. When the Australian press proved uninterested in Vanunu's leaks, the former nuclear technician contacted The Sunday Times with the help of the Australian reporter. He flew to Britain and aired Israel's nuclear secrets in an interview.

After getting caught in a honey trap, Vanunu appeared before an Israeli court that sentenced him to 18 years in prison. He was released in 2004, but banned from leaving Tel Aviv. He was imprisoned again in 2004, 2007 and 2010. Today, Vanunu remains in an 'open-air prison' in the Israeli capital.

Finally, Turkey conducted one of the most memorable intelligence operations in recent history in the regime-controlled city of Latakia in Syria, where a civil war has been raging since 2011. On 12 September 2018, the Turkish intelligence repatriated Yusuf Nazik, a terror suspect responsible for the May 2013 bombing in Reyhanli, Hatay that killed 50 innocent people, as part of Operation Dagger.

Especially in a war zone, it is more difficult to repatriate a target than to assassinate them. In such cases, field operatives must infiltrate hostile territory, apprehend their target without attracting attention to themselves, and return in one piece. As such, repatriation missions involve higher risk than assassination attempts.

The Assad regime's intelligence service, Mukhabarat, could not discover the names nor find photographs of Turkish operatives that carried out Operation Dagger. There have been no leaks about the identity of Turkish intelligence officers that repatriated the Reyhanli bomber. Hence our original point: The measure of a covert operation's success is to accomplish one's mission without leaving behind traces. From that perspective, the Jamal Khashoggi murder was probably one of the least successful secret operations in the history of espionage.

THE THREE UNKNOWN MEMBERS OF THE SAUDI DEATH SQUAD

Turkish President Recep Tayyip Erdogan announced that the Saudi death squad consisted of 15+3 members. *Sabah* revealed the identity and published photographs of one of the additional three operatives shortly after that announcement. One of the three men was Ahmad Abdullah al-Muzaini, the Saudi intelligence agency's station chief in Istanbul.[5] He was responsible for having Riyadh's orders carried out and the plan implemented.

For the first time ever, this book will reveal the identities of the two remaining members of the Saudi death squad: Saad Muid Al-Qarni, an intelligence officer who was the Saudi consulate's security chief, and Muflis Shaya al-Muslih, who was registered as a security officer but was an undercover intelligence operative. Like Al-Muzaini, those men carried diplomatic passports.

The three men's voices could not be heard on the 7.5-minute audio recording of Jamal Khashoggi's murder. That's because they oversaw recon missions rather than the execution itself.

According to profilers in the Turkish intelligence, the audio re-

---

5   Al Muzaini's critical role in the Khashoggi assassination is discussed in greater detail in Chapter IV.

cording featured a conversation in Arabic between the team leader, Mutreb, and Al-Tubaigy, the forensic expert who dismembered Jamal Khashoggi's body.

That conversation, which captivated the Turkish and global public, took pace in the scene of the crime – Saudi Arabia's consulate general in Istanbul.

CHAPTER II

Where?

1

THE AUDIO RECORDING

Behind Intelligence-to-Intelligence Diplomacy

Hakan Fidan, Turkey's powerful spy chief, slowly turned to his last foreign counterpart that he hosted at the National Intelligence Organization headquarters in the Turkish capital's Yenimahalle district:

> "You can listen to the tape now. I have already heard it, and I don't need to listen to a gruesome murder over and over again. My colleagues will inform me when you're done. We will talk again after to hear the audio recording."

Obviously, Fidan hadn't grown tired of hearing the Khashoggi murder. He was merely trying to convey the message to his guest and their colleagues about the gravity of the tape's content – of diplomatic savagery.

A group of Central Intelligence Agency officials, led by Director Gina Haspel, was the first foreign delegation to listen to the notorious tape. After meeting the Americans, the Turkish intelligence made the audio recording available to Saudi, British, French, Canadian and German intelligence chiefs. With the exception of the MI6 delegation, which heard the tape at the National Intelligence Organization's Istanbul Field Office, all spooks had to make the trip to the Turkish capital for the listening session.

Turkey's top spy hosted each foreign delegations personally and had them listen to the tape, in line with Turkish President Recep Tayyip Erdogan's 'intelligence diplomacy' strategy.

Simply put, the Turks believed that making the audio recording available to foreign secret services was the most effective way of shedding light on the Saudi journalist's murder, whose location and methodology was unlike any other violent crime that they had encountered. In other words, a significant part of the answer to the question –where?— remained unclear.

It was indeed noteworthy that the crime took place inside Saudi Arabia's consulate general in Istanbul. Jamal Khashoggi's killers did not go after him in the United States or London, but instead chose to take his life in Turkey. That leads us to the second key question about the mysterious incident: Where?

ARISTOTLE: THE INVENTOR OF 5W1H

The rule of 5W1H dates back to Aristotle. That rule applies to not just journalism but also police investigations and even the work of intelligence agencies. As a matter of fact, some intelligence agencies teach the 5H1W rule at their academic institutions.

The rule itself is quite simple. It helps us understand what happened, where and when it happened, how it happened, why it happened and, finally, who was involved in it.

Thomas Aquinas, a prominent thinker of the Middle Ages, stated that the 5W1H rule was the brainchild of Aristotle. After all, those questions can be found in Aristotle's Nicomachean Ethics. Some claim that Hermagoras of Temnos, an Ancient Greek master of rhetoric who lived in the second century B.C., used the same rule. In Latin, the same six questions are known as:

quis (who), *quid* (what), *quando* (when), *uni* (where), *cur* (why), and *quem ad modum* (how).

Yet it was William Cleaver Wilkinson, a 19th century American professor of theology, who helped 5W1H become popular.

THE UNBEARABLE LIGHTNESS OF IMPUNITY

The Saudi death squad's choice of crime scene, their country's consulate in Turkey, a country with rapidly growing clout in the Middle East and around the world, was not random at all.

Before engaging in a more detailed discussion of the Khashoggi murder's significance, let us describe its legal framework. Provided that the Washington Post columnist's slaying took place inside the Saudi consulate in Istanbul and that incident was virtually unprecedented, the Turkish authorities took all relevant legal steps with extraordinary care.

Article 31 of the Vienna Convention on Consular Relations stipulates that consular premises are untouchable:

1. Consular premises shall be inviolable to the extent provided in this Article.

2. The authorities of the receiving State shall not enter that part of the consular premises which is used exclusively for the purpose of the work of the consular post except with the consent of the head of the consular post or of his designee or of the head of the diplomatic mission of the sending State. The consent of the head of the consular post may, however, be assumed in case of fire or other disaster requiring prompt protective action.

3. Subject to the provisions of paragraph 2 of this Article, the receiving State is under a special duty to take all appropriate steps to protect the consular premises against any intrusion or damage and to prevent any disturbance of the peace of the consular post or impairment of its dignity.

4. The consular premises, their furnishings, the property of the consular post and its means of transport shall be im-

mune from any form of requisition for purposes of national defence or public utility. If expropriation is necessary for such purposes, all possible steps shall be taken to avoid impeding the performance of consular functions, and prompt, adequate and effective compensation shall be paid to the sending State.

Moreover, Article 41 of the Convention imposes significant restrictions on the personal violability of consular officers:

1. Consular officers shall not be liable to arrest or detention pending trial, except in the case of a grave crime and pursuant to a decision by the competent judicial authority.

2. Except in the case specified in paragraph 1 of this Article, consular officers shall not be committed to prison or liable to any other form of restriction on their personal freedom save in execution of a judicial decision of final effect.

3. If criminal proceedings are instituted against a consular officer, he must appear before the competent authorities. Nevertheless, the proceedings shall be conducted with the respect due to him by reason of his official position and, except in the case specified in paragraph 1 of this Article, in a manner which will hamper the exercise of consular functions as little as possible. When, in the circumstances mentioned in paragraph 1 of this Article, it has become necessary to detain a consular officer, the proceedings against him shall be instituted with the minimum of delay.

In accordance with Article 31(2), Turkish investigators entered Saudi Arabia's consulate general in Istanbul with Riyadh's permission and conducted a detailed search on the premises. Turkish officials also inspected the official residence of Consul General Mohammed Al-Otaiba, who rushed back to the Saudi capital on Oct. 16, with Saudi consent and under the supervision of Saudi officials.

A SECRET NOTE TO THE CIA

The Turkish claim –that Jamal Khashoggi was the victim of a gruesome murder that the Saudis planned in Riyadh and committed in Istanbul— rested firmly on credible intelligence. The strongest piece of evidence, in turn, was an audio recording of his final moments alive.

Turkey's diplomatic offensive in the wake of the Khashoggi murder was based on the body of evidence at its disposal. That strategy was born inside the Turkish presidential palace under Erdogan's instructions. In line with the the Turkish leader's orders, MIT Director Hakan Fidan held talks with the Kingdom and third parties, including the United States.

When the Turks caught wind of U.S. Secretary of State Mike Pompeo's Oct. 16 visit to Riyadh, President Erdogan summoned his intelligence chief. At the time, the Turkish effort to force Saudi Arabia into an admission of guilt had not yet succeeded. Pompeo was reportedly going to meet King Salman, hoping to learn more about what happened in Istanbul.

In a phone call around the same time, Erdogan and U.S. President Donald Trump discussed the powerful evidence that the Turks had on Khashoggi's killers. The first direct contact between the two leaders after the *Washington Post* columnist's death was on Oct. 22. In addition to counter-terrorism efforts and the situation in Syria, a Turkish readout announced, Erdogan and Trump had talked about the Khashoggi murder.

Ahead of Mike Pompeo's visit to the Kingdom, the Turkish president gave the National Intelligence Organization to brief the CIA's Ankara station chief at its headquarters on Oct. 15. The American was instructed to pass a note to the U.S. Secretary of State before he set foot in Saudi Arabia. That was how the Agency obtained a list, containing the names of 15 Saudi operatives that killed Jamal Khashoggi, and information about their arrival at Ataturk International Airport. The Turks also shared detailed information with the CIA's man in the Turkish capital about the role that each member of the Saudi death squad played as part of the lethal plot. Finally, Turkey's secret note explained for which department Khashoggi's killers worked: the General Intelligence Presidency, the Saudi Arabia Armed Forces, the Ministry of Foreign Affairs and the Interior Ministry. The Turks added that some members of Crown Prince Mohammed bin Salman's security detail were also among the slain journalist's executioners.

AN ENCRYPTED MESSAGE TO LANGLEY

The Turkish intelligence did not attach an official transcript of the notorious audio recording, which documented Jamal Khashoggi's final moments alive, to its message to the Central Intelligence Agency. Yet the authors explicitly stated that everything they included in the note was backed by credible intelligence.

Provided that Turkey handed the secret note to the CIA station chief, it was clear to all parties involved, including Mike Pompeo, that Gina Haspel was going to know about it. The U.S. Secretary of State had served as CIA Director between January 2017 and April 2018, and was therefore aware that official protocol required MIT to share information with the CIA liaison in the Turkish capital, who would encypt the message and forward it to Langley. Finally, the Agency would share the note with the State Department.

During his stint as CIA Director, Secretary Pompeo had met Fidan, Turkey's spy chief, on multiple occasions. They had known each other for a long enough time to be on a first-name basis. Yet the State Department did not know about the murder inside the Saudi consulate until they received Turkey's message from Langley. From the Turkish standpoint, the important point was to ensure that Pompeo knew everything there was to know before setting foot in Saudi Arabia. That was why he flew to Ankara on Oct. 17 after making a quick stop in Riyadh.

The reason that the Turkish intelligence excluded information about the content of the murder tape from their initial message to the United States was Ankara's plan to show the hand in good time – like a good poker player. To be clear, that move was in line with the country's original gameplan. Moreover, it only made sense for the Turkish spooks to keep their cards close to the chest: information, in their world, was power.

Out of courtesy, Turkey wanted to give the Saudis an opportunity to come clean before sharing evidence with the international community. It was therefore that Hakan Fidan told his Saudi counterpart, Abdulaziz bin Mohammed Al-Hawairini, to "cut off the gangrene-plagued arm" of the Kingdom's state apparatus. In other words, Ankara gave Riyadh some time to think. When it became clear that the Saudis weren't going to do the necessary thing, Turkey placed its cards on the table.

THE KHASHOGGI MURDER'S AUDIO RECORDING

A common misconception about the audio recording of Jamal Khashoggi's final moments alive was that it covered nothing but the 7.5 minutes that it took for the Saudi assassins to take the *Washington Post* columnist's life. In truth, there were much more detailed information on the tape.

One of the most interesting parts of the notorious audio recording related to a conversation among Jamal Khashoggi's killers before the 59-year-old Saudi citizen walked into his country's consulate. Caught on tape were Maher Abdulaziz Mutreb, a general in the Saudi intelligence, the forensic expert Al-Tubaigy and intelligence officer Al-Harby. On November 3, 2018, *Sabah's* Special Intelligence Unit revealed that those three men were part of the core team that murdered and dismembered Khashoggi.[1]

According to their conversation, which took place less than an hour before the *Washington Post* columnist entered the building, Riyadh's plan was to have the Saudi dissident killed and his body dismembered on the spot. That information was what convinved CIA Director Gina Haspel that the Saudis had Khashoggi's blood on their hands and the murder was indeed premeditated.

Haspel arrived at the Turkish capital Ankara on Oct.23 together with a large group of CIA officials. Thanks to Turkey's skillful

---

1   Abdurrahman Şimşek and Nazif Karaman, "İşte cesedi yok eden cellatlar" [Here Are The Executioners That Destroyed The Body], *Sabah*, 3 November 2018.

moves since the Saudi journalist disappeared into his country's consulate in Istanbul, she was already aware that MIT had some evidence at its disposal.[2] Yet the Americans couldn't be sure what to expect.

The CIA Director was eager to listen to the murder tape that everyone talked about, yet only a handful of individuals, including Turkish President Recep Tayyip Erdogan and his powerful spy chief, had actually heard. It was clear that she did not wish to have flown halfway across the world in vain, especially because she'd have to brief U.S. President Donald Trump through the Director of National Intelligence.

CIA IMPRESSED BY PRE-MURDER CHATTER

Haspel and her colleagues took a private jet to Ankara. Hakan Fidan and his associates hosted the U.S. delegation at the National Intelligence Organization headquarters. That day, the Turkish intelligence shared the audio recording of Jamal Khashoggi's slaying with a foreign secret service for the first time and told their guests what took place before and after the murder. At that point, not even the Saudi intelligence knew what exactly was on the tape.

First, Haspel heard the conversations among the Saudi assassins between noon and Jamal Khashoggi's arrival at 1.14 p.m. local time. The Agency's Arabic interpreter began to translate the audio: "We will first tell him that we are taking him to Riyadh. If he fails to comply, we will kill him here and get rid of the body."

At the time, only MIT officials knew that the man who uttered those words was Maher Abdulaziz Mutreb, the death squad's leader. The Turks immediately shared the conclusion, at which they had arrived after a comprehensive examination by MIT's audio experts, with the CIA delegation. The Americans then learned which operative said what in the lead-up to the Khashoggi murder.

Mutreb's words were addressed to Salah Muhammad Al-Tubaigy, who was the head of Saudi Arabia's Forensic Med-

---

2   Turkish officials had verbally confirmed to U.S. Secretary of State Mike Pompeo on Oct. 17 that they were in possession of said audio recordings.

icine Institute. Tubaigy was a key member of the assassination team because the killers needed him to chop the *Washington Post* columnist into small pieces.

According to the audio recording, the autopsy expert turned to his co-conspirators before they killed Jamal Khashoggi and said:

> *"I always work on cadavers. I know how to chop them up quite well. I have never worked on a warm body before, but I will take care of it easily. When I cut cadavers, I usually put on my headphones and listen to music. At the same time, I drink coffee and smoke."*

Al-Tubaigy continued:

> *"Jamal is quite tall – around 1.80 meters. It is easy to take apart the offering's [sic.] joints, but it will take time to chop it into pieces. Usually, one hangs the animal on a hook after butchering them to tear them into pieces. I have never done that on the ground. When I'm done chopping up, you will wrap the pieces in plastic bags, place them in suitcases and take them out."*

That the Saudi autopsy expert referred to the victim as an offering was significant because it revealed just how gruesome the murder really was.

What the assassins discussed in and around Consul General Mohammed Al-Otaiba's office revealed that the Khashoggi murder was planned in the Saudi capital and the operatives were determined to execute the *Washington Post* columnist if he resisted his extraordinary rendition. As a matter of fact, several members of the Saudi death squad took the Saudi journalist from the visa section to Al-Otaiba's office upstairs at 1.15 p.m. – just one minute after he walked through the consulate's door.

When the Saudis grabbed him to take him upstairs, Jamal Khashoggi asked them what they thought they were doing and told them to let his arm go. His captors did not comply with that request.

Once Khashoggi was in the room, Mutreb told him to sit down and informed the Saudi journalist that he would be taken to the Kingdom. The victim's response was brief and clear: "I am not going to Riyadh."

The Saudis then instructed the *Washington Post* columnist to text his son, Salah, who was in de facto captivity in Riyadh. Defying his captors, Khashoggi asked: "Are you going to kill me? Will you choke me?"

In an attempt to conceal his true intentions until the last possible moment, Mutreb told the journalist that all would be forgiven if he agreed to cooperate.

KHASHOGGI'S LAST STAND

According to the murder tape, Jamal Khashoggi remained dignified and determined when he faced the Saudi death squad. He was a seasoned journalist with enough experience to know, without a doubt, what the Saudi regime had dispatched its henchmen to Turkey to do. Still, the journalist did not show his killers any fear or seem hesitant in their presence. Khashoggi stood tall, even in his final breath – even at the expense of his life.

The message that the Saudis wanted Khashoggi to send to Salah was as follows: *"My son, I am in Istanbul. Do not worry if you cannot get through to me for a while."*

That the Saudi journalist refused to text his son caught his killers by surprise. At that very moment, there was a brief, deafening silence in the room. The tape kept rolling, documenting everything – including silence. Throughout the operation, none of the Saudi operatives spoke on an open line.

The killers had no intention of pleading with Khashoggi. Nor did they respond to the journalist's protestations. On Mutreb's orders, the men began to take out their tools and place them on the large desk. The victim remained seated. The sight of murder weapons did not seem to intimidate him. Even though the *Washington Post* columnist was about to meet his end, he did not bow to the Saudi regime. He did not try to leave the room either, even though the henchmen were clearly going to kill him. Under those circumstances, not many people would have shown the same kind of courage, dignity and calm.

All of a sudden, five Saudi agents attempted to choke Jamal Khashoggi to death – again, on Mutreb's orders. One of them, possibly Al-Harby, tried to block the victim's mouth, yet the journalist escaped his grasp.

Four men proceeded to attack the 59-year-old all at once. One of them, analysts concluded with absolute certainty, was Al-Zahrani.

The *Washington Post* columnist, who was going to die right there, in that room, just 7.5 minutes later, resisted his captors with a seemingly endless will to live. The henchmen, however, were physically stronger than Khashoggi and trained in this lethal art. The victim kept trying to liberate himself from the tight grasp of his killers' strong and merciless hands than squeezed his arms and legs.

JAMAL KHASHOGGI'S FINAL WORDS

In the end, the Saudis managed to block Khashoggi's mouth. *"Do not close my mouth,"* he pleaded with them. *"Let go of my mouth. I have asthma. Stop, you are choking me."*

Those were the Saudi journalist's last words. The executioners placed a plastic bag over Khashoggi's head, which would eventually claim his life.

For the next five minutes, the defiant victim put up a fierce resistance. The audio recording of those moments was so graphic and inhumane that even intelligence officers, whose tolerance is higher than ordinary citizens due to their professional backgrounds, were unsettled by what they heard.

As a matter of fact, CIA Director Gina Haspel, whom critics have repeatedly accused of torturing prisoners, was visibly moved by the murder tape when she heard it in the Turkish capital. The audio brought tears to the Arabic interpreter's eyes and they kept translating the killers' words with a broken voice.

It took the CIA delegation several minutes to recover from the horror. One could hear a pin drop inside the large room at the Turkish intelligence headquarters. The Americans were staring at each other.

The last thing on the murder tape was the wheezing of a man about to leave this world. By that moment, Khashoggi had no power left to fight back and there was not enough air inside the plastic bag, still over his head, to keep him alive.

At 1.24 p.m. on Oct. 2, Jamal Khashoggi passed away.

THE BONE SAW

With their victim choked to death, it was time for the Saudis to dismember his body. But first, they had to strip the journalist naked and hand his clothes to a body double. Two operatives, Al-Madani and Al-Qahtani, took the dead man's clothes. Since Khashoggi suffocated, there was no blood on his personal belongings. Al-Madani proceeded to put on the *Washington Post* columnist's still-warm clothes.

Tubaigy, the forensic expert who watched the Khashoggi murder from across the room, was responsible for chopping the victim's body into small pieces. The Saudi journalist was dismembered right where he died – in the Saudi consul general's office. Within minutes, the head of Saudi Arabia's Forensic Medicine Institute had transformed the room into an autopsy lab. Over the next 30 minutes, he chopped up the body with some help from Al-Harby and Al-Zahrani.

Blood would spray everywhere during the dismemberment process. Obviously, Tubaigy was aware of that problem. He proceeded to drain blood from Khashoggi's naked body with medical tools and flushed the fluid down the drain.[3]

The audio recording documented that the Saudis used a cleav-

---

3   Abdurrahman Şimşek and Nazif Karaman, "Cemal Kaşıkçı cinayetinde dehşet detaylar" [Horrible Details Of The Jamal Khashoggi Murder], *Sabah*, 23 November 2018.

er-like tool to break the dead journalist's bones. Every once in a while, the forensic expert switched on an electric autopsy saw. Tubaigy used the blender-like, handheld device to mercilessly tear the victim's body into pieces within a matter of minutes. He was possibly as excited as the ancient Egyptians who invented the bone saw and as calm and collected as modern practitioners.

Turkish analysts had concluded upon hearing the sound of a running engine that the killers used a bone saw to dismember Jamal Khashoggi. Forensic experts concurred.

During the dismemberment process, Tubaigy could be heard shouting instructions and yelling at the thugs: "What are you waiting for?" As the Saudi operatives put on a performance, whose savagery was matched by Hannibal Lecter from the *Silence of the LaMBS* alone, at the consulate in Istanbul, some members of the consular staff fell ill.

To be clear, Tubaigy was in no position to tell his fellow murderers to "listen to music" – as some news outlets reported. He concentrated fully on the unprecedented task at hand. The forensic expert was caught on tape before the murder, however, as saying that he usually listened to music at work. Yet his gruesome task was nothing like chopping up cadavers. Indeed, Tubaigy did not listen to music at 'work' that day.

At some point, the U.S. media began to describe Jamal Khashoggi's murderers as rogue killers. That term was attributed to Turkish officials.[4]

HASPEL: A FIRST IN THE HISTORY OF ESPIONAGE

The CIA Director was visibly moved by what she'd heard. She was aware that the chatter among the Saudi operatives before Khashoggi's arrival at the consulate amounted to proof of premeditation.

A moment of silence followed the listening session. Gina Haspel turned to her Turkish counterpart, Hakan Fidan, and told

---

4   Ertuğrul Özkök, "Kadavra uzmanlığından kemik testereli cinayete" [From Cadaver Specialization To A Bone-Saw Murder], *Hürriyet*, 18 October 2018.

him that gaining access to that evidence was one of the most significant accomplishments in the history of tradecraft. She proceeded to congratulate the Turkish spy chief.

Although the Turkish intelligence kept the audio file to itself, it shared an official copy of the transcript with the Central Intelligence Agency.

On the morning of her return trip to the United States, on Oct. 23, the CIA Director shared her findings with U.S. President Donald Trump at the President's Daily Briefing.[5] Secretary of State Mike Pompeo was also in the room.

Three days later, White House Spokeswoman Sarah Sanders confirmed that Trump was briefed by Haspel, who had met her Turkish counterparts in Ankara, on the murder tape. She added that the administration was yet to decided how to move forward.[6]

The Washington Post, citing anonymous sources, reported three weeks after the CIA Director's visit to the National Intelligence Organization headquarters on Langley's conclusion that Saudi Crown Prince Mohammed bin Salman had ordered the hit on Jamal Khashoggi.

Another U.S. official told the Associated Press that the intelligence community was confident about MBS's culpability.

The Washington Post story stressed that the CIA assessment was credible and had the potential to undermine the Trump administration's effort to maintain a strong relationship with Mohammed bin Salman.

CIA analysts, the newspaper wrote, took into consideration a phone call between Jamal Khashoggi and Khaled bin Salman, the Saudi ambassador to the United States and Mohammed's brother, that the U.S. intelligence had intercepted.

During that phone call, anonymous sources told *The Washington Post*, Prince Khaled instructed the Saudi journalists to pick up his official papers from the Saudi consulate in Istanbul and reassured him that it would be safe for him to visit the dip-

5   Serdar Turgut, CIA Başkanı Gina Haspel'in Türkiye dönüşünden sonraki ilk başkanlık brifinginin konusu Türkiye'ydi [Turkey Was The Subject Of The First Pdb After Gina Haspel's Return From Turkey], *Habertürk*, 26 October 2018.
6   Beyaz Saray'dan Cemal Kaşıkçı açıklaması [White House Statement On Jamal Khashoggi], *Timeturk*, 29 October 2018.

lomatic mission.

Fatimah Baeshen, a spokeswoman for the Saudi Embassy in Washington, promptly denied the claim that Khaled bin Salman had spoken with Jamal Khashoggi and claimed that the CIA was wrong.

The same newspaper also reported that the U.S. Government knew in advance that the *Washington Post* columnist could be in trouble, yet did not know about the specific threat prior to his Oct. 2 disappearance.

In other words, the CIA, like its Turkish counterpart, was not engaging in real-time surveillance at the time of the Khashoggi murder. They uncovered the truth retroactively.

"CUT OFF THE GANGRENE-PLAGUED ARM"

In his first meeting with the Saudi intelligence chief, Abdulaziz bin Mohammed Al-Howeirani, after the Khashoggi murder, Hakan Fidan –whom the Saudi addressed as "Doctor"— did not talk about the evidence at Turkey's disposal. Yet he made it clear to his counterpart that Ankara had a strong hand.

"You did it. You are suffering from gangrene. You must cut off the gangrene-plagued arm," said Turkey's top spy and added: "You get to decided when and where you will cut. If you're too late, however, the disease will spread to all parts of the body."

In retrospect, Fidan was right. With Saudi Arabia issuing denial after denial, the problem got bigger and bigger. In the end, Riyadh had to pay a heavy price to survive the crisis. That Jamal Khashoggi's killers included officials from the Saudi intelligence, military, diplomatic corps, interior ministry and the Forensic Medicine Institute placed the immense political responsibility of what happened on Mohammed bin Salman's shoulders.

Without the crown prince's knowledge, it would have been impossible for so many Saudi officials from such diverse professional backgrounds to work together on any mission. Even the head of the General Intelligence Presidency lack the political power to make that call. One way or another, there must have been a political decision-maker involved. That puppetmaster was Mohammed bin Salman – a.k.a. *MBS*.

To be clear, the Turks knew the truth from the start. Yet they wanted their western counterparts, including the United States, to appreciate the gravity of the situation and come to terms with the fact.

The reason that the Kingdom dispatched four intelligence operatives to Turkey shortly after the Khashoggi murder was to figure out whether the Turks were aware of Mohammed bin Salman's involvement and what Ankara could actually prove. That was why one of the Saudi representatives stayed in the Turkish capital for a while and monitored the criminal investigation underway.

It wasn't until later that Saudi Arabia learned about the audio recording at Turkey's disposal. Had they known earlier, during or even after Jamal Khashoggi's slaying inside the Saudi consulate on Oct. 2, Riyadh would have certainly been more cautious. Knowing that the Turkish intelligence had proof of what exactly happened, Riyadh proceeded to bury all evidence of the crime with extra care.

Upon receiving a formal request from Turkish investigators to search the consulate and the consular residence per the Vienna Convention, the Saudis cleaned up the crime scene. Their actions, to say the least, amounted to a grave abuse of international law.

Saudi Arabia delayed the search for ten days after the Chief Public Prosecutor's Office in Istanbul filed the request on Oct. 10. The Turks had been asking to look for criminal evidence using luminol.

The Saudis did everything in their power to delay the search. First, they demanded that Turkish investigators scanned the premises visually and without using luminol. Saudi officials raised that issue in a meeting with the Turkish prosecutor and police officers at the Turkish National Police headquarters in Istanbul. Turkey responded negatively. The Saudi officials then asked Turkey to state in advance who would be on the search party and on what grounds. In the second meeting, the Turks agreed to that request in line with the Vienna Convention.

By asking the Turkish authorities for more information about the investigators and the use of luminol, Saudi Arabia did more than gain time. It also determined what it would have to do in order to prevent the Turks from finding the murder evidence.

Throughout that process, international law seriously impeded Turkey's efforts to discover incriminating evidence against the murderers. Unlike Riyadh, the Turks strictly adhered to the Vienna Convention – which the Saudis used as an excuse to bury the physical evidence.

HOW TO CONTAMINATE A CRIME SCENE
IN FOUR SIMPLE STEPS

Saudi officials covered up the evidence of Jamal Khashoggi's slaying in four steps. In the immediate aftermath of the murder, the 15-member death squad cleaned up the crime scene to a limited degree. Hours later, in the afternoon of Oct. 2, diplomatic staff at the Saudi consulate swept the crime scene a second time.

Yet two Saudis, whom Riyadh dispatched to Turkey ostensibly to cooperate with the Turkish investigation, were responsible for the destruction of all criminal evidence. Called 'erasers' in intelligence jargon, this specialized team, which consisted of a toxicologist and a chemist, flew to Istanbul nine days after the Khashoggi murder to bury the evidence.

Among the 11 Saudi officials that traveled to Turkey on Oct. 11 were chemist Khaled Yahya Al-Zahrani and toxicologist Ahmad Abdulaziz Al-Janubi. Their mission was to cover up criminal evidence – under the pretext of helping Turkish investigators.

The two men checked into the S, a luxury hotel on the Western bank of the Bosphorus, under fake names and visited the Saudi consulate every day for a whole week.

Al-Zahrani and Al-Janubi conducted the fourth and final 'sweep' at the Saudi consulate and official residence. After visiting the building repeatedly until Oct. 17 along with nine other officials on a faux research mission, the chemist and the toxicologist left

Turkey on Oct. 21.

Saudi Arabia did not permit Turkish investigators to search either building until the two operatives were done burying the evidence. On Oct. 16, just before the search began in the residence, Riyadh recalled its consul general, Mohammed Al-Otaiba, from Turkey.

THE FIVE MEN AT THE HEART OF THE PLOT

The Turkish police searched Saudi Arabia's consulate in Istanbul on Oct. 15-16. The residence was searched on Oct. 17. According to Turkish officials, the chemist and the toxicologist kept cleaning both buildings until those dates.[7]

That was possibly the most diligent cleaning job since the birth of alchemy, in the history of chemistry and since the discovery of toxins.

In later meetings with Saudi officials, the Turkish intelligence told them bluntly that Riyadh's efforts to bury the evidence was not lost on anyone. The Saudi response was also straightforward: "We know that you need criminal evidence. We are merely taking precautions."

The infamous conversation among the chief suspects – Mutreb, Tubaigy and Al-Harby— was caught on tape around noon on Oct. 2. According to CCTV footage that the Turkish police obtained, the forensic expert entered the Saudi consulate at 10.43 a.m. Yet the aforementioned conversation took place after the team gathered at Al-Otaiba's office. According to the murder tape, the Saudi consul did not actually tell the killers to "do that thing somewhere else."

Turkish officials assess that the murder suspects, including the body double, Al-Madani, are in an isolated place, but not behind bars, in the Kingdom. In a written statement, the Saudi attorney general announced that the prosecution demanded the death penalty for five suspects. Turkey believes that those individuals are kept isolated in an attempt to keep them under control.

---

7   Abdurrahman Şimşek and Nazif Karaman, "Delilleri silici ekip kararttı" [The Eraser Team Buried The Evidence], *Sabah*, 5 November 2018.

The obvious reason for limiting culpability to just five operatives is to save anyone that was not directly involved in the Khashoggi murder. Although Saudi Arabia refuses to identify the murderers, who might face capital punishment, those individuals are probably Mutreb, Tubaigy, Al-Harby, Al-Madani and Al-Zahrani.

2

WHERE IS KHASHOGGI'S BODY

"This Isn't a Banana Republic."

One of the most significant –yet unanswered—questions that surround the Khashoggi murder relates to the whereabouts of the victim's remains. Under Islamic law, the body (or parts thereof) must be buried and there must be a tomb, where the deceased's loved ones can recite prayers. Although Saudi Arabia admitted to the murder, it did not help the Turks locate the body. If anything, Saudi officials have been actively blocking efforts to find the *Washington Post* columnist's remains.

The National Intelligence Organization and the Turkish National Police continue the search, leaving no stone unturned. Yet that effort is yet to produce clear answers. There are possible and probable answers, but no concrete results.

The closest thing to an actual answer is that Khashoggi's remains are at the bottom of a well at the consular residence. With less certainty, Turkish officials assess that the body parts are buried elsewhere around the residence.

Provided that Turkish intelligence and law enforcement agents leave nothing to chance, they have looked in other places as well. Most recently on Nov. 26, the security forces raided a luxury villa in the city of Yalova, but could not find any traces of the murdered journalist. To be clear, the Turkish authorities had told the authors of this book prior to that raid that they were not hopeful.

Turkey continues to believe that the body parts are in the well. That is because intelligence analysts and law enforcement agents were able to track the body from the Saudi consulate to the consular residence, yet no further. The Turks haven't been able to search the well at the Saudi consul general's official home, because Riyadh refuses to permit Turkish investigators to conduct the search.

The same Saudi official that are blocking the search for the body were responsible for delaying the initial sweep. In response to the Turkish request to inspect the crime scene with forensic equipments, they said that the police was only welcome to search the premises visually. A senior police officer, outraged by the Saudi response, ticked off: "This isn't some banana republic. We won't be coming to your building to sip tea and sample pastries. A visual search is out of question. The only way we can conduct the search is with forensic gear."

The Saudis told the Turkish police to send them information about the evidence discovery team and how exactly they would conduct the search. They said that Riyadh would have to sign off on the Turkish request.

Saudi officials did not actually need any of that information, but could really use the extra time. Either way, the two sides could not make any progress. It took a phone call between the Turkish president and the King of Saudi Arabia on Oct. 15 to get the green light.

When the search began, the police had no prior knowledge about the layout of the Saudi consulate or the consular residence. Citing the Vienna Convention, Saudi minders followed the discovery team's every footstep.

A piece of marble, which could not be spotted at first sight, was next to the pool's engine room down a long aisle. A former consulate employee, who shared information with the police, told the authorities about that well.

Prior to the search, the police pulled the social security records of all former and current employees of the Saudi consulate and proceeded to question them. It was a former employee, who worked with the Saudis for two year, that told law enforcement about the well.

Thanks to the confidential informant's testimony, police officers were quick to spot the well on Oct. 17 and asked the Saudis allow firefighters to access the facility and drain the water for an inspection. The Saudis refused to cooperate yet again: "You have permission to search the building. Riyadh must sign off on your request to inspect the well separately."

Although Saudi officials reassured their Turkish counterparts that they asked for Riyadh's permission, the Turks are yet to hear back from the Kingdom. The well, which the Saudis seemed hell-bent on keeping away from prying eyes, was 21 meters deep. The water was an estimated nine meters deep. It resembled the infamous wells found in Hollywood horror films, but it was actually one of some 200 wells that Istanbulites dug in the Levent district during the water shortage of the early 1990s.

THE SECRET AT THE RESIDENCE'S WELL

The Turkish investigator collected a water sample from the well, yet they did not find any DNA there. Nor did Turkey's Institute of Forensic Medicine detect any acid in the well.

Those findings, however, are not conclusive. The killers may have dumped the body inside a waterproof container. In other words, it is still highly likely that Jamal Khashoggi's body remains at the bottom of the well.

The investigation into the whereabouts of Khashoggi's remains led investigators and the Turkish police to the well below the Saudi consulate's residence. That was a critical lead. The first-ever story on the well, too, appeared in *Sabah*:

On Oct. 17, the day after Consul General Mohammed al-Otaiba returned to Riyadh, crime scene investigators began their search at the consular residence. Since the police knew about the well beforehand, they easily found where it was.

Keeping in mind that current employees working at the residence could be reluctant to disclose information, fearing that they could lose their jobs, the Turkish authorities questioned former employees as well.

The Police Crime Scene Investigation Department used information obtained from a former employee to create a three-dimensional illustration of the well.

When Saudi officials did not consent to a search of the well, the Turkish police notified the Chief Prosecutor's Office in Istanbul. The prosecution filed a report indicated that the police could not search the well. The Chief Prosecutor's Office, through the Justice Ministry, filed a request with the Saudi government. Yet the Saudis refuse to permit the search.[1]

The most likely scenario is that the body is in the residence's well. It is impossible, however, to search that area illegally or secretly – which would be a violation of the Vienna Convention.

The public debate on the whereabouts of Khashoggi's remains rekindled when the police searched a villa in the city of Yalova on Nov. 26.[2] Like the earlier discovery of a Mercedes-Benz vehicle registered to the Saudi consulate in a parking garage in Sultangazi, the search excited the public.

On Nov. 26, the Chief Prosecutor's Office in Istanbul issued a written statement regarding the search in Yalova. According to that statement, a member of the Saudi death squad, Mansour Othman Aba Hussein, contacted Mohammed Ahmed A. Al-Fowzan (codename Ghozan) on Oct. 1, 2018.[3] The authorities conducted the search based on that intercepted call, which led them to think that Khashoggi's body may have been taken to Yalova.

---

1   Abdurrahman Şimşek and Nazif Karaman, "Kuyudaki sır" [The Secret at the Well], Sabah, 25 November 2018.

2   Yalova'da lüks villada Kaşıkçı'nın cesedi için arama yapılıyor [Search underway for Khashoggi's body at luxury villa in Yalova], Milliyet, 26 November 2018.

3   It is unclear why the individual had a codename.

The prosecution's statement made references to earlier written statements. An Oct. 31 statement provided the public with the gist of the prosecution's argument:

Within the framework of the investigation into the murder of journalist Jamal Khashoggi inside the consulate of the Kingdom of Saudi Arabia in Istanbul on Oct. 2, 2018,

As mentioned in detail in statements to the press dated Oct. 7, Oct. 18 and Oct. 31, 2018,

Jamal Khashoggi was killed inside the Kingdom of Saudi Arabia's consulate in Istanbul, according to a plan conceived by the suspect(s) in advance, through choking and dismemberment.

As part of the Republican Chief Prosecution's multi-dimensional investigation,

It has been detected that Mansour Othman M. Aba Hussein, who was among the suspects that arrived at [Turkey] on Oct. 1 and Oct. 2, 2018 for the purpose of killing Jamal Khashoggi, contacted on Oct. 1, the day before the incident, Mohammed Ahmed A. Al-Fowzan (codename Ghozan), a citizen of Saudi Arabia who resided in the village of Samanli in Yalova.

We believe that said phone call was related to the disappearance/concealment of the murdered journalist Jamal Khashoggi's body upon dismemberment. Therefore,

The Istanbul Police Department is conducting a search, under the supervision of the Republican Chief Prosecutor's Office, based on the Istanbul 7th Penal Court's ruling No. 2018/5664. Updates will follow.[4]

---

4   Statement by the Chief Prosecutor's Office in Istanbul, dated 26 November 2018.

The prosecution would have certainly shared updates with the public if the investigators had found body pieces in Yalova. Yet no such statement was made. The search was inconclusive, because – as mentioned in this section— Khashoggi's remains are most likely in the well under the Saudi consulate's residence.

THE PARADOX OF REAL TIME INTELLIGENCE

One of the most controversial aspects of the Khashoggi murder is whether the audio of the murder was obtained in real time – in technical terms, whether the intelligence relied on HUMINT, or human intelligence, in addition to ELINT, or electronic intelligence.

Regardless of which authority eavesdropped on the Saudi consulate, it is certain that no official was listening to the audio with headphones by the recording equipment. Such recordings are made automatically.

The HUMINT stage began after 6 p.m. on Oct. 2, when it became clear that Khashoggi was missing and the tape was rolled back for the investigation.

As such, there is no reason to believe that the audio was obtained as real time intelligence – no matter who was listening and how.

Here's why that piece of information matters: Turkey obtained the entire audio recording through an undisclosed method and analyzed the tape to access information about the murder as well as its lead-up and aftermath. In other words, there was no system that eavesdropped on the consulate in real time and shared that information with the authorities simultaneously. Clearly, any secret service that used such an equipment would step in and prevent the murder instantly.

The authors of this book, however, have obtained information about the audio recording from primary sources and that information is clear enough to end all speculation. What we know includes answers to some critical questions that Ertuğrul Özkök, a columnist for *Hürriyet*, posed in an Oct. 24 column:

The world curiously awaits that audio recording. Three claims have been made regarding the 7-minute audio recording of Khashoggi's death.

FIRST: It was recorded on an Apple Watch. Shortly afterwards, it became clear that that was a technical impossibility.
SECOND: The Turkish intelligence had bugged the place a long time ago.
THREE: The Turkish intelligence had a very solid informant inside.

Judging by the international media coverage, if there is an audio recording [at Turkey's disposal], Turkey could face the following questions in coming days:

-       If there is an audio recording, did [Turkey] detect the conversation in real time or after the murder?
-       Khashoggi was told to come back four days after [his first visit to the consulate]. During that time period, was there no information regarding a plan to commit murder from the inside?
-       If [Turkey] conducted real-time surveillance, why were the 15 individuals allowed to leave? Why were their bags never searched? Why did [Turkey] not start monitoring the consulate's exit immediately?

We answered the third question above. Let us, however, state it again: The audio recording was not real time intelligence. There is no reason to explain that this kind of surveillance cannot be conducted through the intermediary of informants either.

The Saudis dismissed the possibility that Turkey could access the audio recording, whose content we have shared in this book, since the beginning. Therefore, they had no problem talking about ways to bury the evidence after the murder.

On Oct. 26, Özkök wrote another column that contained false information:

CIA Director Gina Haspel's visit to Turkey was the most significant event in the last 48 hours. Let me share some hidden details about that visit.

Question 1: *Did the CIA Director listen to the audio recording in Istanbul or Ankara?* Neither U.S. nor Turkish media outlets reported on that aspect with certainty. According to my research, she listened to it in Istanbul.

Question 2: *Who played the recording of torture to the CIA Director?* Again, according to my research, MIT President Hakan Fidan himself played the tape [for Haspel]. Foreign Minister Mevlüt Çavuşoğlu, too, suggested the same thing by telling reporters to ask Fidan about it.

Question 3: *Did Turkey hand over the recording of torture to the CIA Director or just play it for her?* According to Turkish and U.S. outlets, the recording was not shared but only played.

Question 4: *Did the CIA Director hear the entire recording or part thereof?* The Turkish media reported that the tape was played. Yet the New York Times published a confusing story yesterday, claiming that the Americans could authenticate the tape if the entire recording were given to them.

There is no question about the authenticity of the audio recording. Moreover, I could not understand why the New York Times would write that sentence, provided that the Washington Post, which has been following the incident very closely, has no doubt about the tape's authenticity.

CIA Director Gina Haspel is known as a woman who can use every single cell in her brain. The U.S. media first heard her name in 2002, when she led a team that questioned Al Qaeda operatives Abu Zubaydah and Abd al-Rahim al-Nashiri.

The media reported that the prisoners were waterboarded. Zubaydah was allegedly waterboarded 83 times in a month, his head was hit against a wall and he consequently lost his left eye.

In other words, she reminds people of Carrie Mathison, an agent and interrogator from the TV series *Homeland*. Therefore, I wondered what her face looked like and what her comments were as she listened to the tape. Given her professional background, she is among the best individuals to assess the recording.

I wondered about one more thing: *Could she have brought along an Arabic speaker, who worked with her in past interrogations?*[5]

Let us begin with the last question: We wrote that an Arabic interpreter was with Haspel. Yet it is highly unlikely that the same person was with her in interrogation rooms. To answer the third question, the media reports were accurate: Haspel heard the audio recording yet did not receive a copy. The Turkish authorities shared with her a transcript – which we wrote above.

Let us now correct Özkök, who wrote that the Turks played the murder tape for Haspel in Istanbul:

The CIA Director and her colleagues listened to the tape in Ankara. The only secret service to hear the audio recording in Istanbul was the British intelligence.

The answer to the second question is correct. An MIT delegation, led by Hakan Fidan, played the tape.

As for the fourth question: The CIA Director heard not the entire tape but a 7.5-minute section related to the murder and chatter among Saudi operatives prior to the killing.

MIT CRACKS THE CASE IN TWO HOURS

Hatice Cengiz reported the incident to the police at 5.50 p.m. That was when the Turkish intelligence became aware of Jamal Khashoggi's disappearance. 10 minutes later, Yasin Aktay called Hakan Fidan, the Turkish intelligence chief, who notified the or-

5   Ertuğrul Özkök, "CIA Başkanı'na o kaydı kim ve nerede dinletti?" [Who played the tape to the CIA Director, and where?], Hürriyet, 26 October 2018.

ganization's field office in Istanbul. Around the same time, audio analysts and Arabic language specialists listened to the audio recording, including the Washington Post columnist's final moments alive and the pre-murder chatter among the Saudi operatives, and filed their initial report.

By 8 p.m., two hours after MIT obtained the murder tape, Fidan had learned that Khashoggi was killed inside the Saudi consulate. He shared everything he knew with the Turkish president. That was the first time that the Turkish intelligence briefed Erdogan on the incident.

Over the following days, Fidan informed Erdogan that the intelligence was in possession of an audio recording of what happened before, during and after the murder. The spy chief arrived at the meeting with a USB flash drive that contained the audio file, which Erdogan heard together with Fidan and received a copy of the transcript.

After that meeting, the Turkish president formed a special team –consisting of Fidan, his communications director Fahrettin Altun and senior aide Ibrahim Kalin, to investigate all aspects of the murder. Erdogan's meeting with the three men kicked off Turkey's public diplomacy offensive.

KHASHOGGI THE ZIONIST

Convinced by the Turkish offensive that Ankara knew who had killed Khashoggi and was in a position to prove it, the Saudi intelligence chief came up with the following excuse: "Jamal Khashoggi was a Zionist. He worked for them. Hatice Cengiz is a Qatari agent. They were trying to undermine Saudi Arabia's relations with its sister Turkey."

The Turks responded that there was no evidence to support that claim and even if that were the case, it would not justify Riyadh sending 15 operatives to murder the *Washington Post* columnist.

For the record, the Turkish intelligence did look into the Saudi allegation that Hatice Cengiz had links to Qatar's secret service. As a matter of fact, they investigated potential ties between the dead journalist's fiancée and any intelligence agency.

The Turkish investigation revealed that Cengiz had made contact with diplomats from an undisclosed Middle Eastern country, for which she worked as a translator. Yet there was nothing to suggest that she was an agent or an informant. In other words, there was no contact between Khashoggi's fiancée and any active foreign spy. As such, the Turks concluded that Cengiz wasn't a professional spook.

The authorities did not specify which country's diplomatic mission was in touch with Hatice Cengiz, but it was certainly a Middle Eastern country. Based on that limited knowledge, it would be unreasonable to think that Khashoggi's fiancée worked for the Egyptians (just because she studied there) or the Saudis (just because she spoke Arabic).

Either way, the Saudi claim about Khashoggi and his fiancée raised two red flags: Branding the slain journalist as a zionist behind closed doors, Riyadh was trying to cozy up to Israel. At the same time, the Saudis portrayed Hatice Cengiz as a Qatari spy in an attempt to discredit her and to fuel tensions between Turkey and a close ally, which happened to be on bad terms with the Kingdom. In the end, MIT could not confirm the claim about Hatice Cengiz.

WHO BUGGED THE SAUDI CONSULATE?

The revelation that Turkey possessed an audio recording of the Khashoggi murder compelled the Saudis to take a range of counter-intelligence measures.

Riyadh dispatched a group of specialists to Istanbul and checked the consulate for hidden listening devices. They discovered around ten pieces of equipment in various parts of the compound.

Having located the bugs, Saudi officials urged the Turkish police to mention them in their official reports. A law enforcement agent, who was around the Saudi consulate at the time, turned that request down – in line with their instructions. After all, they did not wish to take responsibility for listening devices that an unknown third party had planted: "We do not know anything about those devices, so we won't sign anything. You didn't let us search the building for a whole month. How are we supposed to know that you didn't plant the bugs yourselves?"

Intelligence agencies around the world are united by their concern for the safety of their nation's diplomatic missions abroad. Yet that particular type of surveillance had never made headlines until the Khashoggi murder – when the only evidence was an audio recording.

The Khashoggi tape qualified as evidence from the intelligence community's standpoint. Turkey used its finding to shed light on the Saudi journalist's murder as part of a masterful diplomatic gameplan.

Intelligence-to-intelligence diplomacy has been crucial throughout history and it will never cease to be important. Yet it is noteworthy that relations between rival secret services are more significant today than ever.

Thanks to Turkish President Recep Tayyip Erdogan's political skill, vast experience and iron will, Turkey remains one of the most effective players in the area of intelligence-to-intelligence diplomacy. Independent observers concede that Erdogan has proved highly successful in this particular area since Turkey's fight against FETÖ, a unique and unprecedented national security threat, began in 2012. That accomplishment strengthens the country's hand in the face of extraordinary challenges like the Khashoggi murder.

Obviously, the Turkish diplomatic offensive did not go unanswered abroad. Yet critics failed to rain on Turkey's parade. For example, shortly after *Sabah* published the names and photographs of Jamal Khashoggi's murderers, certain U.S.-based think tanks responded by accusing the Turkish government of politicizing the incident. Those accusations, however, fell on deaf ears.

What the Saudi agents discovered in their consulate were high-tech listening devices. It is possible to eavesdrop on any given location using the so-called passive pieces of equipment - which costs up to $2 million per device. Once installed, that tool facilitates remote audio surveillance via GSM base stations.

The authors of this book have not heard the murder tape. Yet they obtained vast information from trusted government sources and that information is included in this book.

Here is what we can say about the audio recording: Until now, all news organizations including Turkish media outlets, reported on the tape based on second-hand information. Over time, the audio recording evolved into an urban legend. By contrast, our sources have personally listened to the infamous tape and, as such, we do not doubt their credibility.

If any international media outlets would like to report on the findings mentioned in this book and confirm the veracity of our claims first, all they would have to do is to contact their own sources in relevant government agencies – which know everything there is to know about the audio recording and therefore are in a position to confirm or deny the details made public here.

Provided that the Turkish authorities used intelligence-based evidence to crack the case, it would not be wrong to credit the Turkish intelligence for this accomplishment. All available evidence shows that the Turks did not receive any help from foreign intelligence agencies. That includes the Central Intelligence Agency and Mossad.

The Saudis planned and carried out the Khashoggi murder. It is possible that some clique within the Saudi state, anticipating the fallout from the journalist's death, may have talked MBS into ordering the hit. Yet there is no evidence that supports that claim and we have no intention of entertaining a remote possibility that is not backed by the facts.

GONE WITH HIS SECRETS

By contrast, there was an actual development, which took place after the Khashoggi murder, that many observers dismissed as fake news:

Mashaal Saad Al-Bostani, a member of the 15-strong team

that murdered journalist Jamal Khashoggi inside Saudi Arabia's consulate in Istanbul, died in a mysterious accident in Riyadh. Al-Bostani, a lieutenant in the Royal Air Force, thus took his secrets to the grave.[6]

That the Saudis attempted to take Khashoggi's cell phones, which he had handed to Hatice Cengiz before walking into the consulate, upon realizing the strength of the evidence at Turkey's disposal made perfect sense. As a matter of fact, before the Saudi attorney general's office asked the Turks to hand over the journalist's two cell phones, MIT received the same request from the Saudi intelligence chief.

In that meeting, Fidan told Al-Howairani that the Turkish intelligence did not have Khashoggi's phones – and even if it did, he could not just hand over criminal evidence to the Kingdom. To the best of our knowledge, the two cell phones reamin in the custody of the Turkish National Police and their passwords remain unknown.

Like the Turkish spy chief, Irfan Fidan, the chief public prosecutor in Istanbul, had to turn down Saudi Arabia's request.

Instead of cooperating with the Turkish investigation, the Kingdom's spies and jurists, under the crown prince's orders, tried to find out what else Turkey knew about the killers in an attempt to cover up the crime.

That Turkey shared intelligence with western spy agencies, including the CIA, left the Saudis increasingly worried. Although the Turks kept the audio recording to themselves, they provided the British, Canadian, French and German secret services with the transcript.

MBS TRIES TO MEET HAKAN FIDAN

Turkey knew plenty about the Khashoggi murder and was in a position to change the conversation at will. Therefore,

---

6   Burak Doğan, "Riyad birini susturdu" [Riyadh silenced one of them], *Yeni Safak*, 18 October 2018.

Mohammed bin Salman requested an audience with Hakan Fidan, Turkey's top spy, in Riyadh. At Erdogan's request, Fidan rejected the Saudi offer.

As an intelligence officer, Fidan usually could afford to be more flexible when it came to taking meetings. Yet meeting MBS under the circumstances could have conveyed the unintended message to the Saudis that Turkey was open to negotiation. It was the same concern that informed the Turkish prosecutor's decision to decline an unconventional invitation by his Saudi counterpart to visit Riyadh.

Up until the Khashoggi murder, Mohammed bin Salman, who unsuccessfully attempted to meet Hakan Fidan, was a leader of the anti-Turkey bloc that included Saudi Arabia and the United Arab Emirates.

Something akin to the Shia resistance line that stretches from Iran to Lebanon via Iraq and Syria has emerged in western-dominated Arab countries. As part of that group, the Kingdom has been engaging in anti-Turkey activities. That alliance brings together unlikely bedfellows: U.S. Evangelicals, Israel, Egypt, Mohammed bin Salman and the UAE Crown Prince Mohammad bin Zayed.

The Turks are fully aware that the emerging axis, whose primary purpose was to undermine Iran's regional influence, has been working against Turkish interests as well. For the record, the United States has openly sided with those countries – just as Turkey took cross-border precautions against the national security threat that PYD/YPG, the terrorist organization PKK's Syrian affiliate, poses.

Prior to the Khashoggi murder, the Turkish government knew that the Kingdom was using its vast financial resources to spread anti-Turkey sentiment in the Middle East, and urged Riyadh to cease those attacks. Removing MBS from his post, however, was something that the Turks were unwilling and unable to do. Nonetheless, it is no secret that Turkey orchestrated a media campaign in the United States to mount pressure on Saudi Arabia.

oday, U.S. President Donald Trump knows, based on what MIT told the Central Intelligence Agency, that MBS was the highest-ranking Saudi politician to sanction the murder, and continues to look for ways to defuse the crisis. When the anti-Iran/anti-Turkey bloc proves too high-maintenance for Washington's taste, the Trump administration could cut them loose to save itself. The way that the Turks managed the aftermath of the Khashoggi murder turned Mohammed bin Salman into the bloc's weakest link. His fate, therefore, hinges on Trump's decision.

According to intelligence analysts, it was Mohammed bin Salman that ordered the hit on Jamal Khashoggi. The slain journalist's columns were full of unpleasant things for the Kingdom's crown prince.

One of those critical essays appeared in *The Washington Post*, which made a reference to it in an Oct. 4 editorial. There, Khashoggi accused Mohammed bin Salman of imposing restrictions on the freedom of conscience in Saudi Arabia:

> MBS has full control over the broadcast and digital content that is produced in the kingdom. While it is still possible to access Google, Facebook, Twitter and other sites, the highly orchestrated campaign to align behind him and his 2030 vision has sucked the oxygen from the once-limited but present public square. You can read, of course, but just think twice about sharing or liking whatever isn't fully in line with the official government groupthink[7].

In the end, Jamal Khashoggi, who told the world that Mohammed bin Salman has left Saudi society without oxygen, lost his life inside that country's consulate with a plastic bag over his head. After he passed away, the murderers drained his blood and chopped him into small pieces.

---

7   https://www.washingtonpost.com/news/global-opinions/wp/2018/02/07/
saudi-arabias-crown-prince-already-controlled-the-nations-media-now-hes-squeezing-it-
even-further/?noredirect=on&utm_term=.aaee6f54d433

3

TURKEY'S LEGAL DIPLOMACY

A Declined Invitation

In addition to skillful intelligence-to-intelligence diplomacy, Turkey conducted 'legal diplomacy' in the wake of the Khashoggi murder to get results. The Turkish justice system worked hard to issue arrest warrants for the Saudi journalist's killers – just as it did to catch Israeli operatives who stormed the Mavi Marmara years ago.

Saudi Crown Prince Mohammed bin Salman came up with the idea to send the Saudi attorney general, who was supposedly investigating the journalist's killing, to Turkey. In a phone call with Turkish President Recep Tayyip Erdogan, MBS offered to dispatch Saud Al-Mujeb to Istanbul. Erdogan accepted what seemed like a genuine offer of help.

On Oct. 28, Mujeb arrived at Ataturk International Airport's VIP Terminal together with eight Saudi officials. He visited Chief Public Prosecutor Irfan Fidan twice, on Oct. 29 and 30, at Istanbul's main courthouse. The meetings took place in Fidan's office on the first floor of the building.

The first meeting between the Turkish and Saudi prosecutors was little more than an introduction. Accompanied by a general from the Saudi intelligence, Abdullah Al-Qahtani, Mujeb was visibly nervous and concerned. Yet the second meeting set the stage for an especially heated argument due to the Saudi delegation's attitude.

In addition to Fidan, the Turkish delegation included Deputy Chief Prosecutor Hasan Yilmaz, Investigator Ismet Bozkurt, Police Counter-Terrorism Chief Kayhan Ay and Ambassador Murat Tamer on behalf of the Ministry of Foreign Affairs.

At the first meeting, the two parties expressed their demands. The second time around, when they met to meet those demands, the Saudis refused to comply with the Turkish requests. Having failed to meet Turkish demands, the Kingdom's representatives added insult to injury by repeatedly requesting Jamal Khashoggi's cell phones. When they asked for a copy of the case file, the Turks shared select documents with their counterparts.

The Saudi attorney general also urged the Turkish authorities not to make statements to the press during the course of the investigation. Yet the Chief Prosecutor turned down that request straight away. Instead of listening to the Saudis, he proceeded to issue several statements to keep the public posted on the murder investigation.

Another item on Mujeb's wish list was a copy of statements by the Saudi consulate's employees to the Turkish police. The Turkish prosecutors also turned down that request, because the Saudi attorney general did not seem to be cooperating with the Turkish investigation.

Until then, the Kingdom had failed to respond to a Turkish request for the extradition of 18 suspects in connection with the Khashoggi murder. The only thing that the Saudis shared with Turkey was a list of 18 names, which they had received from Turkey in the first place, and a notification that 5 suspects were under arrest.

During the search of the Saudi consulate and the consular residence, a total of 30 officers, including ten ranking officials, divided into five teams to look for evidence. They were accompanied by Deputy Chief Prosecutor Hasan Yilmaz, Investigator Ismet Bozkurt and police liaisons – Deputy Police Chief Ali Tuna Coskun, Deputy Police Chief Kayhan Ay and Crime Scene Investigation Lead Burak Bal.

When Turkish officials entered the 5-storey consulate, each investigator was accompanied by two Saudis at all times. As such, the search took place in a tense atmosphere. The Saudis allowed Turkish investigators to look at certain parts of the building. Other places, including the well, were declared off limits.

The Saudi attorney general spent three days in Istanbul and offered absolutely no insights into the whereabouts of Jamal Khashoggi's remains to the Turkish authorities. The purpose of trip was to discover what the Turks knew, rather than make new evidence available to investigators or cooperate with the investigation. The Chief Prosecutor's Office issued a written statement after Mujeb's departure to make that point clear.

AN INDICTMENT-LIKE STATEMENT

On Oct. 31, the Chief Public Prosecutor's Office issued its clearest statement on the Khashoggi case to date. In that statement, the prosecution announced for the first time that the Saudi journalist was choked to death by Saudi operatives who proceeded to dismember him inside the consulate. The text read like a formal indictment.

Irfan Fidan's written statement, which the prosecutor wrote personally, was something for history books. That day, the Turkish prosecution announced that the Saudis denied to have mentioned a local collaborator who was reportedly responsible for getting rid of Khashoggi's body. At the same time, Turkey made it clear that it would not let Riyadh manipulate the public opinion.

The full text of Fidan's statement was as follows:

Saudi public prosecutor Saud Al-Mujab, together with a group of Saudi officials, paid a working visit to the Chief Prosecutor's Office in Istanbul on October 29, 2018.

In said meeting, the Turkish side stated that Turkish courts had jurisdiction over the case in line with Turkish law and principles of international law, provided that Jamal

Khashoggi was killed in Turkey. The Turkish officials also reiterated their request for the extradition of suspects that have reportedly been arrested in Saudi Arabia.

Furthermore, the Turkish officials have asked, verbally and in writing, (a) where Jamal Khashoggi's body was, (b) whether the Saudi investigation had discovered anything regarding the planning stage of Khashoggi's killing, and (c) who the reported 'local cooperator' was.

The same questions were asked during the Saudi delegation's second visit the following day, when the Turkish side highlighted that they were awaiting answers. The Saudi public prosecutor has stated that they would answer those questions within the same day.

On October 31, 2018, the Saudi prosecutor's office sent a written answer to the Chief Prosecutor's Office in Istanbul to invite the Turkish prosecutor and his delegation to Saudi Arabia along with the evidence that they have obtained. They added that what happened to Khashoggi's body and whether the killing was premediated could only be discovered as a result of a joint interrogation with Saudi Arabia. The Saudi prosecutor also noted that no statement had been made by the authorities of the Kingdom of Saudi Arabia regarding the existence of a "local cooperator."

Despite our well-intentioned efforts to reveal the truth, no concrete results have come out of those meetings.

In this regard;

The Chief Prosecutor's Office is obliged to share the following details regarding the seriousness of the incident based on evidence discovered as part of its investigation.

1- In accordance with plans made in advance, the victim,

Jamal Khashoggi, was choked to death immediately after entering the Consulate General of Saudi Arabia in Istanbul on October 2, 2018 for marriage formalities.

2-	The victim's body was dismembered and destroyed following his death by suffocation – again, in line with advance plans.

In conclusion;

The investigation, which the Chief Prosecutor's Office has launched immediately after a relative of the victim, Jamal Khashoggi, informed the authorities about his failure to exit the Consulate General of Saudi Arabia, continues into all dimensions and depth.

The cornerstone of Turkey's legal diplomacy, like its intelligence-to-intelligence diplomacy, was the murder tape – even though it was not admissible in court. It was Turkish President Recep Tayyip Erdogan who, on Nov. 10, announced that representatives of several foreign intelligence services had heard the audio recording. It was noteworthy that Erdogan made that statement before visiting France for the centennial of Armistice Day.

After all, World War I started shortly after Archduke Franz Ferdinand and his wife were killed by a Serbian nationalist in Sarajevo on 28 June 1914. That was the assassination that led to a devastating war. Even though there was many structural reasons behind that war, which fall outside of this book's scope, the irony was not lost on anyone.

Luckily, the Khashoggi murder did not start a conventional war in the Gulf, the Middle East or elsewhere. Yet there has been no shortage of comparisons between that event and the Franz Ferdinand assassination since Oct. 2.

Erdogan worked hard to prevent the Khashoggi murder, which closely resembled the assassination that changed the world 104 years ago, from resulting in war. Making the audio recording, which we have described in detail, available to foreign intelligence agencies was part of that carefully managed diplomatic effort.

CHAPTER III

When?

1

DIARY OF KHASHOGGI'S MURDER

Erdogan: "We gave them the tapes."

On November 10, Turkish President Recep Tayyip Erdogan, the country's first popularly elected head of state, was due to attend a commemoration to mark the 80th anniversary of the death of Mustafa Kemal Ataturk, Turkey's founding president, before flying to France for the commemoration of the centennial of Armistice Day.

Ataturk, the country's founder, had served in World War I as an Ottoman lieutenant on multiple fronts. The devastating conflict ended twenty years before Ataturk's death on November 10, 1938.

In a press conference at Esenboga International Airport in the Turkish capital Ankara, Erdogan made perhaps his most significant statement on the murder of Jamal Khashoggi: "We gave the tapes pertaining to the incident to the United States, Germany, the United Kingdom and Saudi Arabia."[1]

"The murderers are definitely among the 15 [Saudi operatives] and there is no point looking for them elsewhere," added Erdogan. "They know who the murderer or murderers are and the Saudi Arabian government can reveal it by making the 15 [men] talk."[2]

---

1   "Kaşıkçı tapelerini verdik" [We handed over the Khashoggi tapes], *Sabah*, 11 November 2018.

2   "Cumhurbaşkanı Erdoğan: Kaşıkçı'nın katilleri gelen 15 kişinin içindedir" [President Erdogan: Khashoggi's killers were among the 15 individuals that arrived in Turkey], NTV, 10 November 2018.

Shortly afterwards, the French foreign minister Jean-Yves Le Drian made an odd statement on Khashoggi: "France does not have the audio recordings regarding the slaying of the Saudi journalist Jamal Khashoggi."[3]

There is a subtle nuance here, which the French minister opted to ignore in an attempt to twist Erdogan's words.

The Turkish word tape refers to a transcript of an audio recording. By saying that Turkey gave the aforementioned countries "the tapes," Erdogan actually meant the transcript rather than the audio recording.

As we have explained elsewhere in this book, Turkey allowed representatives of several foreign intelligence agencies listen to the audio recording, yet did not give them a copy of the tape. Instead, the Turkish intelligence shared a transcript of the recording with their counterparts. To be clear, it would have been pointless for the Turks to provide a copy of the audio file at their disposal to others, provided that spy chiefs from the United States, Saudi Arabia, the United Kingdom, France, Canada and Germany had already listened to the recording.

Having made the evidence available to the French intelligence already, Turkey issued a harsh response to the French foreign minister's comments. Mevlut Cavusoglu, Le Drian's Turkish counterpart, said the French diplomat was "out of order" and "must know how to address a president." Fahrettin Altun, Erdogan's communication director, issued a written statement to note that Le Drian's accusations were unacceptable.

THE TURKISH PRESIDENCY'S COMMUNICATION STRATEGY

For the record, it was Altun who implemented the Turkish presidency's communication strategy and streamlined the flow of information – just as the National Intelligence Organization conducted effective diplomacy regarding the Khashoggi case per Erdogan's instructions.

3   "Fransa: Cemal Kaşıkçı'nın öldürülmesine ilişkin ses kayıtları elimizde değil" [France: We do not have audio recordings pertaining to the Jamal Khashoggi murder at our disposal], Al Sharq al Awsat Turkish, 13 November 2018.

How else could anonymous police and intelligence officials share information with international media outlets? After all, it is virtually impossible for a bureaucrat to do things without the knowledge of their superiors and hide their identity from the authorities. A system known as HTS enables the authorities to discover who met whom, when and where, based on a range of information including GSM base station logs.

Today, the British author George Orwell's 1984 no longer qualifies as a piece of dystopian fiction. The Big Brother is an unmistakable, undeniable fact.

As such, Fahrettin Altun –and, by extension, the Turkish presidency— was fully aware of the statements that senior police and intelligence officials made to reporters. Had it not been for Turkey's skillful communication strategy, the Khashoggi murder would have been covered up in no time, and the Saudi death squad and their superiors would have literally gotten away with murder.

Therefore, Altun included the following sentence in his response to Le Drian: "Let us not forget that this case would have already been buried, had it not been for Turkey's determined efforts." Altun's written statement continued:

"A representative of the French intelligence listened to the audio recording on 24 October 2018 and received detailed information, including a copy of the transcript. If there is a lack of communication between the various parts of the French state, the French authorities, not the Republic of Turkey, should be expected to resolve that problem."[4]

From an intelligence standpoint, the final sentence in Altun's statement meant that Turkey could not be held responsible by French politicians if their intelligence community withheld information from them or shared with them inaccurate information.

In light of Turkey's response, the French Foreign Ministry proceeded to issue a second statement, noting that Le Drian's re-

---

4   "Altun: Eğer Fransa devletinin muhtelif kurumları arasında iletişim kopukluğu varsa bu sorunu..." [Altun: If there is a lack of communication among the various institutions of the French state...], *Habertürk*, 12 November 2018.

marks on the Khashoggi murder had been misunderstood.[5]

Shortly afterwards, Canadian Prime Minister Justin Trudeau told reporters that his country's intelligence agency had listened to the audio recording at Turkey's disposal and refuted Le Drian's claim.[6] Trudeau proceeded to thank the Turkish president for his handling of the Khashoggi affair.

Steffen Seibert, the German government's spokesman, also confirmed that the German intelligence had been briefed by their Turkish counterparts.[7]

THE INTELLIGENCE COMMUNITY'S CRYPTIC LANGUAGE: ASSASSINATION

In truth, neither France nor Germany –not any other country, for that matter— could have predicted a covert operation of this nature. For the record, the Turks were caught by surprise as well. Yet a careful analysis of CCTV footage and audio recordings enabled the Turkish authorities to crack the case almost immediately.

To appreciate the nature of the covert operation that claimed Jamal Khashoggi's life, one must be familiar with the secret, cryptic language of intelligence agencies. Spies conducted countless covert operations throughout history – especially during the Cold War. Murder and even acts of terrorism can serve as encrypted messages between rival intelligence agencies.

Some intelligence organizations tend to send messages to other spy networks through assassinations and terror attacks. In other words, acts of terrorism represent a means of communication between competing intelligence agencies. More specifically, some

5   "Fransa Dışişleri: Kaşıkçı tapeleriyle ilgili açıklamamız yanlış anlaşıldı" [French Foreign Ministry: Our statement on the Khashoggi tapes was misunderstood], *Sputnik*, 13 November 2018.
6   "Kanada Başbakanı Trudeau: İstihbaratımız Kaşıkçı cinayetinin ses kayıtlarını dinledi" [Canadian Prime Minister Trudeau: Our intelligence heard the audio recordings of the Khashoggi murder], *Euronews*, 12 November 2018.
7   "Alman Hükümet Sözcüsü Seibert: Kaşıkçı olayında Türkiye ile Almanya arasında bilgi alışverişi oldu" [German Government Spokesman Seibert: There was exchange of information between Turkey and Germany on the Khashoggi affair], *Sputnik*, 12 November 2018.

secret services adopt those methods and resort to them.

For example, a series of attacks that ISIS, PKK and FETÖ carried out against Turkey in 2013-2016. The Turkish authorities, hardened by the bitter experiences of the past, cracked those cases with relative ease. According to them, ISIS and PKK attacks in 2014-2016 were part of an attempt to incite a civil war in Turkey by encouraging the two organizations to fight on Turkish soil. The Turkish authorities interpreted that message correctly and responded as required.

OPERATION DAGGER: AT THE HEART OF SPY PARADISE

Turkey's intelligence strategy is firmly based on counter-terrorism. Until recently, the Turks took intelligence and military measures to protect themselves from terrorists within their country's borders. Yet a new approach enabled Turkey to target terrorism at its source. Operation Dagger, a covert operation that the Turkish intelligence carried out in Latakia, Syria to capture terrorist Yusuf Nazik, reflected that change. In a way, the operation was a message to rival intelligence networks that undoubtedly interpret it.

Real-life secret service operations look nothing like the stuff of Hollywood movies. There are no superhuman spooks, like Ethan Hunt from the Mission Impossible film series, in the real world. Instead, intelligence operatives risk their lives and tap into their professional experiences to overcome challenges on the ground.

Since the Syrian civil war kicked off in 2011, two places – Antakya in Turkey and Latakia in Syria— have set the stage for the harshest battles among spies. Just as Istanbul was a capital of espionage during the Cold War, those cities are currently densely populated by spooks.

It was a major accomplishment for the Turkish intelligence to convince Talal Silo, a former spokesman for the YPG-dominated Syrian Democratic Forces, to defect.[8] Likewise, capturing and

---

8   "SDG Sözcüsü ÖSO'ya teslim oldu" [SDF Spokesman Surrenders to FSA], Sabah, 16 November 2017.

repatriating Yusuf Nazik was a successful intelligence operation. In the wake of that mission, the Syrian regime could not reveal the identities and photographs of the agents involved – unlike what Turkey did with Jamal Khashoggi's killers.

The 15-member Saudi death squad's cover was blown as soon as they left Turkey. Moreover, the Turkish authorities found out what exactly each man did, and when.

According to the Turkish investigation, the nine Saudi operatives led by the intelligence general Maher Abdulaziz Mutreb entered the country at 3.38 a.m. on October 2. Mutreb himself was caught on camera by the passport control counter at Ataturk International Airport's General Aviation Terminal at 3.37 a.m. Upon leaving the terminal, the Saudi operatives waited for a short while, before exiting General Aviation at 4.29 a.m.

By 5.20 a.m., the Saudis were at the M Hotel in Istanbul's Levent district, which was home to the Saudi consulate. Two groups of men left the building at 9.40 a.m. and 10.50 a.m., and made their way to their country's consulate. Mutreb was seen at the entrance of the Saudi mission at 9.55 a.m.

At 1.14 p.m., Saudi journalist Jamal Khashoggi walked into the building, which he would never get to leave. The Saudi team was caught on camera again at 3.08 p.m., rushing out of the consulate with two diplomatic vehicles.

Mutreb appeared at 4.53 p.m. in front of the consular residence down the road. By 5.15 p.m., Mutreb and his men left their hotel in Levent carrying a large suitcase. At 5.58 p.m., the men cleared passport control at Ataturk Airport's General Aviation Terminal and departed Turkey shortly afterwards.

After finishing 'the job', the Saudi operatives left the country on two private jets and a commercial flight. Some of the killers departed at 6.30 p.m. aboard the private jet with the tail number HZ SK1, which had arrived at Ataturk International at 5.15 p.m. Others took HZ SK2 out of Ataturk International at 10.45 p.m.

Most of this book is based on information that the authors have obtained from trusted government sources. Here, however, we will directly quote an official document pertaining to the Saudi death squad:

Activities pertaining to the matter:

1)   [With regard to] the individuals who left aboard the private jets with the tail numbers HZ SK1 and HZ SK2, owned by a Saudi aviation company, it has been discovered that the aircraft with the tail number HZ SK1 left the country at 1830 hours on 2 October 2018, before the authorities learned about the incident. Upon inspection of camera footage and X-Ray images, it has been concluded that the missing person was not present.

Prior to the departure of individuals, who departed about the aircraft with the tail number HZ SK2 at 2250 hours on 2 October 2018, all individuals and their passports were inspected by officials one by one, as the authorities had been notified and suspected an abduction, and their belongings were scanned by an X-Ray machine. There was no sign of the missing person.

2)   An inspection of camera footage from the vicinity of the [Saudi] consulate general revealed that certain papers, which cannot be identified at this time, and an accompanying bag were burned in a barrel in the building's backyard at 1638 hours on 4 October 2018.

3)   The authorities assess that Ahmad Abdullah al-Muzaini, who serves as intelligence attaché at the consulate general, drove the diplomatic vehicle with the plate number 34 CC 2404 into the Belgrade Forest on 1 October 2018 for reconnaissance purposes. [The authorities] continue camera inspection and research in the area.

4)   It has been discovered that S.K., a Turkish citizen employed by the consulate general, rehearsed at 0138 hours on 2 October 2018 whether he could back the [Mercedes-Benz] Vito [van] with the plate number 34 CC 1865 into the ramp (tunnel), which vehicle except the consul-gen-

eral's official vehicle [usually] enters, and parked the vehicle in front of the police checkpoint at 0200 hours before leaving on foot. The vehicle was taken to the rehearsed location at 1200 hours by another individual and departed from said location at 1500 hours to enter the consular residence's indoor garage.

5) Consular staff were told that the delegation, which arrived on various flights on 1 and 2 October 2018, were [in Turkey] for auditing purposes, and gethered in a room inside the building for a meeting. It has been discovered that the employees resumed their regular duties upon the departure of said vehicles.

6) [The authorities] have learned that the staff of the consular residence, including a cook and a cleaner, were instructed "not to show up for work until further notice" on 1 October 2018, citing the arrival of inspectors for an audit.

7) An inspection of cameras in the consulate's vicinity revealed that Mustapha Mohammed al-Madani, who walked into the consulate from the front door at 1057 hours, left the building wearing a jacket, a shirt and pants –which, we assess, belonged to Jamal Khashoggi— as well as a fake beard and glasses. He was accompanied by Saif Saad al-Qahtani, who wore a hood –unusual for the season— and covered up his face, left from the rear door carrying a plastic bag. It has been detected that the suspects went to the Blue Mosque, where Mustapha Mohammed al-Madani changed back into his own clothes, and subsequently to the M Hotel. They left the country at 0020 hours on 3 October 2018, separately from the team [members] that arrived with them.

8) Within the framework of the legal investigation into the incident and per the chief public prosecutor's instructions, teams of specialists conducted a search at the consulate, which started at 2000 hours on 15 October 2018

and continued for 8.5 hours, and the consular residence, which started at 1700 hours on 17 October 2018 and continued for 12 hours, to discover forensic traces and clues. The materials that [the investigators] deemed potential evidence were delivered to the Forensic Medicine [Institution] for further study.

9)   An interview with a former employee of the consulate general, who worked there for two years, [the authorities] have learned that the engine room for the pool was located on the lower floor of the residence, that a piece of marble covered up a well "whose bottom they could not see despite using a flashlight repeatedly." During the search, a 21-meter-deep well was discovered with water up to nine meters high. A sample was collected from the well for inspection, yet the well could not be searched due to the objections of the Saudi officials.

10)   23 individuals have been questioned as part of the investigation.

That information was gathered in the wake of Jamal Khashoggi's slaying – just as the Saudi operatives were members of the so-called Tiger Team that Riyadh used to neutralize dissidents or force them into returning to the Kingdom.

2

THE TIGER TEAM'S COVERT OPERATIONS

The Saudi operatives, whom the Turkish police and intelligence caught red-handed after the Jamal Khashoggi murder, have a long history of conducting covert operations without covering up their footprints. Until today, the Kingdom carried out a large number of 'reckless' assassinations and abductions.

The Saudi government has been involved in this particular type of covert actions since the early 2000s. Yet there has been an uptick in the number of dissidents, who became the target of abductions and assassination attempts, since Crown Prince Mohammed bin Salman perpetrated a palace coup to seize power in February 2018.

Let us begin with the abduction of Prince Sultan bin Turki – the prototype of the new generation of covert Saudi operations.

Prince Sultan was abducted twice, in 2003 and 2016, by Saudi operatives in Europe as part of covert operations akin to what the general public tends to witness in spy movies. Back in 2003, when King Fahd bin Abdulaziz was still in power, Prince Sultan was openly talking about the Saudi royal family's corruption and called for reform from Europe.

One day, Sultan bin Turki received an invitation from Prince Abdulaziz, his cousin and the king's son, for a breakfast meeting at a luxury hotel in Geneva, Switzerland. There, he received reassurance that the Saudi authorities would not harm him if he chose to return to Riyadh. For obvious reasons, Prince Sultan did not believe Abdulaziz and told him that he would rather stay in Europe. When his cousin left the room to take a phone call, a group of Saudi operatives attacked Sultan bin Turki – like journalist Jamal Khashoggi inside the country's consulate in Istanbul. Storming the hotel room, masked men beat up the prince, cuffed him up and injected him with a sedative. The Saudis took him to a private jet awaiting their arrival at Geneva International Airport. When Prince Sultan opened his eyes, he was already in Riyadh.

Abducted in broad daylight from a European capital, Sultan bin Turki was placed under house arrest for the next six years. In 2010, when the Saudi authorities allowed him to leave the country to receive medical treatment, the prince went back to Europe. Six years later, he boarded a plane in Paris to visit his father in Cairo, only to end up in Saudi Arabia again. Prince Sultan has been missing ever since.

A similar fate awaited Prince Turki bin Bandar, who was a senior member of the Saudi law enforcement agency. He knew many secrets about the Saudi royal family as part of his job. The prince was arrested over an inheritance dispute and moved to Paris upon being released from prison in 2012. There, he started producing videos about the Saudi royal family's corruption and uploaded them on YouTube. The former law enforcement official thus became a target of the Saudi government.

In 2015, Turki bin Bandar received a phone call from his country's deputy interior minister, who told him that it was safe to come home. "Everyone's expecting you with their arms wide open," said the Saudi minister. Prince Turki answered: "They're expecting me with open arms? How about the public officials sending me letters, threatening to repatriate me?" The deputy minister responded by assuring Turki bin Bandar that he would be untouchable: "I am your brother."[1] The prince wasn't convinced. He told the minister that the threats came directly from the Interior Ministry, and proceeded to release the phone call on YouTube. After a business trip to Morocco, Prince Turki was arrested before boarding a flight to Paris and subsequently extradited to Saudi Arabia. Like Prince Sultan bin Turki, Turki bin Bandar's where-

1   Reda El Mawy, "Saudi Arabia's Missing Princes," BBC News, 15 August 2017.

abouts are unknown.

The two men weren't alone. Prince Saud bin Saif al-Nasr loved luxury and gambling. He did not care about making money, and authored tweets from his home in Italy that criticized the Saudi royal family for supporting the Egyptian coup leader Abdel Fattah el-Sisi. In September 2015, Prince Saud publicly endorsed two anonymous letters calling for the overthrow of King Abdulaziz to become a high-priority target for Riyadh. Shortly afterwards, a private company with Italian and Russian partners contacted the runaway prince, asking for an audience in Rome. They told him that they wanted to do business in the Gulf and needed help from a member of the family. Under the agreement, Prince Saud would receive three-percent commission. The company dispatched a private jet to Paris to pick him up – or so the prince thought. The plane landed in Riyadh rather than Rome. The rest is –hardly—unclear. Like the other princes, Saud was detained by the Kingdom and probably executed.

A more recent Saudi operation involved Saad Hariri, the Lebanese prime minister who was detained in Riyadh and forced into resigning his post under house arrest. When Hariri arrived at the Saudi capital on November 3, 2017, he was greeted by the security forces instead of a diplomatic delegation. The law enforcement agents confiscated the Lebanese prime minister and his security detail's phones. Hariri was taken to an undisclosed location, where he recited a resignation letter, whose author was clearly not himself.

Another murder with Saudi links took place in New York in October 2018, when Jamal Khashoggi was killed and dismembered inside the Saudi consulate in Istanbul. The authorities discovered the bodies of Tala and Rotana Farea, both Saudi citizens, in the Hudson River. Their mother stated that they had received a phone call from the Saudi Embassy in Washington, urging them to leave the United States immediately. The two girls filed for political asylum in the United States upon receiving the threatening call from the Saudi authorities. Together with their brother, a college student, the Farea sisters left their Virginia home on September 24. They requested political asylum from the U.S. authorities and went off the grid shortly afterwards. Their bodies were discovered a month later, on October 24, in the Hudson River. The dead girls were tied together.[2]

Experts believe that the Farea family, which fled Saudi Arabia in 2015, when King Salman came to power, and moved to the United States, may have been targeted by members of the notorious Tiger Team – a group of operatives tasked by the Kingdom to 'hunt down' dissidents abroad. It is nearly certain that the two girls were executed by the Tiger Team.

Like the Khashoggi murder, the Saudi operatives acted recklessly in this case. Obviously, the death squad's biggest mistake in the Khashoggi affair was to ignore the possibility that there was proof of their conversations inside the consulate. Needless to say, all diplomatic missions around the world are at risk of surveillance by foreign intelligence agencies. Hence the construction of so-called vaults in U.S. diplomatic missions abroad.

SUCCESSION FIGHTS AND MURDERS IN HISTORY

Historian Murat Bardakçı posits in his Oct. 22 column for *Habertürk* that the Saudis committed this type of murder to end succession fights, citing a recent example:

Let me tell you about a murder that Saudi princes instigated in the past – the 1979 execution of Princess Mishaal bint Fahd bin Mohammed al-Saud.

Mishaal was the daughter of Fahd, one of the sons of Mohammed – the oldest son of King Abdulaziz, the founder of Saudi Arabia. Although Prince Mohammed, his grandfather, was one of the oldest surviving sons of King Abdulaziz, the family council opposed his coronation, citing his love of alcohol and lifestyle, which they deemed incompatible with the crown. In Mohammed's stead, Khaled, his younger brother, ruled the

2   Victoria Bekiempis, "New York police investigate deaths of Saudi sisters found bound together," *The Guardian*, 31 October 2018.

Kingdom.

When Mishaal (born 1958) told her family that she wanted to receive a good education, she was sent to Beirut, where she enrolled at the American University and rented a small villa by the sea. The Saudi ambassador to Lebanon watched over the young princess. He frequently invited her to the embassy, inquired about her needs, asked her to stay for dinner, and had his driver take her to home.

One of the Saudi ambassador's cousins, Khaled, lived in Beirut. Over time, Mishaal and Khaled developed warm feelings for each other.

One day, Mishaal received a phone call from her grandfather, Prince Mohammed, in Riyadh, who instructed her to return home immediately. Upon flying back to Riyadh, Mishaal learned that she was about to marry an old, rich Saudi man. She showed unusual courage for a Saudi woman at the time by opposing the arrangement, told her family that she loved another man, and rushed off her grandfather's side.

Khaled, too, was in Riyadh at the time. That night, they fled to Jeddah together and went to the home of a sheikh, whom Mishaal had been following for years. The young princess begged the man and convinced him to officiate their wedding.

Mishaal and Khaled were now man and wife, yet Mishaal's grandfather was hanging over their heads. Before even consummating their marriage, the couple made an escape plan. Mishaal cut her hair, dressed like a man, and they checked into a hotel in Jeddah like two strangers. They made a deal with two Armenian flight attendants, who promised to take them to the airport. The couple was going to fly to their freedom with false identity papers.

As soon as they stepped out of the hotel the next morning, they encountered Prince Mohammed's armed men. The flight attendants were killed on the spot, but Mishaal and Khaled made it to the airport and even boarded their flight. Armed men stormed the aircraft just before takeoff and dragged the screaming couple out of the flight under the watch of shocked passengers.

Mishaal and Khaled appeared before a judge loyal to Prince Mohammed. Mishaal's grandfather was present, yet did not look his granddaughter in the eye. He only said that the couple engaged in adultery and, under Islamic law, must be executed.

For the first time ever, the judge objected. "They got married," he said. "They didn't commit adultery. As such, they are not guilty."

Yet the grandfather was determined to have Mishaal and Khaled killed. Prince Mohammed wasn't crowned king, yet he was the most senior prince and the head of his family. He didn't even blink when he ordered their killing.

Even though it wasn't illegal for two adults to get married –even without parental consent— under any legal system, Prince Mohammed's order had to be executed!

The arbitrary sentence that Prince Mohammed handed down was carried out in Jeddah on July 15, 1977. Prior to the execution, there was a dispute within the family over how they were going to kill the couple. They could not stone Mishaal to death, as she wasn't guilty under Islamic law. Nor could an executioner for the state carry out the order, since the princess wasn't convicted by a Saudi court.

They decided to shoot them dead. Mishaal and Khaled were taken to a parking garage, and a gunman fired a single bullet to the back of Mishaal's head. Next up was Khaled, who had just watched the killers execute his wife and was no longer himself. He did not even notice as the executioner struck him with a sword to the back of his neck.

Three years later, British journalist Anthony Thomas produced a documentary about the murder, which aired on December 9, 1980. The Saudis raised hell and King Khaled declared the British ambassador to Riyadh *persona non grata*.

The situation got worse when it became public that the Saudi king had offered an $11 million dollar bribe to the producers not to air the documentary. The Kingdom proceeded to boycott British goods, cancel trade agreements, and suspending public tenders. As a matter of fact, the American company that co-produced the documentary had to issue an apology. The oil giant Mobil, heavily invested in Saudi Arabia, took a full-page ad in *The New York Times* to warn that the documentary could hurt Washington's relations with the Kingdom.

It took months for British Prime Minister Margaret Thatcher to resolve the crisis. Under pressure from big business, the Iron Lady covered her head and made the trip to Jeddah in order to apologize to the Saudi king and save her country's investments.

Thus ended Princess Mishaal's miserable life. Let us not wonder how the Saudis dared to commit such a crime inside their consulate. What wouldn't someone, who'd have their granddaughter killed, do to others?[3]

SAUDI ARABIA'S GREAT LIES

Judging by Murat Bardakçı's account, the Saudis were carrying out executions and assassinations as early as the 1970s. Yet the location of the Khashoggi murder distinguished it from all other crimes. Indeed, the murder of journalist Jamal Khashoggi was unique in terms of its methodology, purpose and aftermath.

Some commentators falsely claimed that the Turkish authorities wouldn't have found out about the Khashoggi murder, had it not been for his fiancée's complaint. Let us take a moment to refute those claims.

It is true that the authorities established in retrospect that Jamal Khashoggi was killed inside the Saudi consulate. Yet the crime couldn't have been kept secret for days or perhaps hours, even if Hatice Cengiz did not make the phone call to report that Khashoggi was missing. Either way, Turkey would have discovered that Khashoggi was dead –and even how and when he was killed. After

3   Murat Bardakçı, "Kaşıkçı cinayetinden hayretteyiz, ama torunu olan 19 yaşındaki kızı bile öldürtenlerle karşı karşıyayız!" [We are shocked by the Khashoggi murder, but we are faced with people that killed even their own 19-year-old granddaughter!], Habertürk, 22 October 2018.

all, the authorities would have inspected CCTV footage from the consulate's vicinity and figured out that Khashoggi never walked out of the building to shed light on the gruesome murder. Without the audio recordings at Turkey's disposal, however, it would have been impossible to shed light on the murder itself.

Unaware that the Khashoggi murder was caught on tape, Saudi officials adopted a communication strategy that the Nazi propaganda minister Joseph Goebbels famously described as follows: *"When one lies, one should lie big and stick to it!"* Despite their incessant denials, the Saudis had to confess to the crime in the end and dismissed five senior intelligence officers – Ahmad al-Assiri, Mohammed bin Saleh al-Rumaih, Abdullah bin Khalifa al-Shaya, Saud al-Qahtani and Rashed bin Hamad al-Mohammady.

In the immediate aftermath of the Khashoggi murder, Saudi Arabia resorted to a big lie. When it became clear that Khashoggi had gone missing inside the country's consulate in Istanbul, the Saudi consulate issued a written statement claiming that the journalist went off the grid after exiting the building and noting that it worked closely with the Turkish authorities to uncover the truth. The Saudi consulate took to social media to lie to the entire world:

> The Kingdom of Saudi Arabia's consulate in Istanbul announced that it monitors media reports regarding the disappearance of KSA citizen Jamal Khashoggi upon leaving the consular building and continues to follow-up and coordinate [its actions] with the brotherly local Turkish authorities to reveal the truth about the circumstances of Khashoggi's disappearance after leaving the consular building.[4]

The Turkish Ministry of Foreign Affairs had summoned the Saudi ambassador on October 4 to request information regarding the incident. The Turks told Walid bin Abdulkarim Al-Khuraiji that Riyadh needed to shed light on what happened without delay. The Saudi ambassador responded that Saudi Arabia did not know

---

4   "Suudi Arabistan Başkonsolosluğu'ndan son dakika Cemal Kaşıkçı açıklaması" [Last minute statement from the Saudi Arabian Consulate General on Jamal Khashoggi], *Sabah*, 7 October 2018.

anything and kept looking for information.

The day after the Saudi consulate claimed that Khashoggi had walked out of the compound prior to his disappearance, Turan Kışlakçı, the slain journalist's friend and president of the Turkish-Arab Media Association, told the television channel A Haber that Jamal Khashoggi was dead:

> We thought that he was kept inside the consulate and moved out later. Yet we confirmed with several sources that Khashoggi was killed. My condolences to everyone. We are making preparations for a funeral service in absentia. It will be Saudi Arabia versus the world's conscience from now on.[5]

The same day, Mohammed Al-Otaiba, the Saudi consul general in Istanbul, took a Reuters crew on a tour of the compound. During the theatrical performance, the diplomat opened cupboards and falsely claimed that the consulate's security cameras did not record footage and the Saudis therefore could not prove that Khashoggi had left the building.

The first reference to Khashoggi's slaying could be found in a news story published two days before Kışlakçı's TV interview. The British news agency Reuters broke the news on Oct. 6 that the Turkish authorities believed that Jamal Khashoggi was killed inside the consulate:

> "The initial assessment of the Turkish police is that Mr Khashoggi has been killed at the consulate of Saudi Arabia in Istanbul. We believe that the murder was premeditated and the body was subsequently moved out of the consulate," one of the two Turkish officials told Reuters.[6]

On October 7, Turkish President Recep Tayyip Erdo-

---

5   Nazif Karaman, Emir Somer and Kenan Kıran, "Sır perdesini camı film kaplı siyah minibüs aralayacak" [The black van with tinted windows will crack open the curtain of mystery], *Sabah*, 8 October 2018.

6   https://www.reuters.com/article/us-saudi-politics-dissident/exclusive-turkish-police-believe-saudi-journalist-khashoggi-was-killed-in-consulate-sources-idUSKCN-1MG0HU

gan told reporters that he was "monitoring the process" and pledged to "share our findings with the entire world."[7]

The following day, Erdogan called on Saudi Arabia to prove that the missing journalist Jamal Khashoggi had indeed walked out of its consulate in Istanbul.[8] Obviously, he was already aware that Riyadh could not prove anything. Erdogan had been briefed about Khashoggi's fate, but he wanted to force the Saudis into an admission of guilt.

What happened to Khashoggi was no longer a mystery for the Turks, but the world was still asking questions. Before long, U.S. officials started receiving questions about the Washington Post columnist. On October 7, U.S. Secretary of State Mike Pompeo called his Saudi counterpart to urgently request information about what happened.

The following day, the State Department said it was monitoring the situation.[9] Fred Hiatt, an editor with *The Washington Post*, stated that, if Khashoggi were indeed murdered, it would be horrific and inexplicable.

On October 6, the chief public prosecutor's office in Istanbul announced that it had launched a formal investigation into the Khashoggi murder: "An investigation was launched immediately on the day of the incident and [we] continue to deepen the inquiry into all dimensions [of what happened]."[10]

THE TIMELINE

Here's a summary of what happened each day in the week

7   "Cumhurbaşkanı Erdoğan: Bu işin takibindeyim" [President Erdoğan: I am monitoring this incident], Milliyet, 7 October 2018.
8   "Erdoğan: Suudi Arabistan, Cemal Kaşıkçı'nın konsolosluktan çıktığını ispatlamalı" [Erdoğan: Saudi Arabia must prove that Jamal Khashoggi left the consulate], BBC Turkish, 8 October 2018.
9   "Trump: Cemal Kaşıkçı'nın akıbeti hakkında endişeliyim" [Trump: I am concerned about Jamal Khashoggi's fate], Sabah, 9 October 2018.
10   Nazif Karaman, "Suudi gazeteci Cemal Kaşıkçı'nın kaybolması ile ilgili soruşturma" [The investigation into Saudi journalist Jamal Khashoggi's disappearance], Sabah, 7 October 2018.

following Jamal Khashoggi's death:

Tuesday, October 2: Jamal Khashoggi went missing upon entering Saudi Arabia's consulate general in Istanbul. The chief public prosecutor launched an investigation into what appeared to be the *Washington Post* columnist's detention by the Saudi authorities.

Wednesday, October 3: A group of activists gathered outside the Saudi consulate to call for the release of Jamal Khashoggi, who, they said, had been detained inside the compound. Ibrahim Kalin, the spokesman for the Turkish presidency, told reporters that "the Saudi citizen remains at the Saudi consulate in Istanbul to the best of our knowledge."

Thursday, October 4: The Saudi government announced that it was monitoring news of Khashoggi's disappearance and working with the Turkish authorities to locate him. Turkish officials maintained that the journalist was still in the building and noted that a formal invitation from Saudi Arabia was necessary to search the consulate.

Friday, October 5: In an interview with Bloomberg, Saudi Crown Prince Mohammed bin Salman said the Turkish authorities were welcome to search his country's consulate general in Istanbul. He did not say whether Khashoggi was charged with any crime in Saudi Arabia and told the interviewees that he would know if Khashoggi were in the Kingdom.

Saturday, October 6: The Turkish police announced that 15 Saudi citizens, who took a private jet and two commercial flights to Turkey, were inside the consulate at the same time as Jamal Khashoggi, and returned to the Kingdom.

Sunday, October 7: Turkish President Recep Tayyip Erdogan told reporters that he was "still optimistic that we won't encounter an undesirable situation."

Monday, October 8: During a press conference in Hungary, Erdogan said it was "very important to us that this incident took place in our country and especially inside Saudi Arabia's consulate in Istanbul" and added that it was his "political and humanitarian duty as president to monitor this process."

The Turkish Ministry of Foreign Affairs summoned the Saudi ambassador for the second time and submitted Turkey's formal request to search for Khashoggi inside the country's consulate in Istanbul. The Turks also urged the Saudi authorities to cooperate fully with the investigation.

The United Nations, the European Union, Germany, France and the United Kingdom stated that the accusation against Saudi Arabia was quite serious and expressed concern.

Tuesday, October 9: Hami Aksoy, the spokesman for the Turkish Ministry of Foreign Affairs, told reporters that the judiciary, the police and the intelligence were monitoring the situation closely and announced that Saudi Arabia had agreed to a search of its consulate in Istanbul. Aksoy said that "the Saudi authorities have expressed their willingness to cooperate and agreed to a search at their consular building."

The United Nations expressed concern about Khashoggi's disappearance.

British Foreign Minister Jeremy Hunt reportedly urged his Saudi counterpart to cooperate fully with the Turkish investigation.

Wednesday, October 10: Sabah published the names and photographs of the 15-member Saudi death squad. According to the story, nine assassins had arrived at Istanbul Atatürk Airport at 3.28 a.m. on October 2.

Turan Kışlakçı was never wrong about the Khashoggi case. We mentioned above that he was first to announce that the *Washington Post* columnist was dead:

"Here's the only thing we haven't been able to confirm: The 15 people that came here sedated and dismembered Mr. Jamal immediately and, like the dogs they are, took a piece of his body with them. I do not wish to go into the details. I hope that no such thing has happened."[11]

Kışlakçı made that statement on October 7th. Three days later, Sabah's Special Intelligence Unit released the names and photographs of the Saudi operatives that he mentioned.

The same day, on October 10, a source claimed that the U.S. intelligence had intercepted a conversation featuring Saudi Crown Prince Mohammed bin Salman instructing his men to talk Khashoggi into returning to Saudi Arabia, only to be placed under arrest upon his return.[12]

AN ADMISSION 18 DAYS TOO LATE

In the wake of the Khashoggi murder, Saudi Arabia refused to acknowledge that the 15 intelligence operatives had killed the *Washington Post* columnist inside the country's consulate in Istanbul. Turkey gave Riyadh some time to think by leaking information to international news outlets through anonymous officials, yet could not get anywhere. The eventual admission of guilt came 18 days after Jamal Khashoggi's death. It was an insincere, half-baked acknowledgement.

11   "Turan Kışlakçı: Bize ulaşan bilgi öldürüldüğü yönünde" [Turan Kışlakçı: The information that we received suggests that he was killed], *Hürriyet,* 7 October 2018.
12   "Veliaht Prens, Kaşıkçı'nın Suudi Arabistan'a çekilip tutuklanmasını mı emretti?" [Did the crown prince order Khashoggi's repatriation and arrest?], Habertürk, 11 October 2018.

On October 20, the Saudi government was compelled to tell its state news agency SPA that Saudi operatives were responsible for the murder. Yet Saudi officials claimed that Khashoggi's death was the result of a brawl. A series of important developments had taken place in the ten days preceding the Saudi confession.

In other words, what happened on October 10-20 paved the way to Saudi Arabia's confession of guilt.

Thursday, October 11: Turkish Foreign Minister Mevlüt Cavusoglu announced that the public prosecutor's office had launched an "intensive and comprehensive investigation" into the Khashoggi case. Ibrahim Kalin, the Turkish presidency's spokesman, said that Turkey and Saudi Arabia had agreed to the formation of a joint working group at the latter's request.

Friday, October 12: The Washington Post claimed that the Turkish authorities had proof of Khashoggi's murder inside the Saudi consulate and shared them with the United States.

Saturday, October 13: UN Secretary General Antonio Guterres demanded the truth about Jamal Khashoggi's death: "We need to know exactly what has happened and we need to know exactly who is responsible and, of course, when we see the multiplication of this kind of situation I think we need to find ways in which accountability is also demanded."

Sunday, October 14: Turkish President Recep Tayyip Erdogan spoke by phone with King Salman bin Abdulaziz of Saudi Arabia and stressed the importance of forming a joint working group to facilitate the murder investigation.

The foreign ministers of France, Germany and the United Kingdom issued a joint statement to call on all sides to shed light on the incident.

Hatice Cengiz, the late Khashoggi's fiancée, penned an

OpEd essay for *The New York Times*: *"If we have already lost Jamal, then condemnation is not enough. The people who took him from us, irrespective of their political positions, must be held accountable and punished to the full extent of the law."*

Monday, October 15: Turkish and Saudi members of the joint working group held talks with counter-terrorism police at the Turkish National Policy field office in Istanbul. The meeting was followed by a criminal inspection of the consulate.

The United States announced that Secretary of State Mike Pompeo was going to visit Saudi Arabia and Turkey.

Tuesday, October 16: Specialists from the joint working group searched the Saudi consulate until the morning. Public prosecutors, police chiefs and crime scene investigators left the compound after nine hours.

King Salman received U.S. Secretary of State Mike Pompeo.

Diplomatic sources from Turkey told reporters that the Turkish investigators were going to search for clues at the Saudi consul general's residence.

Mohammed Al-Otaiba, Riyadh's consul general in Istanbul, left the country on a commercial flight at 1700 hours.

Wednesday, October 17: U.S. Secretary of State Mike Pompeo visited the Turkish capital Ankara after making a stop in Riyadh to hold talks on the Khashoggi affair. He was received by the Turkish president and subsequently met Foreign Minister Cavusoglu and MIT Director Hakan Fidan.

Thursday, October 18: The New York Times reported that U.S. intelligence officials were convinced that Saudi Crown Prince Mohammed bin Salman was behind the Khashoggi murder.

The chief public prosecutor's office in Istanbul issued another written statement: "The investigation continues diligently and into all dimensions of the incident in compliance with international law, customs, treaties and conventions. The prosecutor's office will issue additional statements if necessary to inform the public about the investigation."

Friday, October 19: U.S. President Donald Trump acknowledged that Jamal Khashoggi was dead, citing intelligence sources.

Saturday, October 20: The Saudi government claimed that Khashoggi was killed during a brawl inside its consulate in Istanbul. The Saudi news agency SPA reported that the journalist argued with other Saudi citizens who were at the consulate when he arrived and lost his life when that argument evolved into a fight.

The Saudi statement was completely devoid of content. As a matter of fact, Riyadh would have to reject its own version of events later. Even the dismissal of Ahmad Al-Assiri and other senior officials hours later meant that the Saudi account was did not reflect the truth. Among the Saudi officials who lost their jobs was Saud Al-Qahtani, an advisor to the Saudi crown prince.

Qahtani was responsible for Mohammed bin Salman's propaganda efforts on social media. After Prince Mansour bin Muqrin, one of the high-profile targets of the crown prince's unofficial coup, perished in a helicopter crash (in which, some claim, the aircraft was hit by missiles) along with seven of his advisers on November 8, 2017, Qahtani deployed the Saudi troll army to spread disinformation. Jamal Khashoggi's 'bees' were intended to counterbalance the regime's 'flies'.[13]

---

13   https://www.middleeasteye.net/news/saudi-prince-mansour-killed-helicopter-crash-near-yemen-border

THE SAUDI ATTORNEY GENERAL CAME TO SEE OUR HAND

What took place between Oct. 20 and 30 compelled the Kingdom to dispatch Saud Al-Mujib, the Saudi attorney general, to Turkey.

Sunday, October 21: President Erdogan said that he was going to make an important statement about the Khashoggi murder at his parliamentary address on Tuesday:
"We are determined to shed light on what happened. God willing, I will make a statement about that issue at the [AK Party] caucus on Tuesday. After all, we seek justice here. All of the naked truth will come out – not just some ordinary steps. 15 people came here, so why did [Saudi Arabia] arrest 18 people? Those issues must be clarified in detail."

The same day, the Saudi foreign minister appeared on Fox News to deny that Crown Prince Mohammed bin Salman knew anything about the Khashoggi murder or was responsible for the incident in any way.

Monday, October 22: Erdogan spoke by phone with U.S. President Donald Trump. The two leaders exchanged views on bilateral issues as well as the Khashoggi murder and the situation in Syria.

King Salman bin Abdulaziz and Crown Prince Mohammed bin Salman reportedly called Jamal Khashoggi's son, Salah, to offer their condolences.

CNN International aired CCTV footage of Al-Madani, a member of the Saudi death squad who served as Khashoggi's body double.

Tuesday, October 23: In his weekly address to the Turkish Parliament, Erdogan shared information about the various developments that took place since Jamal Khashoggi's ill-fated visit to the Saudi consulate in Istanbul. In the same speech, which many international outlets carried live, the Turkish president maintained that the murder suspects must be extradited to Turkey: *"The crime was committed in Istanbul. As such, I propose that the 18 detainees be brought to justice in Istanbul. It is up to [Saudi Arabia] to decide, but this my personal proposal and demand. This is important because the crime took place here."*

Recalling that certain media outlets attempted to discredit Turkey and distract attention from the Khashoggi murder, Erdogan pledged to uncover the truth:

"Such assassination attempts against our country's reputation have never stopped us from seeking the truth. Nor will they in the future."

Erdogan called the Khashoggi family to offer his condolences.

British Foreign Minister Jeremy Hunt said that his country was concerned to hear that Erdogan described the Khashoggi murder as *premeditated*.

Wednesday, October 24: British Prime Minister Theresa May announced that the United Kingdom would revoke visas held by Jamal Khashoggi's murder suspects.

Thursday, October 25: It became clear that the Kingdom rejected a Turkish request to search the well inside Saudi Arabia's consular residence in Istanbul. The Saudis conceded that, in light of information that Turkey shared with Riyadh, the Khashoggi murder was indeed premeditated.

Friday, October 26: Turkish President Recep Tayyip Erdogan called on the Kingdom to identify the whereabout of Jamal Khashoggi's remains:

"Here's what we're saying: it has been established beyond doubt that [Khashoggi] was murdered. You have to show where the body is. You told us that he left [the consulate] and we told you to prove it. In the end, [KSA] admitted that 18 people were under arrest. I learned it personally from the Servant of the Holy Mosques. Here's the question: those 18 individuals must know who killed Jamal Khashoggi. There is no other explanation. After all, the killer is one of them. If he isn't, then you must identify the local collaborator. Saudi Arabia can't clear the air until it agrees to provide that explanation."

Saturday, October 27: Saudi Foreign Minister Adel Al-Jubeir stated that Jamal Khashoggi's killer would appear before a Saudi court.

In a joint press conference with Russian President Vladimir Putin, German Chancellor Angela Merkel and French President Emmanuel Macron, Erdogan said that the leaders "discussed the issue in bilateral meetings" and he "shared necessary information" with his counterparts. "Our intelligence agencies had been briefed earlier," added the Turkish president. "We delved into the details in today's bilateral meetings."

Sunday, October 28: The Turkish authorities established that diplomatic vehicles registered to the Saudi consulate in Istanbul were cleaned after the Khashoggi murder.

Monday, October 29: The Saudi attorney general arrived at Istanbul's main courthouse to meet Chief Public Prosecutor Irfan Fidan. The meeting lasted 75 minutes.

Tuesday, October 30: Saud Al-Mujib visited his country's consulate in Istanbul as part of the investigation into Jamal Khashoggi's slaying. Three days later, he left Turkey, without sharing any valuable information with his Turkish counterpart, taking back five boxes of nuts to the Kingdom.

Wednesday, October 31: The Chief Public Prosecutor's Office in Istanbul issued its most straightforward statement on the Khashoggi murder to date and announced that Khashoggi's body was "dismembered and destroyed" by the assassins. The clarity of the prosecution's statement caught the attention of global media outlets.

THE GLOBAL MEDIA COVERAGE

U.S. News Outlets

The Washington Post quoted the Turkish prosecution as saying that Khashoggi was choked to death and dismembered, and stressed that the whereabouts of the victim's body remain unknown. Citing a senior Turkish official, it added that Turkey was entertaining the possibility that the Saudis dissolved Khashoggi's body in acid somewhere around the consular residence.

The New York Times reported that the Turkish prosecutor accused the Saudi killers of choking Khashoggi to death, warning that the high-profile murder strained Turkey's bilateral relations with the Kingdom.

The Wall Street Journal stated that the Turkish investigators criticized Saudi Arabia for failing to clarify what happened to Jamal Khashoggi's body.

CNN, one of the leading U.S. news channels, highlighted that the Khashoggi murder, according to the prosecution, was premeditated.

Finally, the *Associated Press* distributed the Turkish prosecution's statement immediately and noted that Turkey mounted pressure on the Kingdom to volunteer additional information about the whereabouts of Khashoggi's remains.

European News Outlets

The British public broadcaster BBC reported that Turkey officially revealed new details about journalist Jamal Khashoggi's death, quoting the prosecution as saying that the murder was premeditated and the killers choked their victim to death immediately after the slain journalist walked into the consulate.

The Guardian stressed that the Turkish prosecution's statement was the first public acknowledgement of the way in which Jamal Khashoggi lost his life inside the Saudi consulate in Istanbul.

The Independent noted that the Turkish authorities were dissatisfied with the Saudi attorney general's visit and recalled that Turkey continued to ask key questions: Who ordered the hit on Jamal Khashoggi? What happened to the victim's body? The Turks, the newspaper reported, were yet to receive a satisfactory answer from Riyadh.

The Financial Times reported that the Turkish authorities accused their Saudi counterparts of failing to cooperate with the murder investigation in Istanbul.

French newspapers *Le Figaro* and *Le Monde* shared Turkey's first official statement on the Khashoggi murder with their readers and reminded them of the prosecution's conclusion that Khashoggi was choked to death and dismembered.

In a story about the Khashoggi murder, the German newspaper *Frankfurter Allgemeine Zeitung* recalled that the Saudi crown prince was suspected to have orchestrated the Khashoggi murder and made references to direct links with the slain journalist's potential killers.

El Mundo, a Spanish newspaper, announced that the Turkish prosecution had finally issued an official statement about Jamal Khashoggi's slaying by 15 Saudi suspects with premeditation after weeks of leaks to the press. The prosecutor's statement, it said, confirmed the claim that Khashoggi's body was dismembered and recalled that the Saudi officials were refusing to cooperate with the murder investigation.

Another Spanish newspaper, *El País,* reported that Turkey requested the Saudi attorney general to share the statements of the

18 murder suspects in the Kingdom, explain where Khashoggi's body was, and identify the local collaborator. It added that Saud al-Mujib refused to answer those questions and claimed that the Saudi authorities never mentioned a local collaborator.

Blick, Switzerland's largest and sole national newspaper, wrote that Turkey asked Saudi Arabia to extradite Jamal Khashoggi's murder suspects, yet Riyadh refused to comply.

Finally, the Dutch news outlet *NOS* announced that Jamal Khashoggi was choked the death shortly after walking into the Saudi consulate in Istanbul and stressed that Turkey issued its first official statement about the Saudi journalist's final moments.

Russian Media Outlets

Vedomosti, Russia's leading financial newspaper, reported on the Turkish prosecutor's written statement and stressed that the assassins choked Jamal Khashoggi to death before dismembering his body.

Kommersant shared the prosecution's statement with its readers and reported on the details of the Khashoggi murder.

The Russian daily *Izvestia* announced that "Turkey shed light on the Saudi journalist's death" and wrote that Khashoggi was choked to death and dismembered inside the Saudi consulate in Istanbul. It added that Turkey's meeting with the Saudi attorney general yielded no results, as the Kingdom refused to reveal who ordered the hit on Khashoggi and where the slain columnist's body was.

The state news agency *TASS* said that "the Chief Prosecutor in Istanbul announced that Khashoggi was choked to death" and shared the prosecution's conclusion that the murder was premeditated.

Middle Eastern News Outlets

The Turkish prosecutor's statement sent shockwaves through the Middle East – albeit in different ways. Media outlets in Iraq, Lebanon and the Gulf states, with the notable exception of Qatar, did not report on the statement. News outlets in other parts of the region included excerpts from the prosecution's written statement in their stories.

Al-Shorouk, a pro-government Egyptian daily newspaper that seeks to follow a more independent editorial line, and *Al-Masry Al-Youm*, which opposes the Egyptian leadership, shared the statement on their front pages.

Al-Shorouk reported that the Saudi attorney general's visit to Istanbul had ended and the Turkish investigator issued a statement acknowledging that Khashoggi was choked to death and dismembered. *Al-Masry Al-Youm* added that the Saudi prosecutor's meetings did not yield concrete results.

The Qatar-based *Al Jazeera* news website claimed that Turkish intelligence officers had Saud Al-Mujib listen to the audio recording of Jamal Khashoggi's final moments.[14]

Iran's official and semi-official news agencies, including *IRNA, FHA, Mehr* and *Tasnim*, shared the prosecution's statement with their subscribers and social media followers immediately.[15]

---

14   That information was inaccurate. Turkey played the audio recording for Qahtani, the intelligence general, in Ankara (not Istanbul) together with the Saudi domestic intelligence chief Howayrani.

15   "Başsavcılığın açıklaması dünya basınında" [The chief prosecutor's statement in the world media], *Sabah*, 2 November 2018.

3

TRUMP'S DILEMMAS

"King – We Are Protecting You!"

"I love the king, King Salman, but I said: 'King, we are protecting you! You might not be there for two weeks without us. You have to pay for your military."

Less than 24 hours after the Khashoggi murder, U.S. President Donald Trump, whose administration reduced Washington's national security strategy to money like a CEO that cares only about their company's financial status, uttered those words at a campaign event in Southaven, Mississippi.

According to official statements, Trump, like the rest of the world, was yet unaware that the Washington Post columnist was no longer alive. Nonetheless, he attempted to mount pressure on the Kingdom by using those words, hoping that he could pave the way to new high-volume arms deals – like the Washington and Riyadh concluded next to the infamous orb in May 2018.[1]

To be clear, Saudi Arabia was no stranger to buying the loyalty of others in return for national security – or, to be more specific, ensure the Saudi royal family's political survival. It was therefore that the Kingdom recently signed a $350 million arms deal with the United States.[2]

---

1   "Trump, Sisi ve Kral Selman dünya küresine ellerini koydu" [Trump, Sisi and King Salman place their hands on the orb], Hürriyet, 22 May 2018.
2   "Suudi Kral'dan Donald Trump'a 4 milyar dolar" [The Saudi king pledges $4 bil-

Several days before making the trip to Mississippi, on Sept. 20, Trump issued a veiled threat against the Saudi regime. The U.S. president complained that the Gulf states, including the Kingdom, refused to lower the price of oil even though "we protect the countries of the Middle East [and] they would not be safe for very long without us."[3]

Trump made a number of contradictory statements when it became clear that journalist Jamal Khashoggi went missing inside Saudi Arabia's consulate general in Istanbul. The asymmetrical alliance that he formed with Mohammed bin Salman through the proxy of Jared Kushner, his son-in-law, and his administration's lucrative arms deals with King Salman left the U.S. president on the fence. In the end, Trump made it perfectly clear that he thought of what happened in terms of money.

On Oct. 17, Nedret Ersanel, a veteran foreign policy columnist for the Turkish daily newspaper *Yeni Safak*, claimed that Trump's son-in-law could have been complicit in the Khashoggi murder, which the Saudi crown prince instigated:

> If the negotiations lead anywhere, the infamous and inauspicious *'orb coalition'* will collapse. Otherwise, it will be crippled. That's why I wrote and said that Turkey grabbed Riyadh by the throat. Now let the bigger piece sink in: [Turkey] also caught the United States. In other words, we must understand where the White House stands.
>
> …
>
> If it becomes clear that Saudi Arabia and the United Arab Emirates were directly or indirectly involved in the Khashoggi murder –and it should—, you can be sure that President Trump's son-in-law, Jared Kushner, will face a political reckoning at the very least – which would pose a huge risk to the White House in the November elections. That's *The Washington Post* factor!

After all, it was curious that the U.S. President talked about

lion to Donald Trump], Sabah, 19 March 2018.
3   Taha Dağlı, "Kral Selman'ın sert hamlesinin ardından tehdide başladı" [Trump issues threats after King Salman's harsh move], Haber7, 4 October 2018.

'rogue elements' in an attempt to protect all suspects.[4]

THE U.S. PRESIDENT'S CONTRADICTORY STATEMENTS

Trump's Oct. 15 statement, which Ersanel quoted, was nothing short of extraordinary. Just five days earlier, the U.S. president had told reporters that the White House deeply cared about the Khashoggi murder and was committed to get to the bottom of what happened. Trump added that he discussed the Khashoggi case with a senior Saudi official and added: "We cannot let this happen, to reporters, to anybody."[5]

Yet the U.S. president failed to keep his promise and flip-flopped on the Khashoggi murder repeatedly.

His initial statement was as follows: "I am concerned about it. I don't like hearing about it. Hopefully that will sort itself out. Right now nobody knows anything about it, but there's some pretty bad stories going around. I do not like it."[6] Later the same day, Vice President Mike Pence called on the Saudi government to cooperate with the investigation into Jamal Khashoggi's disappearance and be transparent about its findings.

The following day, however, the United States extended an unconventional offer of support. Pence, a leader of the evangelical movement, told reporters that Washington was prepared to send an FBI team to Turkey if the Saudis call for help.[7]

It should go without saying that the U.S. vice president's statement made little sense. Why would Washington dispatch FBI agents to Turkey if the Kingdom needed help? Obviously, it would take a formal request from the Turks for U.S. law enforcement officials to fly over there and help with the case. Indeed, Ankara did

---

4   Nedret Ersanel, "Kaşıkçı cinayetinde Kushner bağlantısı" [Kushner's connection to the Khashoggi murder], Yeni Şafak, 17 October 2018.

5   "Beyaz Saray'dan Cemal Kaşıkçı açıklaması" [The White House statement on Jamal Khashoggi], Sabah, 10 October 2018.

6   https://www.washingtonpost.com/politics/president-says-he-is-concerned-about-missing-saudi-journalist/2018/10/08/28a1a8c2-cb1a-11e8-a360-85875bac0b1f_story.html?utm_term=.8a645711473c

7   https://thehill.com/homenews/administration/410716-pence-open-to-sending-fbi-team-to-turkey-to-investigate-missing

not need any form of U.S. assistance – neither in the area of intelligence nor regarding the criminal investigation. Quite the contrary, it was the Turkish government that shared credible intelligence about Jamal Khashoggi's death with intelligence agencies in the United States and elsewhere.

On Oct. 11, the U.S. president told Fox News that the United States had "investigators over there and we're working with Turkey [since] we want to find out what happened."[8] To the Turks, Trump's statement was cryptic at best. If anything, Turkey's only request from the United States regarding the Khashoggi murder was not to meddle with the criminal investigation.

Hours later, Trump responded to his administration's critics, who called on the White House to suspend military aid to the Kingdom, by saying that "we don't like it, but whether or not we should stop $110 billion in this country knowing [Saudi Arabia has] four or five alternatives – that would not be acceptable to me."[9]

Again, on Oct. 12, the U.S. president contradicted himself when he told reporters that Saudi Arabia created jobs in the United States by purchasing $110 billion worth of military equipment[10] and "we would be punishing ourselves" by punishing the Kingdom.

The following day, Trump spoke by phone with King Salman of Saudi Arabia to discuss the Khashoggi murder and announced that Secretary of State Mike Pompeo would fly to Riyadh on Oct. 15 to hold talks with the Saudi leadership. He added that Washington would be frustrated if the Washington Post columnist died at the hands of Saudi officials and promised to have an answer in the near future.

Appearing on *60 Minutes* on Oct. 14, Trump said that the Saudis denied any involvement in the Khashoggi murder "every way you can imagine" and added: "Could it be them? Yes." He also stated that he hoped to know the answer "in the not-too-distant

8   https://www.theguardian.com/world/2018/oct/11/jamal-khashoggi-saudi-arabia-under-pressure-from-trump-administration
9   https://www.defensenews.com/congress/2018/10/11/trump-doubles-down-hes-not-stopping-saudi-arms-sales/
10   https://www.theguardian.com/us-news/video/2018/oct/12/trump-khashoggi-case-will-not-stop-110bn-us-saudi-arms-trade-video

future" and figure out what happened inside the Saudi consulate in Istanbul. If Saudi Arabia was behind Khashoggi's disappearance, said Trump, "there will be severe punishment."[11]   When asked whether his administration would suspend an arms deal with Riyadh over the Washington Post columnist's death, however, the U.S. president stressed that "I don't wanna hurt jobs. I don't wanna lose an order like that. There are other ways of – punishing, to use a word that's a pretty harsh word, but it's true."

Having announced that he did not wish to cancel Saudi Arabia's $110 billion agreement with the United States over Khashoggi's death on Oct. 11, Trump was now saying that he could inflict "severe punishment" on the Kingdom.[12]

For the record, that was hardly the first time that the U.S. president walked back his comments about Saudi Arabia. In retrospect, one could easily speculate that Trump was forced to make some of those statements. After all, U.S. defense contractors were quick to throw their weights behind the White House when Trump came out against letting the Khashoggi affair impact existing arms deals.[13]

The Saudi government responded to Trump's words on 60 Minutes with a written statement to the state news agency SPA, in which Riyadh said it would not bow to threats and retaliate against any negative step that Washington could take.[14]   The ceremonial sword dance, which Trump and King Salman performed during the former's maiden trip to the Kingdom, had just become reality.[15]

When asked about the Khashoggi murder on Oct. 17, Trump told the White House press corps that the United States requested any audio or video recording related to the Khashoggi murder

---

11   "Trump'tan Suudi Arabistan'a Cemal Kaşıkçı tehdidi" [Trump threatens Saudi Arabia over Jamal Khashoggi], TRT Haber, 13 October 2018.

12   https://www.usatoday.com/story/news/world/2018/10/13/jamal-khashoggi-trump-saudi-arms-deal/1630693002/

13   "Trump, Selman ile Cemal Kaşıkçı'yı görüşecek" [Trump will talk to Salman about Jamal Khashoggi], Posta, 13 October 2018.

14   "Suudi Arabistan'dan Trump'a Cemal Kaşıkçı resti!" [Saudi Arabia doubles down on Jamal Khashoggi], Sabah, 14 October 2018.

15   https://www.theguardian.com/us-news/video/2017/may/21/trump-joins-ceremonial-sword-dance-in-saudi-arabia-video

from the Turkish government. The U.S. president also said that he would not be surprised if the audio and video recordings actually existed: "I want to find out what happened, where is the fault, and we will probably know that by the end of the week. But Mike Pompeo is coming back, we're gonna have a long talk."[16]

Four days later, Trump announced that he was going to talk to congressional leaders about the Khashoggi murder, recalled that he was working closely with Turkey and Saudi Arabia, and pledged to find all the answers.[17]

Speaking to reporters at the White House on Oct. 23, U.S. President Donald Trump described what happened as "the worst cover-up in history." The Saudis had a "very bad original concept," he said. "Whoever thought of that idea, I think is in big trouble. And they should be in big trouble."[18] Asked what his administration was planning to do about the slain journalist, Trump deferred to Congress and called for a bipartisan recommendation on penalties: "In terms of what we ultimately do I'm going to leave it very much -- in conjunction with me -- up to Congress."[19]

On Oct. 24, *The Washington Post* reported that CIA Director Gina Haspel listened to an audio recording of columnist Jamal Khashoggi's final moments. That report contradicted Trump's earlier statement about being unsure whether or not the recording actually existed. Speaking to the Post, Bruce Riedel, a former CIA official and scholar at the Brookings Institution, said:

"This puts the ball firmly in Washington's court. Not only will there be more pressure now from the media but Congress will say, 'Gina, we would love to have you come visit and you can tell us exactly what you heard.'"[20] If the U.S.

16   https://www.theguardian.com/world/2018/oct/17/jamal-khashoggi-pompeo-to-meet-erdogan-as-gory-reports-of-killing-emerge
17   "Kaşıkçı'nın katledilişinin 40. günü" [The 40th day since Khashoggi's slaying], Anadolu Agency, 10 November 2018.
18   https://www.bbc.com/news/world-us-canada-45960865
19   https://www.bloomberg.com/news/articles/2018-10-23/trump-leaves-u-s-response-to-khashoggi-killing-up-to-congress
20   https://www.washingtonpost.com/world/national-security/cia-director-listens-to-audio-of-journalists-alleged-murder/2018/10/24/b07af451-7422-4fea-b0cd-ae9ad70df3e2_story.html?utm_term=.2d4b3dd5f2f1

Congress summoned the CIA Director, he added, her comments could leak before long.

WHERE THE U.S. MAINSTREAM MEDIA STOOD

Like *The Washington Post*, the leading U.S. news outlet CNN adopted an anti-Trump stance in its coverage of Jamal Khashoggi's death. In an Oct. 29 OpEd essay, Nic Robertson, the network's international diplomatic editor, warned that "Trump could pay a political price for keeping [Mohammed] bin Salman close." Recalling that the U.S. president was already under pressure for his close relationships with Russian President Vladimir Putin and the North Korean leader Kim Jong-Un, he speculated that the administration's handling of the Khashoggi affair "would open [Trump's] amiable antics with those autocrats to even more scrutiny." Robertson also wrote about his brief encounter with Turkish Foreign Minister Mevlut Cavusoglu, who said that Turkey was going to handle the evidence "step by step."[21]

The New York Times, too, was among the Trump administration's harshest critics in the wake of the Khashoggi murder. On Nov. 19, the liberal newspaper published a story, in which Mark Landler accused the U.S. president of standing with the Kingdom despite their criminal conduct and stressed that Trump began to ignore a report by the Central Intelligence Agency, which linked MBS to the incident, before it was even published.[22] A denial from Prince Mohammed over the phone, the *Times* claimed, was enough for the White House and complained that Trump refused to listen to the audio recording due to its graphic content.

Landler added:

The president's remarks were a vivid illustration of how deeply Mr. Trump has invested in the 33-year-old heir,

21   https://edition.cnn.com/2018/10/29/opinions/trump-khashoggi-stand-off-opinion-intl/index.html
22   https://www.nytimes.com/2018/11/20/world/middleeast/trump-saudi-khashoggi.html

who has become the fulcrum of the administration's strategy in the Middle East — from Iran to the Israeli-Palestinian peace process — as well as a prolific shopper for American military weapons, even if most of those contracts have not paid off yet.[23]

Noting that the Trump administration was "desperate," Riedel warned that the U.S. president may have no choice but to admit to the Saudi crown prince's complicity in the Khashoggi murder: "They're now staring at the fact that they're not going to be able to deny Mohammed bin Salman's culpability."[24]

DEFENDING RIYADH IS HARD – EVEN FOR TRUMP

Trump complained on Oct. 26 that whoever thought of murdering Jamal Khashoggi and responding to the backlash in this particular manner must find themselves in trouble. Speaking to reporters at the White House, he made a reference at the CIA Director's visit to Turkey and said that he hoped to know more about the incident soon.

Bercan Tutar, a foreign policy columnist for *Sabah*, wrote on Oct. 21 that the Khashoggi murder was the embodiment of Washington's long-standing disagreements with the Kingdom:

We have finally glanced behind the veil of secrecy before the Khashoggi murder. When Riyadh broke its silence after 18 days to claim that Khashoggi was killed in a brawl at the Saudi consulate in Istanbul, all eyes turned to the United States.

The first response by U.S. President Donald Trump, who had been waiting for the Saudi confession, was business-oriented. In an attempt to profit from Saudi Arabia's desperation, Trump announced that his administration

23   https://www.nytimes.com/2018/11/18/us/politics/trump-khashoggi-saudis.html
24   https://www.nytimes.com/2018/11/18/us/politics/trump-khashoggi-saudis.html

would keep existing arms deals and take other kinds of punitive measures against Riyadh.

As such, many experts believe that the Khashoggi crisis, which broke on Oct. 2, was a turning point in U.S.-Saudi relations. Going forward, the road from Washington to Riyadh won't be covered in rose petals and there will be more thorns along the way.

After all, the Khashoggi murder compelled all chaotic projects, which the U.S. and Israel implemented through the proxy of MBS, to undergo certain changes.

Not just the Middle East but also the 73-year-old American-Saudi alliance, which has been based on the politics of petro-dollars, encounters a major change.

In addition to the CIA's black ops, the United States wants Saudi Arabia to pick up the check for Washington's wars in Syria, Iraq, Afghanistan, Libya and Yemen. Primarily, the Trump administration set its eyes on Aramco's $2 trillion capital. In this sense, the U.S. wants to turn the Khashoggi scandal into a historic amount of money.

It would appear that Riyadh does not wish to sign a new slave contract with the United States and Israel without receiving certain concrete guarantees in return. The Saudis learned their lesson from the Obama administration's pivot to Iran, and they are being extra careful this time around.

Attempting to reverse their dependence on the United States in foreign policy and military technology, the Saudis signed a $130 billion agreement for the construction of weapon and drone factories. At the same time, they broke with tradition by purchasing S-400 missiles from Russia. Understandably, the United States is frustrated with Riyadh's new foreign policy opening – dubbed the Eurasian option.

In this sense, we must view the Khashoggi murder as an expression of the disagreement between the United States and Saudi Arabia. Otherwise, the CIA, which knew about the execution in advance, would have stopped the Saudis from such a miserable conspiracy. Yet Trump indeed waited for the Saudis to dig themselves into a hole.

In the end, Riyadh launched a counter-offensive and, for the first time in 45 years, threatened to use petroleum as a political trump card and to use the Chinese Yuan rather than the U.S. Dollar. Roger Diwan, an OPEC watcher, maintains that the Saudis "broke an essential market taboo" by issuing that threat.

There is no reason to believe that the U.S. will turn its back on its 73-year-old strategy based on Saudi despotism overnight.

U.S. President Trump did not insult King Salman in front of a global audience, by saying that Riyadh would not last two weeks without Washington's support, for no reason. Now, citing the Khashoggi murder, Trump threatens economic sanctions against the Saudis.
It is important to understand how Russia and China helped the Saudis in a geopolitical sense since the Khashoggi crisis broke out.

After all, the problem at hand is far bigger than the death of a Saudi journalist or an effort to tarnish the Saudi crown prince's reputation. Having read the play, Turkey called the shot and dealt a heavy blow against Washington's reliance on Saudi despotism. As such, we strengthen our hand against Riyadh, the United States and Israel simultaneously.[25]

The strongest criticism against Trump's contradictory statements about the Khashoggi murder came from Max Boot, who authored an op-ed essay for *The Washington Post* on Oct. 17 and accused the U.S. president of stalling the public debate and distracting attention from the incident by talking about rogue killers.

---

25   Bercan Tutar, "ABD'nin Suudi despotizminde kırılma noktası" [A tipping point in the Saudi despotism of the United States," Sabah, 21 October 2018.

"How long before he claims that Khashoggi could have been killed by a 400-pound couch potato who somehow waddled into the heavily guarded Saudi Consulate?" asked Boot.[26] He added that it was a great time to be a dictator, as the United States seemed to support all dictators.

On Oct. 19, *The Washington Post's* Moscow bureau chief, Anton Troianovski, and Emily Rauhala, a staff writer covering foreign affairs, published a critical analysis of Trump's contradictory remarks. The authors recalled that the world watched the U.S. president downplay the Khashoggi murder for weeks and warned that Trump's inconsistent statements raised questions about his administration's credibility. "The U.S. is setting a new standard for itself," they quoted Vali Nasr as saying, "[The U.S. response to the Khashoggi murder] signals a very different foreign policy that does not hold governments accountable for things that are outside normal legal or ethical parameters."[27]

The Democrats, too, complained about Washington's double standards. On Nov. 10, several news outlets reported that Representative Brad Sherman was planning to introduce legislation to prevent a nuclear agreement between the United States and the Kingdom.[28]

In a Nov. 18 interview with *Fox News Sunday*, Trump acknowledged the receipt of the Khashoggi murder's audio recording. "I don't want to hear the tape," he added, because it was "very violent, very vicious and terrible."[29]

Let us make a quick correction to Trump's account here. In that interview, the U.S. president probably meant the transcript of the audio recording rather than the audio itself. After all, the Turkish intelligence did not provide a copy of the recording to the Central Intelligence Agency.

---

26   https://www.washingtonpost.com/opinions/global-opinions/trump-has-given-every-despot-on-the-planet-a-license-to-kill/2018/10/17/cf3d6ea2-d211-11e8-8c22-fa2ef74bd6d6_story.html?utm_term=.bf141d23f5f0

27   https://www.washingtonpost.com/world/2018/10/19/world-has-question-white-house-when-do-murders-matter/?utm_term=.d642fbc0be30

28   https://www.vox.com/2018/11/9/18072660/saudi-arabia-nuclear-deal-congress-123-agreement-sherman

29   https://www.theguardian.com/world/2018/nov/18/jamal-khashoggi-killers-may-have-taken-body-parts-out-of-turkey-in-luggage

Two days later, Trump contradicted himself again to claim that the CIA's conclusion was not 100 percent. Hours later, he would tell reporters that the U.S. intelligence community was still reviewing the evidence: "Our intelligence agencies continue to assess all information, but it could very well be that the Crown Prince had knowledge of this tragic event – maybe he did and maybe he didn't!"[30]

The U.S. president faced heavy criticism from the media over those comments. On Nov. 21, Fred Ryan, the publisher and chief executive officer of the Washington Post, and Karen Attiah, the newspaper's Global Opinions editor, issued strongly-worded statements against Donald Trump's remarks on the Khashoggi murder.

U.S. news outlets described Trump's statement as a reiteration of Washington's support for Saudi Arabia. The Washington Post accused the U.S. president of placing "personal relationships above the United States' strategic relationships."[31]

The next day, Trump threw his weight behind the Kingdom yet again: "Israel would be in big trouble without Saudi Arabia. So what does that mean, Israel is going to leave? You want Israel to leave? We have a very strong ally in Saudi Arabia."[32] Implicitly, he conceded that Mohammed bin Salman's position was aligned with Tel Aviv.

Finally, the U.S. president doubled down on his support for the Saudi crown prince, announced that there was not enough evidence to hold Mohammed bin Salman accountable for Jamal Khashoggi's death and made the case that "maybe the world" ought to be held accountable instead.[33]

---

30   https://www.telegraph.co.uk/news/2018/11/20/trump-says-crown-prince-may-have-known-khashoggi-killing-says/
31   https://www.washingtonpost.com/opinions/trumps-dangerous-message-to-tyrants-flash-money-and-get-away-with-murder/2018/11/21/4202e69e-edc2-11e8-8679-934a2b33be52_story.html?utm_term=.7744e4bbd962
32   https://www.timesofisrael.com/trump-israel-would-be-in-big-trouble-without-saudi-arabia/
33   https://www.independent.co.uk/news/world/americas/us-politics/trump-khashoggi-murder-blame-vicious-world-saudi-journalist-a8647701.html

TURKEY'S RED LINE

Turkish President Recep Tayyip Erdogan's administration managed the crisis carefully and strived to protect the rights of Jamal Khashoggi, whom the Turkish leader knew personally and to whom he gave an interview after the July 2016 coup attempt in Turkey.

Repeatedly urging the Saudis to determine the whereabouts of Khashoggi's remains and highlighting the human and religious aspects of the murder, Erdogan made it clear that he was not going to exploit the tragedy in diplomatic negotiations – unlike Donald Trump's America and Mohammed bin Salman's KSA. The way he saw it, Turkey had no choice but to speak for the man, who was murdered brutally, destroyed and disappeared. That was Turkey's red line.

Saudi Arabia, in turn, drew its own red line around the political survival of Crown Prince Mohammed bin Salman, who was politically responsible for the Khashoggi murder. They did not go to great lengths to hide that fact either.

In a Nov. 22 interview with BBC, Saudi Foreign Minister Adel Al-Jubeir said that efforts to hold the Saudi crown prince accountable for Jamal Khashoggi's slaying would constitute a "red line," for the Kingdom. He proceeded to urge the Turks to stop leaking information to the press – which meant that Turkey's plan was working.[34]

Erdogan's most important statement on the Khashoggi murder came after an official visit to France. The Turkish president shared valuable information with journalists covering his trip. Here's what Erdal Safak, *Sabah's* editor-in-chief, wrote on Nov. 13:

As we talked about the Khashoggi murder over dinner, we included [German Chancellor Angela] Merkel and [French President Emmanuel] Macron as well. It is clear that the murder was premeditated and the order came from the highest levels of the Saudi government. As I mentioned

---

34   https://www.middleeasteye.net/news/MBS-red-line-khashoggi-murder-probe-saudi-foreign-minister-says-2045123307

in my op-ed essay for *The Washington Post*, it would be impossible for me to think such things about the Servant of the Holy Mosques, whom I respect greatly.

Yet we want to find out who gave the orders. They must tell us who gave the order and what the murder suspects said [in their statements to the prosecution]. I told President Trump, too, that it was unnecessary to look for the killers here and there. First and foremost, the killers are among the 18 [detainees]. Did the [Saudi operatives] who arrived before Friday come to make preparations? After all, Khashoggi visited the consulate on Friday and he was received warmly. He was then invited to come back on Tuesday. A team arrived in the early hours on Tuesday. They, too, made preparations for the next day.

Immediately after the murder, [Saudi] officials claimed that Khashoggi walked out of the consulate. Is such a thing even remotely possible? After all, his fiancée was waiting outside. How is it possible that Khashoggi used that door or another door to leave and did not take his fiancée with him? It is obvious that something fishy is going on. Saudi Foreign Minister Adel Al-Jubeir reportedly talked about a local collaborator. Later, [the Saudis] claimed that Jubeir said no such thing. We played the audio recordings for anyone that asked to listen. Our intelligence agency did not hide anything. We played it for whoever asked to listen: the Saudis, the United States, France, Canada, Germany and the United Kingdom.

...

The audio is truly terrible. As a matter of fact, the Saudi intelligence agent was so shocked upon listening to the tape that they said: "This person must have taken heroin. Only someone on heroin would do such a thing." Yes, he was shocked when he heard it. The truth is out there. Nonetheless, some people are still trying to distort the facts.

When the Crown Prince called me, he asked me if he could send his attorney general [to Turkey]. I said that he was welcome to visit, of course. He came and talked to the chief

141

prosecutor in Istanbul. When he asked for an audience with me, the chief prosecutor told [the Saudi attorney general] that he was his counterpart and he alone would see him.

Unfortunately, the attorney general was inclined to slow things down. All those things happened and there is all this information available. It is unacceptable that the [Saudi] prosecutor could be still undecided. The Crown Prince says that he will shed light on the incident and do what is necessary. He said that to my special representatives. We are patiently waiting.

A journalist was murdered. We must shed light on what happened and identify the assailants. 18 people are under arrest in Saudi Arabia. The killers are absolutely among those 18 detainees. Who else was there? Who gave the order? We must establish who gave them the order to kill. What happened to Khashoggi's body? If it was buried, where was it buried? Or was it dismembered and spirited away? We will follow up on this incident at the international level as well. That murder took place in Istanbul. The Chief Prosecutor's Office in Istanbul already submitted a request to the Saudi authorities to hold the suspects accountable in Turkey.

A CLEAR WARNING TO THE TIGER TEAM

In an op-ed essay for the Washington Post, the Turkish president stated that he did not believe King Salman to have ordered the hit on Jamal Khashoggi:

Jamal Khashoggi, a Saudi journalist and a family man, entered Saudi Arabia's Consulate in Istanbul on Oct. 2 for marriage formalities. No one – not even his fiancee, who was waiting outside the compound — has ever seen him again.

Over the course of the past month, Turkey has moved heaven and earth to shed light on all aspects of this case. As a result of our efforts, the world has learned that Khashoggi was killed in cold blood by a death squad, and it has been established that his murder was premeditated.

Yet there are other, no less significant questions whose answers will contribute to our understanding of this deplorable act. Where is Khashoggi's body? Who is the "local collaborator" to whom Saudi officials claimed to have handed over Khashoggi's remains? Who gave the order to kill this kind soul? Unfortunately, the Saudi authorities have refused to answer those questions.

We know the perpetrators are among the 18 suspects detained in Saudi Arabia. We also know those individuals came to carry out their orders: Kill Khashoggi and leave. Finally, we know the order to kill Khashoggi came from the highest levels of the Saudi government.

Some seem to hope this "problem" will go away in time. But we will keep asking those questions, which are crucial to the criminal investigation in Turkey, but also to Khashoggi's family and loved ones. A month after his killing, we still do not know where his body is. At the very least, he deserves a proper burial in line with Islamic customs. We owe it to his family and friends, including his former colleagues at The Post, to give them an opportunity to say their goodbyes and pay their respects to this honorable man. To ensure that the world will keep asking the same questions, we have shared the evidence with our friends and allies, including the United States.

As we continue to look for answers, I would like to stress that Turkey and Saudi Arabia enjoy friendly relations. I do not believe for a second that King Salman, the custodian of the holy mosques, ordered the hit on Khashoggi. Therefore, I have no reason to believe that his murder reflected Saudi Arabia's official policy.
In this sense, it would be wrong to view the Khashoggi slaying as a "problem" between two countries. Nonetheless, I must add that our friendship with Riyadh, which goes back a long time, doesn't mean we will turn a blind eye to the premeditated murder that unfolded in front of our very eyes. The killing of Khashoggi is inexplicable. Had this atrocity taken place in the United States or

elsewhere, authorities in those countries would have gotten to the bottom of what happened. It would be out of the question for us to act any other way.

No one should dare to commit such acts on the soil of a NATO ally again. If anyone chooses to ignore that warning, they will face severe consequences.[35]

In the world of intelligence-to-intelligence diplomacy, the two final sentences quoted above meant one thing: "You won't be able to do such things here in the future either." Had the Turks not cracked the Khashoggi case and revealed the truth, Saudi Arabia's Tiger Team could have carried out other attacks against dissidents in Istanbul. Turkey's success in the area of counter-intelligence foiled such plots – at least for now. You can find additional, previously unknown information about Tiger Team and its plans in the relevant section.

Here's a clue: The Saudi regime created ten cells in Turkey to carry out attacks akin to Iranian assaults against dissidents in the 1980s and the assassinations of Chechen dissident by the Russians in 2008-2015. The Turkish intelligence was watching the Saudi cells around the clock. Where the illegals lived and which dissidents they were monitoring was known to the Turkish authorities, which waited for them to take action before picking them up – just as they did when the Saudis killed Jamal Khashoggi on 'their' soil and tried to blame it on Turkey by having a body double walk around Istanbul.

---

35   https://www.washingtonpost.com/news/global-opinions/wp/2018/11/02/recep-tayyip-erdogan-saudi-arabia-still-has-many-questions-to-answer-about-jamal-khashoggis-killing/?utm_term=.848e296c5cf6

CHAPTER IV

How?

1

THE BODY DOUBLE

The Fake Beard

A bearded, heavy-set man, who was approximately 180 cm tall and weighed around 100 kg, entered a public restroom behind the Blue Mosque at 4.50 p.m. on October 2. Five minutes later, he walked out, with no beard yet an irritating grin on his face. The man was also wearing fresh clothes. Gone were his black jacket, grey shirt and dark jeans.

The curious man had arrived at Istanbul's tourist district from Levent in a yellow cab. Just 90 minutes ago, before leaving the Saudi consulate, he had put on the clothes of Jamal Khashoggi, who was killed and stripped naked inside the same building. The middle-aged man had one job: to walk around the city, wearing a dead man's attire, to leave a false trail around the consulate's rear exit and to be seen by Istanbul's CCTV system.

Saif Saad Al-Qahtani, another member of the Saudi death squad, accompanied the man. Together, they walked out of their country's consulate in Istanbul at 2.53 p.m.

Judging by photographs taken at Atatürk International at 3.29 a.m. and near the consulate at 10.57 a.m. earlier that day, the body double was usually clean shaven. Therefore, the Turkish police was quick to flag the man when he exited the building with a fake beard. Moreover, the body double was wearing glasses in an attempt to look like Jamal Khashoggi.

Having exited the consulate from its backdoor and walked down the street for a few minutes, the two Saudi operatives hailed a taxi at 3.15 p.m. At 4.07, the taxi dropped them off near the Blue Mosque. The men visited the mosque between 4.13 and 4.29 p.m. After the body double changed back into his own clothes at the nearby public restroom, the Saudis took another taxi to their hotel at 5.24 p.m. By 6.04 p.m., they were back in Levent. The body double dumped a plastic bag, which contained Khashoggi's clothes, into a garbage bin near the M Hotel at 6.05 p.m. For minutes later, the two men walked into their hotel.

Like Mutreb, the death squad's leader, and his accomplices, the body double left the Saudi consulate from the rear door. He'd taken the private jet with the tail number HZ SK2, which was owned by the Saudi aviation company Sky Prime, to Turkey. In other words, the mysterious man was one of the nine operatives that formed the first component of the 15-strong Tiger Team that Riyadh had dispatched to Istanbul.

After walking around the city in disguise, the man left the country on a commercial flight on October 3.[1] He wasn't alone: Saif Saad Al-Qahtani, his colleague from the Saudi death squad, was with him the whole time. The two suspects arrived at Atatürk International and flew back to Riyadh after clearing passport control at 12.18 a.m.

SOLDIER BY PROFESSION, BODY DOUBLE BY FATE

The body double's full name was Mustafa Mohammed Al-Madani. Born in 1962, he served as a brigadier general in the Saudi military. Although some media outlets falsely described Al-Madani as a security guard, trusted government sources confirm that he was indeed a soldier.

The Saudi death squad included two brigadier generals (including Mutreb), a lieutenant colonel who also happened to be

---

1 Some members of the Tiger Team took private jets to Turkey, but left on commercial flights. Their goal was to mislead the Turkish intelligence and police.

an autopsy expert, three intelligence officers (including an airport security specialist), a colonel from the Saudi intelligence, an Air Force lieutenant, a member of the Royal Guard and an additional intelligence operative with extensive knowledge of strategy, planning and combat. Although the Turkish authorities could not establish what the remaining two assassins did for a living, it was clear that they were senior Saudi officials as well.

Al-Madani's role, however, was crystal clear: he only had to wear Jamal Khashoggi's clothes, walk out of the Saudi consulate and walk around the city – to make it seem like the slain journalist had left the building in one piece. In other words, Al-Madani was a body double alone. It made perfect sense: Al-Madani was around the same age as Khashoggi. The two men could have been mistaken for twin brothers.

The body double spectacle's sole purpose was to mislead the world into thinking that the *Washington Post* columnist exited the compound and went missing on the streets of Istanbul. Raising questions about Turkey's culpability would have been an added benefit.

Obviously, Al-Madani knew all along that Khashoggi was going to die inside the Saudi consulate in Istanbul that day. Nonetheless, there is no evidence linking him to the decision to kill the journalist or the planning and execution of the murder. For some reason, however, Al-Madani was the first member of the death squad to react on Twitter when Sabah published photographs of the Saudi death squad.

At the time, Al-Madani claimed that his photograph on Sabah's front page was taken during an earlier trip to Istanbul. By taking to social media, he indirectly incriminated himself. The Saudi operative was following media reports closely and clearly wondering what the Turkish authorities had on the Tiger Team. As such, he revealed his weakness to the Turks.

Al-Madani's Twitter account, in which he refers himself as Engineer Mustafa Madani, there is no additional personal information about the man – nor a lot of content.[2]

---

2   Abdurrahman Şimşek and Nazif Karaman, "Cemal Kaşıkçı'nın dublörü böyle kaçtı" [This is how Jamal Khashoggi's body double escaped], Sabah, 24 October 2018.

A FRIEND LOOKS YOU IN THE EYE.
AN ADVERSARY LOOKS YOU IN THE FOOT

The body double and his accomplices took everything into account, as they worked diligently on all other aspects of the Khashoggi murder, yet they missed something: the body double's shoes weren't the same as Jamal Khashoggi's footwear.

The Turkish police discovered that detail during a close inspection of the CCTV footage that helped them identify Al-Madani. The man behind the discovery was Mustafa Çalışkan, Istanbul's police chief who oversaw some 750 law enforcement agents working on the case.

Çalışkan instructed Ilker Küçükhidir, who leads the intelligence department, to include 500 officers to the investigation team. An additional 250 law enforcement agents joined the team from the counter-terrorism unit. The intelligence specialists played a significant role in identifying the suspects by repeatedly watching CCTV footage from the vicinity of Atatürk International and various parts of the city.

Police officers watching the video recording found it suspicious that the body double exited the consulate from its rear door. They proceeded to work on the footage more diligently. In light of that close inspection, the Turkish police concluded that Al-Madani was wearing Jamal Khashoggi's clothes.

The body double's attire was almost identical to the Saudi journalist's clothes. The only difference was that Khashoggi had walked into the consulate wearing leather shoes, whereas Al-Madani left the compound with sneakers. In other words, the Saudi operative and the *Washington Post* columnist had different shoe sizes. Khashoggi wore size 42, yet visual experts assessed that Al-Madani's shoe size was 45 or 46. The body double's feet were too big to fit into the slain journalist's shoes.

Mustafa Çalışkan's attention to detail led to the discovery after hours spent watching the CCTV footage with his staff. Khashoggi wore dress shoes, whereas Al-Madani had white sneakers. That split-second revelation resulted in the conclusion that Khashoggi had not left the consulate. Identifying the body double was a major

151

step towards foiling an imminent attack against Turkey.

In light of that discovery, the Turkish police attempted to find out what happened to Khashoggi's clothes, which Al-Madani used to leave a false trail on the day of the murder. Locating those items, which would typically carry traces of sweat and hair, could have resulted in the discovery of DNA evidence necessary to confirm the identities of the body double and his victim. That's why law enforcement agents worked hard to find Khashoggi's clothes.

KHASHOGGI'S CLOTHES, NOT HIS BODY, WERE BURIED

The intelligence unit led by Ilker Küçükhidir reached the following conclusions:

The body double had taken a yellow cab from Sultanahmet to Levent after putting on Khashoggi's clothes and walking around the city like an actor. He took off Khashoggi's clothes at a public restroom in Sultanahmet and dumped them in a garbage container by the subway station near the M Hotel.

The garbage collectors picked up the trash at 6 p.m. that day and took everything to a recycling center in Kemerburgaz. At the recycling center, which employs some 50 women to sort separate reusable items from actual waste, Khashoggi's clothes may have been identified as recyclable. Yet the investigators could not find what they sought in the reusable item storage. Everything else would go to a landfill near Şile in the city's outskirts, where they would be buried underground. It was impossible to find Khashoggi's personal belongings there.

The murder took place on October 2, yet the recycling center wasn't inspected until three days later – when the police discovered CCTV footage of Al-Madani dumping Khashoggi's clothes into the garbage container. Provided that the recycling center sorted through garbage within 12 hours and all waste materials were buried within 24 hours, it was virtually impossible to access the trash after one day.

Nonetheless, a group of approximately 100 officials from the Turkish intelligence and police searched the landfill for clues. The authorities also enlisted the services of paper collectors in the area to increase their chances of success. Yet Khashoggi's clothes could not be located.

2

AT THE CONSULAR RESIDENCE, FIVE BAGS VANISH INTO THIN AIR

3,500 Hours Of CCTV Footage

In the immediate aftermath of the Khashoggi murder, Turkey established a crisis command center and formed a special investigative team, which brought together intelligence officers from MIT's Istanbul field office and law enforcement agents from the Istanbul police, to shed light on what happened. As described in Chapter II, the Turkish authorities were already aware that the Saudi journalist was the victim of a premeditated murder. The newly-established team's objective, however, was to find admissible evidence.

In an attempt to bring the Khashoggi murder into light, the Istanbul police went over footage from a total of 78 security cameras near the consulate and the consular residence, and along the suspects' travel routes in Istanbul between Jamal Khashoggi's first visit to the Saudi consulate on September 28 and October 11. Over the course of the investigation, police officers watched 3,500 hours of footage recorded over a total of 147 days.

Simultaneously, the Terrorism and Organized Crime Bureau at the Istanbul chief prosecutor's office, which oversaw the legal investigation, questioned 38 employees of the Saudi consulate, including drivers, technicians, accountants and switchboard operators. The consular staff did not provide useful information to the authorities.

The authorities identified three vehicles that left the Saudi consulate at approximately 3 p.m. on the day of the Khashoggi murder. Two of those vehicles headed to Büyükdere Avenue, whereas the third vehicle drove to the consular residence. The Saudis intended to use the two cars to distract the Turkish authorities. It was the diplomatic vehicle with the plate number 34 CC 1865 that transported five bags, which contained Jamal Khashoggi's body pieces, to Mohammed Al-Otaiba's residence.

Just as Khashoggi himself had disappeared into the Saudi consulate that day, the five suitcases containing his body pieces vanished into thin air after leaving the consulate at 3.08 p.m. and entering the consular residence two minutes later. The Turkish authorities could see Saudi operatives carrying the body pieces into the consul's home, but there was no footage of those bags leaving the premises.

Three members of the death squad left the Saudi consulate at 3.05 p.m. and drove a diplomatic vehicle to the residence. It became clear that their bags remained inside the consular residence upon inspection of CCTV footage from the area.

The Saudi operatives used the diplomatic vehicle with the plate number 34 CC 1865, which was parked in the consulate's indoor garage, to take the suitcases to the residence. As a matter of fact, a total of six vehicles departed from the Saudi consulate on the day of the murder. Yet the Turkish investigation concluded that the killers used only one of those vehicles.

There is no doubt that the vehicle carried Jamal Khashoggi's body pieces. At 3.09 p.m., it was caught on camera outside the consular residence on Meseli Street. CCTV footage also shows clearly that the Saudis took five pieces of luggage into the building. That those suitcases never left the premises supports the view that Khashoggi's body is in the well under the consular residence.[1]

---

1   Abdurrahman Şimşek and Nazif Karaman, "Cemal Kaşıkçı'nın dublörü böyle kaçtı" [This Is How Jamal Khashoggi's Body Double Escaped], *Sabah*, 24 October 2018.

THE DIPLOMATIC VEHICLE AT THE CAR WASH

The team led by Maher Abdulaziz Mutreb, a general in the Saudi intelligence and one of Mohammed bin Salman's right-hand men, took five suitcases to the consular residence. According to CCTV footage, Mutreb carried Khashoggi's body pieces together with Tubaigy and Al-Harby. The diplomatic vehicle, which transported the bags, remained at the residence for three whole days. The Saudis took it to the car wash right away.

The Turks found traces in two spots when they inspected the van. Yet the luminol test did not reveal biological evidence matching Khashoggi's DNA. It was clear that the Saudi chemist and toxicologist spent some time on that vehicle when it came back from the car wash.

Provided that the Saudis implemented a four-step plan to cover up the murder evidence, Turkish investigators could not find any evidence in the consulate or the residence.

The Turks searched the consulate on October 17, the day after the Saudi consul general, Mohammed Al-Otaiba, suddenly left the country.[2] Although the chemist and the toxicologist took precautions against the luminol test, the Saudis used less refined methods to destroy the suitcases. Turkish officials assess that the bag containing Khashoggi's body parts have been torn into pieces with heavy machinery.

SECRET DOCUMENTS ON THE DEATH SQUAD'S PHONES

Just before this book went to print, the Turkish intelligence shared a crucial piece of information regarding the potential location of Jamal Khashoggi's remains with law enforcement. Moreover, the National Intelligence Organization accessed data from the cell phones of some Saudi operatives, including critical correspondence and photographs linking those individuals to the Khashoggi murder. In other words, the Turkish authorities were

2   "Suudi başkonsolosu ülkesine döndü" [The Saudi consul general returned to his country], TGRT Haber, 16 October 2018.

able to access some key pieces of evidence stored on those individuals' cell phones using an undisclosed method.

If that information, which shows that Khashoggi's body was dismembered by the Saudi operatives, leads to any indication of the slain journalist's remains, Turkey will investigate it. Yet the data that the Turkish authorities have accessed to date hasn't helped them to find where Khashoggi's body is.

At the same time, intelligence analysts worked on hours of audio recordings from the Saudi consulate – including the arrival of the killers and Khashoggi's first visit on September 28. According to sources, there was unusual traffic between Riyadh and the Saudi consulate in Istanbul between September 28 and October 2.

The consular staff that made those phone calls was Ahmed Abdullah Al-Muzaini, the Saudi intelligence agency's station chief in Istanbul. After making several calls to his country's capital, Al-Muzaini flew to his native country. The station chief's phone calls with the center indicate that the Saudis began planning the Khashoggi murder as early as September 28.

A SERPENT BITING ITS OWN TAIL

There is a three-hour gap in what the Turkish authorities know about the Khashoggi murder, when the Saudi operatives remain inside the consular residence with the five suitcases. Whatever happened to Khashoggi's remains happens right there and then. The Saudis probably dumped the body parts to the nearby well. It is less likely that they moved the remains out of the residence and disposed of it elsewhere.

It is a certainty that the Saudi operatives dismembered the slain *Washington Post* columnist's body. Even the Saudi attorney general conceded that point in a statement by his spokesman, Shalan Al-Shalan, on November 15. According to the Saudi authorities, Khashoggi's body was dismembered and moved out of the consulate in Istanbul. The killers, they say, initially attempted to talk the victim into returning to the Kingdom.

A fight broke out between Khashoggi and the assassins, when

the journalist refused to comply with the Saudi request. The operatives proceeded to inject him with a lethal dose of chemicals. Riyadh said that Khashoggi was killed and dismembered after the killers failed to persuade him to go back to the Kingdom. It did not respond to the claim that the body was dissolved in acid. Finally, the Saudis claimed that a local collaborator had disposed of the body, yet failed to support their claim with concrete evidence.

Having ordered a hit on Jamal Khashoggi, the Saudis continued to play for time and cover up the crime by citing the ongoing search for the slain journalist's remains. According to the attorney general's office, the Saudi operatives that moved Khashoggi's body out of the consulate in pieces handed it over to a local collaborator. Riyadh did not provide any information about that individual, who was tasked with eliminating or burying the body, yet pledged to share a facial composite with the Turkish authorities.[3]

Here's how we know that the Saudis were lying through their teeth: If there were indeed a local collaborator, it would be completely unnecessary to produce a facial composite. Maher Abdulaziz Mutreb, the intelligence general who led the Saudi death squad, would be in a position to know to whom his team handed over the victim's remains. It would be unreasonable to think that a group of trained assassins gave body pieces to a random bypasser. No random individual could be trusted to carry out such a sensitive task. In this sense, the Saudi prosecutor's statements contradicted each other.

WHO DID WHAT?

Having studied the Khashoggi murder in detail and examined at length the video footage, from which stills of suitcases entering the consular residence were obtained, the authors of this book must point out the following:

Jamal Khashoggi's dismembered body was placed in five suitcases, moved out of the Saudi consulate in Istanbul and taken

---

3   "Kaşıkçı cinayetinde adım adım inkârdan itirafa giden yol" [In The Khashoggi Murder, The Step-By-Step Road From Denial To Confession], *Sabah*, 16 November 2018.

to the consular residence nearby. Several members of the death squad were already at the residence, waiting for their colleagues to bring the bags from the consulates.

Based on a detailed analysis of the footage that we have obtained exclusively, here's how the body parts vanished into the consular residence at exactly 3.05 p.m. on October 2:

First of all, only some members of the Saudi death squad were inside the consulate at the time of the Khashoggi murder. Others were stationed at consul general Mohammed Al-Otaiba's residence down the street, getting ready to eliminate the slain journalist's remains. We concluded that the following Saudi operatives were in the consulate:

1- Maher Abdulaziz Mutreb
2- Salah Mohammed Al-Tubaigy
3- Sair Ghaleb Al-Harby (who drove the diplomatic vehicle with the license number 34 CC 1865)
4- Badr Lafi Al-Otaiba
5- Waled Abdullah Al-Shahry
6- Mustafa Mohammed Al-Madani (a.k.a. the body double)
7- Sayf Saaf Al-Qahtani (who accompanied Madani to Sultanahmet)
8- Fahd Shabib Al-Balawi
9- Turki Musharrif Al-Shahry
10- Mohammed Saad Al-Zahrani (who checked the night before the murder whether the Mercedes-Benz Vito van would fit into the parking garage – left the consulate alone)

The following men, by contrast, were stationed at the consular residence the whole time. They did not set foot in the consulate:

1- Abdulaziz Mohammed Al-Hossawi
2- Khaled Aiz Al-Tabi
3- Mansour Othman Aba Hussein

4-   Naif Hassan Al-Arifi (who was with Al-Zahrani during the dress rehearsal)
5-   Mashaal Saad Al-Bostani

THE SAUDIS WHO CARRIED THE SUITCASES

A detailed analysis of CCTV footage led to the conclusion that the following operatives spent time in the consulate and the residence alike: Maher Abdulaziz Mutreb, Saleh Mohammed Al-Tubaigy, and Sair Ghalib Al-Harby. After all, those three men transported the five suitcases containing Khashoggi's body parts from the consulate to the residence, where a second group of operatives awaited their arrival. Those men were responsible for carrying the bags into the consular residence and facilitating the elimination of the slain journalist's remains.

According to video recordings, the diplomatic vehicle with the license number 34 CC 1865 parked in front of the Saudi consul's residence at 3.05 p.m. Upon the vehicle's arrival at the site, some members of the death squad walked out of the residence. During those moments, there was a lot of foot traffic outside the building. Before the vehicle drives into the parking garage, several operatives were seen walking there. After spending three whole minutes on the vehicle's front seat, Mutreb got off the van at 3.09 p.m., like a ruthless mob boss or a drug trafficker, and made his way to the parking garage.

The vehicle entered the indoor garage, with Khashoggi's remains on board, at 3.12 p.m. One by one, the Saudi operatives carried the suitcases into the consular residence, as unsuspecting civilians walked by the building and children, playing on the street, were caught on camera.

According to the video recording, Khaled Aiz Al-Taby dragged the first suitcase for seven or eight meters on the ground before carrying it into the residence at 15:19:35. The second and third bags are picked up by Abdulaziz Mohammed Al-Hossawi at 15:19:58. Finally, Saad Al-Bostani carried the remaining two pieces into the building at 15:20:15. Having dropped off the suitcases, Al-Bostani goes back to pick up black plastic bags containing bloody plastic bags, on which the operatives dismembered Khashoggi's body, at 15:21:26.

The Saudi operatives moving the bags into the consular residence were visibly anxious and clearly in a rush. At the time, they were unaware of the CCTV camera, located at the nearby police checkpoint, recording their movements, as they dragged the dismembered body of a world famous journalist like they were going on vacation.

That the public prosecutor in Riyadh falsely claimed that his office was still looking for Khashoggi's remains, even though everything happened in front of CCTV cameras and the Saudi authorities themselves learned it all from the killers, was pathetic to say the least. In other words, the Saudi claim that they do not know the whereabouts of Jamal Khashoggi's body contradicts itself.

THE PRE-MURDER KEBAB SESSION

Another noteworthy aspect of the Khashoggi murder was that the Saudi consulate's Turkish driver was on leave as the killers carried the five suitcases into the consular residence. An additional 28 Turkish employees of the Saudi consulate were told to take the day off. After the murder, Saudi Arabia's consul general in Istanbul, Mohammed Al-Otaiba did not leave his home for three whole days – like the diplomatic vehicle that the killers used to transport Khashoggi's remains.

The Turkish driver, who picked up the Saudi operatives from the airport upon their arrival from Riyadh, told the prosecutor's office that the vehicle was taken away from him on the day of the murder. A member of the death squad, he said, was behind the wheel on October 2.

In an interview with Al Haber, the driver described the moments that he spent with Khashoggi's killers as follows:

Their flight landed at 3.20 a.m. There was nine of them – three in each vehicle. Maher Abdulaziz Mutreb rode in my car. I took him to a hotel near the consulate in Levent. They instructed us to be ready at 8 a.m. Two other consular vehicles were waiting with us in front of the hotel at the time. I arrived at the consulate and dropped them off outside the barricades. They opened the gates and let my vehicle into the consular parking garage. I sat by the security gate and they offered me tea. Some time between 10 and 11 [p.m.] I told them I wanted to go out.

As we waited outside, we were informed that [the officials] were coming out. Khashoggi was told he could come in and searched before going in. His fiancée started waiting for Khashoggi in front of a supermarket.

The driver told the authorities that the assassins, whom he picked up at the airport and dropped off in the afternoon later the same day, were in a good mood. "They smoked and drank alcohol in the car," he said. The following were his remarks on the time period when Khashoggi went disappeared into the Saudi consulate:

Khashoggi walked in, but never came out. As a matter of fact, here's what happened: some other Saudi guests arrived. The security guards told them that an inspection was underway and they could not enter, and instructed them to come back the following day. Approximately two hours after Khashoggi entered, I received a phone call. [The operatives] said they were at the hotel and asked to be picked up. We drove to the hotel. Four people appeared at the door. They did not look like the individuals that I had picked up at the airport. "We are part of your group. We want a car and another vehicle for the bags. We will take two vehicles to the airport," they said. On the way to the airport, they asked me where they could eat, so I took them to a kebab place.[4]

---

4   "Cemal Kaşıkçı cinayetinde infaz timini taşıyan şoför A Haber'e konuştu" [The Driver Who Drove The Death Squad Spoke To A Haber], *Sabah*, 26 October 2018.

The driver described how the vehicle left the consulate, carrying five bags that contained Khashoggi's body parts:

> No more than an hour later, three vehicles exited [the consulate]. They had CC license plates. I gazed into the van carefully to see whether our [passengers] were leaving. I looked at length, but could not see into the van. The windows were extremely dark. One vehicle went left and the others drove straight. There were some Saudi guests arriving before that. Everyone came out within half an hour. Yet the lady [Hatice Cengiz] caught my eye, as she waited for one or two hours.[5]

An eyewitness to this part of the story, Hatice Cengiz, assumed that her fiancée was detained inside the Saudi consulate for questioning and hoped for his immediate release. That was before the public knew about the Khashoggi murder. In an Oct. 26 interview with *Habertürk*, she described those moments as follows:

> *I do not have children, but I believe mothers experience this type of emotion. Police officers arrived from the field office. I headed directly to the police station to file a complaint. They went [to the consulate] and spoke with the officials there, but I do not know what they discussed. That day, I waited until late night.*

> *Within the first hour, I thought that they were trying to scare me. I did not think of something like this. Had I thought about it, I would have walked in with him. I wish he hadn't wanted to marry me, as I am left with an extremely heavy emotional burden. I do not know how to explain what happened to someone who just wanted to get married. It did not occur to me that they could do something like this to a world famous patriot and nationalist like Jamal Khashoggi.[6]*

---

5   Ibid.
6   Transcript of the Habertürk interview with Hatice Cengiz, 26 October 2018.

3

THE STATION CHIEF'S SECRET LINKS

The Unknowns of the Murder Hierarchy

According to Hatice Cengiz, who Jamal Khashoggi's last friend to see him alive, the Saudi journalist assumed that Crown Prince Mohammed bin Salman's men would not dare carry out this type of mission in Turkey. Unfortunately, he was wrong.

That misconception was partly informed by his warm reception at the consulate during his first visit on September 28. Without a doubt, Khashoggi did not know that the superiors of his hosts would decide to kill him on the day of his application.

Saudi Crown Prince Mohammed bin Salman ordered the hit on Jamal Khashoggi. He gave the order to Saud Al-Qahtani, his right-hand man and the keeper of his secrets, and Ahmad Assiri, the Saudi intelligence agency's deputy head who was known as an MBS loyalist. Qahtani and Assiri passed the crown prince's orders to the death squad.

Ahmed Abdullah Al-Muzainy oversaw that process and delivered the order and the mission plan to the assassins within the Saudi hierarchy.[1] In other words, the Saudi intelligence agency's station chief in Istanbul was the person responsible for the implementation of the order to kill.

According to information on the Saudi consulate's official

---

1   On December 3, just before this book went to print, the Chief Prosecutor's Office in Istanbul issued a warrant for Al-Muzainy's arrest.

website, Al-Muzainy began his service on September 11, 2015 as an attaché. Yet his real title was Istanbul station chief. Al-Muzainy traveled to Riyadh after Khashoggi scheduled an appointment with the consulate on September 28. He received his orders and the mission plan, and returned to Turkey on October 1. The Saudi station chief flew back to Riyadh after the Khashoggi murder and never set foot in Turkey again.[2]

On September 28, when Khashoggi arrived at the Saudi consulate in Istanbul to schedule an appointment, Al-Muzainy was in the building. After the Saudi journalist was told to come back on October 2 and flew to London, the station chief departed Sabiha Gokcen Airport at 2.41 p.m. on September 29 for Riyadh. There, he met deputy intelligence chief Ahmad Assiri, whom the Saudis dismissed after the Khashoggi murder.

Muzainy received his orders and the mission plan from Assiri and flew back to Istanbul at 4 p.m. on October 1. He told the consul general, Mohammed Al-Otaiba, about the order to kill and how they were supposed to carry it out. Hours after Khashoggi's slaying, at 9.35 p.m., he took a flight to Riyadh from Atatürk International Airport.

Sources believe that Al-Muzainy probably met the 15 Saudi operatives after holding talks with Assiri in Riyadh. The main reason why Al-Muzainy emerged as the 'brains behind the operation' was that he flew to Saudi Arabia and back to avoid scrutiny – even if the operatives were to encrypt their communications.

Clearly, Al-Muzainy, like the consul general Al-Otaiba, won't ever go back to Turkey. After all, the Saudi station chief knows a lot of secrets about the Khashoggi murder, which he took back to Saudi Arabia. It is out of question that MBS will send him or any other members of the death squad and take the risk of them sharing information with the Turkish authorities.

That Al-Muzainy did not take the private jet with the tail number HZ SK2, which took nine Saudi operatives to Turkey, was a clear attempt to ensure operational security. Instead, the station chief took a commercial flight to Istanbul on October 1, along

2   Abdurrahman Şimşek and Nazif Karaman, "İşte Cemal Kaşıkçı'yı katleden timin beyni" [The Brains Behind The Team That Massacred Jamal Khashoggi], *Sabah*, 23 October 2018.

with three assassins: Mansour Othman Aba Hussein, Naif Hassan Al-Arifi and Mohammed Saad Al-Zahrani.

MIT FLAGS RECON MISSION AT BELGRADE FOREST

Al-Muzainy's contacts raised flags at the National Intelligence Organization and the Istanbul police's intelligence division when Jamal Khashoggi went missing. Law enforcement agents were quick to track down footage of Al-Muzainy at Sabiha Gokcen and Atatürk airports. On October 1, the Saudi station chief arrived at Atatürk Airport with a large handbag.

The Turkish authorities believe that Al-Muzainy's bag contain the order to kill Khashoggi as well as mission plans. Clearly, Riyadh had handpicked the station chief to ensure that the diplomatic staff, including the consul general, would stick to the plan.

It was Al-Muzainy who was seen in a diplomatic vehicle near the Belgrade Forest in Istanbul. The day before the Khashoggi murder, the Saudi spy drove to the forest together with another intelligence operative, Abdulaziz Suleiman al-Gumizi, for a reconnaissance mission. Unknowingly, he was under surveillance.[3]

At the time, the Turkish intelligence assessed that the two Saudi spooks went to the Belgrade Forest for espionage purposes. They did not know that the Saudis were conspiring to murder Jamal Khashoggi. It wasn't until after the journalist's death that the Turks learned about Al-Gumizi was part of the reconnaissance mission. As such, Al-Gumizi could be added to the list of 15+3 intelligence operatives that were complicit in the Washington Post columnist's death.

After *Sabah's* special intelligence unit broke the news[4] about Al-Muzainy, Sedat Ergin, a columnist with *Hürriyet*, penned a noteworthy column:

---

3   Abdurrahman Şimşek and Nazif Karaman, "Belgrad Ormanı'ndaki keşfi infaz timinin beyni yaptı" [The Death Squad's Brains Conducted The Recon Mission At The Belgrade Forest], *Sabah*, 28 October 2018.

4   Abdurrahman Şimşek and Nazif Karaman, "İşte Cemal Kaşıkçı'yı katleden timin beyni" [This Is The Brains Behind The Team That Killed Jamal Khashoggi], *Sabah*, 23 October 2018.

Khashoggi visited the consulate on Friday, September 28, and was told to go back there on October 2. The following day, Abdullah Al-Muzainy, who appeared to be an attaché at the Saudi mission, flew to Riyadh. According to a story by Sabah reporters Abdurrahman Şimşek and Nazif Karaman, Al-Muzainy was actually the station chief in Istanbul. He departed Sabiha Gokcen Airport at 1431 hours on September 29.

An interesting detail was that the station chief returned to Istanbul on October 1, the day before the Khashoggi murder, and entered the country at Atatürk International Airport. Three members of the death squad took the same flight to Istanbul. After the Khashoggi murder, Al-Muzainy cleared passport control at 2135 hours on October 2 and departed Atatürk International Airport to return to Riyadh. The movements of that official alone attests to the Saudi intelligence agency's central role in the Khashoggi murder. It would appear that Saudi Arabia itself finds itself stuck in the well now.[5]

THE DOG THAT REACTED TO THE WARDROBE

In his column, Ergin made a reference to Riyadh's refusal to allow Turkish investigators search the well below the consular residence. In Chapter II, we discussed at length why Khashoggi's body was possibly at the bottom of that well. Moreover, we mentioned above that the five suitcases, which contained Khashoggi's body parts, never left the residence – which, Turkish investigators believe, makes it more likely that the body was in the well.

One of the details that we have omitted from our account of the investigation thus far was that a police dog reacted strongly to a smell near a wardrobe at the Saudi consul's residence. That reaction told the investigators that Khashoggi's body, or part(s) of

---

5   Sedat Ergin, "Konsolosluk kuyusuna sıkışan Ortadoğu jeopolitiği" [The geopolitics of the Middle East – stuck in the consulate's well], *Hürriyet*, 25 October 2018.

it, were inside that wardrobe.

During the search, the Turkish police enlisted the services of Melo, a body-sniffing dog trained to locate dead bodies. Top of his class of seven dogs, Melo was flown into the crime scene from Antalya. Although the Blue Malinois reacted strongly to the wardrobe, the investigators found no concrete evidence of the Khashoggi murder at the consular residence.

THE INCONSEQUENTIAL BUZZING OF 'TROLL' FLIES

Provided that paying one's respects to the dead at their burial site is part of Islamic tradition, the Saudi attempt to prevent the discovery of Jamal Khashoggi's remains was inhumane at best. Although Turkey resorted to a range of methods, including luminol tests and body-sniffing dogs, in the mission to locate the Saudi journalist's remains, Saudi Arabia repeatedly denied knowledge of his body's location, as if to mock the international community.

One such statement was made by the Saudi foreign minister Adel Al-Jubair, who told reporters that Riyadh did not know how Khashoggi died and where his remains were. Noting that the Khashoggi murder was a terrible mistake and Crown Prince Mohammed bin Salman had no knowledge of the incident, Saudi Arabia's top diplomat claimed that they did not know how Khashoggi died and where his body was, even though the Saudi investigation had supposedly established that the journalist was killed inside the Saudi consulate in Istanbul.[6]

As Al-Jubair made that statement, Saud Al-Qahtani's troll army was busy spreading disinformation about Turkey on social media. As soon as Khashoggi's disappearance hit the wires, MBS had deployed his trolls to Twitter. Although that 'army' attempted to disseminate false information on numerous occasions, it failed spectacularly – because Turkey had concrete evidence at its disposal that no amount of trolling could undo.

---

6   "Cesedin nerede olduğunu bilmiyoruz" [We Do Not Know Where The Body Is], *Sabah*, 20 October 2018.

168

HOW THE INTELLIGENCE ASSESSED HATICE CENGIZ

The Saudi intelligence raised the bar by claiming that Hatice Cengiz, Khashoggi's fiancée, was a Qatari agent. That was a claim that the Saudis spread in an attempt to shape the public opinion. Those accusations led some parties to question whether Cengiz, who entered Khashoggi's life suddenly, may have 'honey trapped' the *Washington Post* columnist.

As part of our attempt to uncover all of the truth, we posed that question to trusted sources in the intelligence community. Here's what we know: Wittingly or otherwise, Hatice Cengiz was in contact with the secret service of a Middle Eastern country, which she served as an interpreter. Yet that connection did not amount to the type of relationship that would make Cengiz a spy or an informant. Nor would it mean that she *'honey trapped'* Jamal Khashoggi.

At this point, it is important to recall what Hatice Cengiz told in her first live interview after the Khashoggi murder:

When we met, Mr. Jamal had been living in the United States for 1.5 years. He wrote for The Washington Post. He wasn't a U.S. citizen, but had recently applied for citizenship. Provided that his Saudi citizenship would create problems for him if he wanted to obtain a new passport, he wanted [to obtain U.S. citizenship]. Many Saudi citizens are currently behind bars. He was crushed under an emotional burden. He said that his friends were in jail and could not write. He felt this great solitude and an emotional responsibility.

I do not know much about his family in Saudi Arabia. He didn't want to talk about his marriage, and I didn't wish to ask because he was so lonely. He was alone politically and emotionally. It was difficult for him to accomplish his goals by himself. He mentioned frequently that he felt all alone, that he couldn't hear from his friends, and that he couldn't overcome the situation in which he found himself.

We are talking about an emotionally lonely person, who was mature in terms of age yet away from his native country. He wanted to spend the rest of his life well. At that point, he faced that truth and wanted to get married. We texted and talked on the phone. He visited Turkey several times. We met repeatedly. That I worked on the ground caught his attention.

Earlier in his career, he had served as a war reporter. His experience enabled him to guide me in those areas, and our shared interests made it possible for our relationship to move forward naturally.[7]

AN ISIS-LIKE ATTACK

That's how Hatice Cengiz described what Khashoggi meant to her and how she'd decided to marry him. The Saudi troll army, which could not get anywhere by targeting Khashoggi's fiancée, launched a new campaign to smear the slain journalist. Those accusations were picked up by anti-Turkish conventional media outlets in the Arab world.

On October 6, the Lebanese newspaper Al Akhbar published a story filled with lies. It supposedly quoted an Arab source claiming that Saudi Arabia had informed Turkey that Jamal Khashoggi was in Riyadh. The Lebanese outlet claimed that the *Washington Post* columnist was flown back to Saudi Arabia on October 2 – and the Turks knew about it!

Al Akhbar did not stop there. It spread the lie that the Saudis, in cooperation with the Turkish authorities, had taken Khashoggi out of the consulate in a white vehicle.

Such attempts to disseminate false information automatically failed when it became clear that Jamal Khashoggi had died inside the Saudi consulate and Riyadh was compelled to admit culpability.

By the time the Saudis spread lies via social media to

7   Transcript of the *Habertürk* interview with Hatice Cengiz, 26 October 2018.

the mainstream media, Khashoggi was already dead. Having announced that Khashoggi was killed inside the consulate, Turan Kışlakçı, a close friend of the slain columnist and president of the Turkish-Arab Media Association, compared the murder to ISIS attacks:

> *"Even ISIS did not commit such an act. This was indeed an ISIS-like operation. I hope that the world's conscience will mobilize against it,"*[8]

As Kışlakçı noted, ISIS had shocked the world by burning people alive and committing other atrocities. Yet even that group had not dismembered one of their victims after killing them.

Kışlakçı emerged as one of the most accurate sources of information about the death of his friend Jamal Khashoggi. His involvement was more about paying homage to a close friend than his journalistic duty. As a matter of fact, Kışlakçı's commitment to inform the public received a somewhat strong response from Hatice Cengiz and others. On October 7, when Kışlakçı claimed that Khashoggi was dead, Cengiz still wanted to believe that her fiancée was alive.[9]

In an OpEd essay for *The Washington Post*, which was published five days later, Hatice Cengiz said she prayed to Allah to spare Jamal Khashoggi. Here's what she wrote that day:

More than a week has passed since our last meeting outside the consulate of Saudi Arabia, before his disappearance became global news. We were in the middle of making wedding plans, life plans. After the consulate, we were going to buy appliances for our new home and set a date. All we needed was a piece of paper.

We were going to take my siblings and some of our closest friends to dinner to share the good news. Marriage is an important and special step for all couples. For us, but es-

8 "Turan Kışlakçı: Bize ulaşan bilgi öldürüldüğü yönünde" [Turan Kışlakçı: The Information We Received Suggests That He Was Murdered], *Hürriyet*, 7 October 2018.
9 "Turan Kışlakçı: Cemal Kaşıkçı öldürüldü" [Turan Kışlakçı: Jamal Khashoggi Was Killed], *Milliyet*, 7 October 2018.

pecially for Jamal, it was particularly significant. Spending more than a year in self-imposed exile in the United States — away from his country, his family and his loved ones — had taken a toll on him. *"I miss my country very much. I miss my friends and family very much,"* he told me. *"I feel this deep pain every single moment."*

Now we were about to be married and spend time between Washington and Istanbul. We were so anxious. He had been feeling so lonely, but I could see the clouds clearing. He wanted to build on his years of professional experience to become an influential journalist in Washington, as the Arab world set the stage for major developments. He was thankful to be able to write in The Washington Post, to be the voice of his colleagues who could no longer speak up.

When I asked him why he decided to live in the United States, he said America was the world's most powerful country, where one could feel the political pulse of the planet. Jamal had applied for U.S. citizenship, and his reason to visit to Turkey was our intended marriage. He was hoping to take care of all necessary paperwork before returning to Washington.

On Sept. 28, Jamal visited the Saudi Consulate in Istanbul for the first time, despite being somewhat concerned that he could be in danger. Yet he noted that there was no warrant for his arrest in his native country. Although his opinions had angered certain people, he said, the tensions between himself and Saudi Arabia did not amount to hate, grudges or threats.

He was, however, increasingly worried about an unprecedented wave of arrests in his country. Yet Jamal did not think the Saudis could force him to stay at the consulate in Turkey, even if they wanted to arrest him. In other words, he did not mind walking into the Saudi Consulate in Istanbul

because he did not believe that something bad could happen on Turkish soil. It would be a violation of international
law to harm, arrest or detain people at a diplomatic mission,
he said, and noted that no such thing had ever happened in
Turkey's history. After a positive first meeting with consular staff, who welcomed him warmly and assured him that
the necessary paperwork would come through, Jamal was
hardly concerned ahead of his second visit. He walked into
the consulate of Saudi Arabia, his native country, without
doubting he would be safe there.

After seeing how relaxed he was, I waited patiently and full
of hope. But after three hours I was overcome with fear and
concern. I texted a few friends to inform them, and I asked
about Jamal at the consular building. I received an answer
that further fueled my fears: Jamal had already left, they
told me, possibly without my noticing. Trying to stay calm,
I immediately called Yasin Aktay, an adviser to Turkish
President Recep Tayyip Erdogan and one of Jamal's oldest
friends. Since the incident came to the attention of the press
and law enforcement, I have been waiting fearfully.

This much is true: He entered the consulate, and there's no
proof that he came out. In recent days, I've witnessed the
work of the Turkish authorities as they monitor the situation closely. I am confident in the abilities of Turkish government officials. At this time, I implore President Trump
and first lady Melania Trump to help shed light on Jamal's
disappearance. I also urge Saudi Arabia, especially King
Salman and Crown Prince Mohammed bin Salman, to show
the same level of sensitivity and release CCTV footage from
the consulate. Although this incident could potentially fuel a
political crisis between the two nations, let us not lose sight
of the human aspect of what happened. Jamal is a valuable
person, an exemplary thinker and a courageous man who
has been fighting for his principles. I don't know how I can
keep living if he was abducted or killed in Turkey.

Although my hope slowly fades away each passing day, I remain confident that Jamal is still alive. Perhaps I'm simply trying to hide from the thought that I have lost a great man whose love I had earned. As an individual who believes that life and death are in the hands of God, I pray to God alone for Jamal's safe return.[10]

THE STILL-UNCRACKED CODES

Hatice Cengiz maintained that Jamal Khashoggi was alive until Saudi Arabia stated that the *Washington Post* columnist had "died in a brawl." On the day of the murder, she had surrendered Khashoggi's two cell phones to the police per the prosecutor's request.

Those two devices underwent an extensive review by the Cyber Crimes Unit at the Istanbul police headquarters. Yet no information could be extracted from them, since the specialists could not crack their passcodes.

The Turkish police had encountered the same problem when a Gülenist police officer, Mevlüt Mert Altintas, shot dead Andrei Karlov, the Russian ambassador to Ankara, on December 16, 2016. The assailant's phone could not be accessed, even though the Turkish Scientific and Technological Research Institution (TUBITAK) cloned the iCloud account associated with the device in an attempt to bypass the passcode. Nor could international experts solve that problem.[11] In the end, the Turkish authorities were able to access that information.[12]

The contents of Khashoggi's cell phones could have helped Turkey to discover the motive behind the assassination and to establish who had ordered the hit on the *Washington Post* columnist. The Turkish police, therefore, continues to work on the devices. Perhaps the Turkish authorities will gain access

10   https://www.washingtonpost.com/news/global-opinions/wp/2018/10/09/please-president-trump-shed-light-on-my-fiances-disappearance/?utm_term=.961e9a0de218
11   "Kaşıkçı'nın iPhone şifresi kırılamıyor" [The Passcode Of Khashoggi's Iphone Cannot Be Cracked], *Yeni Şafak*, October 15, 2018.
12   The Karlov assassination indictment.

to Khashoggi's cell phones, as they did with the cell phone of Russian ambassador's killer.

4

DNA EVIDENCE

273 DNA Samples Analyzed

The Istanbul police's Crime Scene Investigation division looked for evidence in six locations as part of their investigation into the Khashoggi murder: Saudi Arabia's consulate general in Istanbul, the Saudi consul general's residence, rooms 515, 611, 615, 1402, 1609, 210, 610 and 903[1] at the M Hotel, rooms 2802, 2809, 2812, 914, 915 and 916 of the WG Hotel, Jamal Khashoggi's apartment in the Topkapi district, and a villa in Yalova. The investigators also inspected diplomatic vehicles with the license plate numbers **34 CC 2342, 34 CC 2404, 34 CC 2646, 34 CC 2280, 34 CC 2464, 34 CC 1736, 34 CC 2460, 34 CC 3071, 34 CC 2254, 34 CC 1696, 34 CC 2248 and 34 CC 1865**.

The Fingerprint Development Laboratory analyzed 257 samples from six locations and identified 1,548 traces based on that material. The authorities submitted their findings to the Automated Fingerprint Identification System, or AFIS, but could not reach any concrete results. The investigators shot 189GB worth of video, took 7633 photographs, used a drone to film 30GB of additional footage and take 132 pictures.

1 According to our sources, Tubaigy stayed at room 515 and Mutreb stayed at room 615 at the M Hotel.

A total of 100 crime scene investigators contributed to Turkey's effort to shed light on the Khashoggi murder. They found 350 DNA samples at the Saudi consulate, the consular residence, the M Hotel, where some assassins stayed, and their vehicles. Jamal Khashoggi's DNA was found during a three-hour search at his apartment.

THE DNA SAMPLE FROM THE BACK OF THE VICTIM'S NECK

The authorities found Jamal Khashoggi's DNA on his razor, toothbrush, underwear, comb, nail clipper and pill boxes as well as the collars of his shirts and other items, such as jackets and shirts, that his family submitted to the authorities.

The authorities attempted to match those DNA samples with evidence from the Saudi consulate, the consular residence, hotels and vehicles. The investigators search the said hotel rooms in case the killers took Khashoggi there. As part of that investigation, Turkish experts compared 273 different DNA samples. That effort was overseen by Yalçın Büyük, the head of Turkey's Forensic Medicine Institution, and carried out by a group of DNA specialists.

Some of the DNA samples, the authorities concluded, belonged to patrons that stayed in those hotel rooms in the past. Yet they could not find Khashoggi's DNA. The Turkish police, however, maintains that "there is no perfect murder" and continues to look for clues.

The Forensic Medicine Institution also analyzed samples from the well under the Saudi consul's residence, yet could not find any traces of the victim's DNA. A subsequent search for acid proved to be a dead end as well. Nor did the authorities find any incriminating evidence in a Mercedes-Benz vehicle, which was found in the Sultangazi district[2] and made many observers think that it could shed light on the murder. That vehicle belonged to the Saudi

---

2   "Suudi konsolosluğuna ait araçta iki bavul bulundu" [Two Bags Found In Saudi Consulate's Vehicle], *Habertürk*, 23 October 2018.

consulate's undersecretary for narco-crime, who placed some of his personal belongings in the trunk of his car when recalled by Riyadh. When those items proved too heavy for air travel, he put them back in his car and had a driver drive the vehicle back from the airport.

The authorities could not find any DNA evidence in the Mercedes-Benz van, which the killers used to move Jamal Khashoggi's body parts to the consular residence. The Saudis had taken that vehicle to the carwash and had a chemical expert detail it before the Turkish investigator were allowed to touch it.

THE ACID THEORY IS AN URBAN LEGEND

One of the Forensic Medicine Institution's most significant findings was as follows: the popular belief that the Saudis used acid to get rid of Jamal Khashoggi's body was misplaced. In other words, that the *Washington Post* columnist's body was dissolved in acid was another common misconception about the murder.

That claim has been the subject of a heated debate in the media and among the general population for two months. Three pieces, which appeared in Turkish newspapers in recent weeks, attest to the dissemination of that false information.

Fatih Altaylı's Nov. 13 column in Habertürk was one of the most noteworthy commentaries on the Khashoggi murder. Highlighting several cases from the history of criminology, the author told his readers "to decide for yourself, in light of that information, whether or not Khashoggi's body was dissolved inside the consulate."[3]

On Nov. 6, Yeni Akit columnist Abdurrahman Dilipak discussed the claim that the Saudi assassins had disposed of the *Washington Post* columnist's body parts using acid and drew parallels between the Khashoggi murder and the assassination of Congolese politician Patrice Lumumba in 1961.[4]

---

3   Fatih Altaylı, "Eritsek de mi saklasak, eritmesek de mi saklasak" [To Melt Or Not To Melt], *Habertürk*, November 13, 2018.
4   Abdurrahman Dilipak, "Kaşıkçı'dan Lumumba'ya" [From Khashoggi to Lumumba], *Yeni Akit*, November 6, 2018.

Finally, Mustafa Ozcan, a columnist for the news website Fikriyat, wrote on Nov. 3 that Jamal Khashoggi's slaying was similar to the murder of Moroccan politician Mehdi Bin Barka on 29 October 1965.[5]

THE COAGULANT INJECTION

Much has been said about the way in which the Saudi death squad disposed of Jamal Khashoggi's body. A popular claim was that the assailants burned the slain journalist's remains in a fireplace at the consular residence. That the police took samples from said fireplace fueled speculation, yet the investigator haven't confirmed that claim.[6]

On Nov. 17, *Hürriyet* published another story seeking to answer popular questions about the evidence. The Saudi assassins, the Turkish paper claimed, had injected Khashoggi with a coagulant chemical immediately after his death to leave no trace of his dismemberment behind them:

Although Saudi Arabia said that Jamal Khashoggi's was killed in a brawl and due to a lethal dose of medicine, Turkish security and court officials posit that a coagulant substance was injected into Khashoggi's body after his death. According to that claim, the killers aimed to leave behind no evidence of the victim's dismemberment.[7]

How the Saudis killed Jamal Khashoggi and what they did to his body was initially leaked to international media outlets by Turkish officials.

CNN International broke the news that Khashoggi's body was dismembered on Oct. 16. Citing a Turkish official, it claimed the the Saudi journalist was killed inside the consulate on Oct. 2 and

---

5   Mustafa Özcan, "İkiz cinayet" [Double Homicide], *Fikriyat*, November 3, 2018.
6   "Cesedi bulunamayan Kaşıkçı hakkında korkunç şüphe" [The Dreadful Suspicion About Khashoggi, Whose Body Is Still Missing], *TGRT Haber*, October 29, 2018.
7   Toygun Atilla, "Pıhtı ilacı verip parçaladılar" [They Dismembered Him After Giving Him A Coagulant Drug], *Hürriyet*, November 17, 2018.

dismembered.[8]

The New York Times made a similar claim in the earlier stages of the investigation and quoted a Turkish official as saying that the Khashoggi murder resembled a scene from Quentin Tarantino's *Pulp Fiction*.[9]

NO LOCAL COLLABORATOR

The Tiger Team's most gruesome act was the murder of Jamal Khashoggi inside the Saudi consulate in Istanbul. There are many rumors about the group's covert operations. Some observers believe that MBS was inspired by Crown Prince Mohammed bin Zayed of the United Arab Emirates to form the assassination team. In the past, some media outlets reported that Prince Mohammed followed in the Emirati crown prince's footsteps to create a 5,000-strong personal army known as Al-Sayf Al-Ajrab. It was therefore that others questioned whether the 15-member Saudi death squad, which traveled to Turkey to kill Jamal Khashoggi on Oct. 2, was inspired by the United Arab Emirates.[10]

At another time, the Saudis attempted to cover up the murder and hide that Khashoggi's body was dismembered by claiming that the operatives wrapped the Saudi journalist in a carpet and moved it out of the consulate. On Oct. 21, a Saudi official told Reuters that the 15-member team was dispatched to Turkey to bring back Jamal Khashoggi, yet murdered the journalist by mistake when he started screaming. The same official claimed that Khashoggi's body was carried out of the building inside a carpet.[11]

That anonymous official mentioned a local collaborator in the same interview, whose identity, the Saudis would later say, had

---

8   "CNN: Cemal Kaşıkçı öldürüldü, cesedi parçalandı" [Cnn: Jamal Khashoggi Was Murdered And Dismembered], *Haberler.com*, October 16, 2018.
9   "Cemal Kaşıkçı ile ilgili korkunç iddia: Özel testere ile geldiler" [The Horrible Claim About Jamal Khashoggi: They Arrived With A Special Saw], *Posta*, October 11, 2018.
10   "Ve Suudi Arabistan itiraf etti" [And Saudi Arabia Confesses], *Akşam*, October 20, 2018.
11   "Suudi Dışişleri Bakanı: Kaşıkçı'nın ölümü korkunç bir hata ve trajedi" [Saudi Foreign Minister: Khashoggi's Death Is A Terrible Mistake And A Tragedy], *BBC Turkish*, October 21, 2018.

been discovered. Yet Riyadh has failed to share information about the so-called local collaborator with the Turkish authorities, as that person does not exist.

The difference between the Saudi source and anonymous sources from Turkey was that the latter relied on credible intelligence. The Saudi official, by contrast, was trying to manipulate public opinion.

All Saudi attempts at manipulation, including the supposed Turkish collaborator, were intended to discredit Turkey and absolve Crown Prince Mohammed bin Salman, who was responsible for Khashoggi's death, of any crime. That the Trump administration and the Saudi government wanted to protect MBS was crystal clear. Yet Turkey risked isolation to approach this unprecedented tragedy from a humanitarian standpoint.

5

TURKEY'S MBS POLICY

A King in the Making

It would not be wrong to make the following point at the beginning of this section: Turkey cannot be expected to look favorably at a prince, who has been engaging in anti-Turkish activities in the Gulf and the Middle East, and could stay in power for five decades after his coronation.

Moreover, Ankara is determined to shed light on all aspects of the Khashoggi murder, no matter who attempts to undermine its investigation into what happened within its borders.

On Oct. 24, Ertugrul Özkök, a columnist for Hürriyet, penned a piece asking whether or not Jamal Khashoggi's death would lead to Mohammed bin Salman's ouster as crown prince, and provided the following answer:

Question I: *Will this savage, inhumane murder end the Saudi crown prince's rule?*
We all know that it is no easy task to overthrow unelected leaders that control all media outlets in Middle Eastern countries. They are particularly immune to outside efforts to overthrow them.

Question II: Will Saudi Arabia change its Qatar policy as

a result of this murder and end Qatar's isolation?
Absolutely not. Quite the contrary, it might adopt a more rigid policy by portraying this incident as a Qatari conspiracy.

Question III: Will Saudi Arabia change its policy on the Muslim Brotherhood as a result of this murder?
No, it won't. Keep in mind that the Saudi media continues to portray Jamal Khashoggi as a 'traitor' every day. Therefore, the Saudi-Egyptian-Emirati axis will probably grow stronger.

- So what will happen?
[The Khashoggi murder] will continue to ruin the reputation of the prince, who has tried to look like a reformist in recent years. Yet do not forget that the Middle East is a place where despotic leaders stay in power despite their terrible reputations.[1]

THE PRINCE AT THE CENTER, THE KING IN THE PERIPHERY

Knowing how things are done in the Middle East, the Trump administration resisted pressure to cut loose the Saudi crown prince, who remains the cornerstone of Washington's Gulf strategy. Whereas MBS found himself at the center of everything, King Salman has been kept in the periphery.

On Oct. 18, Bercan Tutar, a foreign policy columnist for *Sabah*, assessed the Trump administration's plan to deal with the Khashoggi murder and claimed that Washington's MBS-centered foreign policy was officially dead in the water:

The gruesome murder of journalist Jamal Khashoggi has already started to trigger numerous geopolitical quakes at the regional and global levels.

After all, the brutal murder led to a total collapse of U.S. Pres-

---

1   Ertuğrul Özkök, "Bu vahşet, bu kan prensi devirir mi?" [Will The Horror And Blood Overthrow The Prince?], *Hürriyet*, 24 October 2018.

ident Donald Trump's foreign policy, whose centerpiece was Saudi Crown Prince Mohammed bin Salman.

In the wake of the 60-year-old Khashoggi's disappearance, the U.S.-Israel-Saudi bloc's hand has been significantly weakened compared to their adversaries.

Jamal Khashoggi kept the darkest secrets of Prince Turki bin Faisal, who led the Saudi intelligence for 22 years between 1979 and 2001, and submitted his surprise resignation just ten days before the 9/11 terror attacks, and, by extension, knew about the Saudi royal family's dirty business with the United States.

It was perhaps therefore that the U.S. intelligence knew about the plan to kill Khashoggi in advance, yet did not take action. As a matter of fact, Ned Price, a former CIA agent, says that the U.S. administration should have warned Jamal Khashoggi.

***

Yet not everything went as the U.S. administration had hoped. In particular, Turkey's extremely successful diplomatic media strategy foiled all those dirty plans.

At this point, not only Turkey but also China, Russia, Iran and the United Kingdom became empowered vis-à-vis the United States. Russia sent a special delegation to Riyadh, as the Chinese government harshly criticized the West's double standards.

To be clear, not only Trump's critics but also his supporters among American elites are outraged by what happened. Trump's effort to downplay the Khashoggi murder as an act of rogue killers and refusal to weaken his country's relations with Saudi Arabia were the feather that broke the camel's back.

Senator Warren criticized the U.S. president for acting like the

Saudi king's spokesman. As Khashoggi led to a rift between the White House and Congress, Senator Lindsey Graham became a symbol of critics who wanted the crown prince, who ordered the hit on Khashoggi, to be dismissed.

Numerous politicians, businesspeople, athletes and artists, including Oprah Winfrey, Bill Gates, Kobe Bryant, Michael Bloomberg, Morgan Freeman, Henry Kissinger, George Bush and Bill Clinton, are furious at Trump.

Companies like Google, Apple, Disney, Lockheed, Snapchat and AMC joined a boycott against the Saudis. Even Joseph Dunford, the Chairman of the Joint Chiefs of Staff, was compelled to concede that there will be a policy change in Washington's military relations with Saudi Arabia.

***

Having been backed into a corner, the United States seems to have no choice but to make concessions on economic sanctions against Turkey, the situation in the east of the Euphrates River, FETÖ and YPG.

By extension, Jamal Khashoggi's slaying will change the U.S.-Israel-Saudi bloc's policy on Iran, Qatar, Yemen, Syria, Libya, Egypt and Jordan.

Furthermore, the Saudis will no longer be able to make the desired contribution to Washington and Tel Aviv's 'deal of the century', which seeks to undermine Palestine. It would seem that the Khashoggi earthquake's geopolitical aftershocks in the United States and our region won't be limited to what already happened.[2]

---

2   Bercan Tutar, "ABD'de Kaşıkçı depremi büyüyor" [The Khashoggi Crack Deepens In The United States], *Sabah*, 24 October 2018.

RIYADH'S 9/11

As Bercan Tutar posits, the Khashoggi murder was prominent enough to trigger geopolitical changes. The event has been described as Riyadh's 9/11 for good reason. In an Oct. 21 column, Saadet Oruc, a senior adviser to Turkish President Erdogan, referred to the Khashoggi murder as Riyadh's 9/11.[3]

Provided that Khashoggi was killed inside the Saudi consulate in Istanbul, Turkey had to tread most carefully in the international arena. There were several diplomatic options available to the country, which Burhanettin Duran, general coordinator of the SETA Foundation, outlined for Sabah on Oct. 20:

That the United States redefines its global role and the shift in the global balance of power that follows must not allow any country to engage in state terror. At the end of the day, the Khashoggi scandal has a symbolic meaning for the Arab world akin to the Wikileaks effect. Clearly, the stakeholders must be aware of that meaning. That is exactly why Washington sees that this incident cannot be covered up, even if it desperately wants it to go away. Therefore, President Trump dispatched Secretary of State Pompeo to Riyadh to deliver a warning and demanded that Riyadh launch an investigation within 72 hours.

Trump has started to talk about severe consequences for Saudi Arabia. At this point, it is necessary to evaluate Turkey's position. After all, there has been attempts to misportray Turkey's consistent, determined, responsible and commonsensical approach. Let us set aside the question why the Saudis did what they did to Khashoggi in Istanbul rather than Washington, and concentrate on the Turkish position.

Since the first signs of the incident began to emerge, there were four options available to Ankara.

First, Turkey could have taken the fall for what happened,

---

3   Saadet Oruç, "Katil ve itiraflar: Riyad'ın yeni 11 Eylül'ü" [The Murderer And Confessions: Riyadh's New 9/11], *Star*, 21 October 2018.

which would go down in history as an unsolved murder. Perhaps the Saudi intelligence, which sought to abduct or eliminate Khashoggi, hoped to accomplish that result. A violation of our nation's sovereignty, the operation would have made Turkey look like an unsafe place where people went missing. The international community was going to target Ankara within the context of security and human rights. Yet the Turkish intelligence agency's technical accomplishment made it impossible for Turkey to take the fall for the Khashoggi scandal.

The second possibility was to take the evidence and use it as ammunition in an all-out offensive against Saudi Arabia. It was possible to describe this comprehensive operation, which took place in Istanbul, as an attack on Turkey. Keeping in mind the regional competition between the two country, it would have been possible to corner Riyadh. Ankara could not take that road on principle and due to the potential damage to bilateral relations.

The third option was for Ankara and Riyadh to shake hands and cover up the issue. The White House, which stands behind the crown prince's ambitious political project, would have probably welcomed that step. Yet that option would have clearly been incompatible with Turkey's humanitarian foreign policy. Home to 3.5 million Syrian refugees and currently the world's leading humanitarian assistance provider, the country criticizes the UN System's unjust nature and therefore cannot accept [murder]. It would have been impossible for Turkey, which stands for humanity's conscience in case of disasters and massacres, could not shoulder that heavy burden. A crime, which would be inexplicable in world capitals and on the Arab street, could not be ignored. As such, Ankara ruled out that option in the first place.

The fourth option was to shed light on what happened through an international investigation and in cooperation with Riyadh. The goal would have been to hold accountable those responsible without covering up the scandal or launching an anti-Saudi campaign. That is exactly what Ankara has been doing. Ankara is not in a position to play favorites in a power struggle within the Saudi royal family. The Saudi people, King Salman and the dynasty will determine the outcome of the Khashoggi scandal. As a responsible player, Turkey opted to uncover the truth and protect its bilateral relationship with Saudi Arabia in the medium and long term.[4]

WHAT DOES THE KHASHOGGI MURDER HAVE
TO DO WITH GULEN?

The international media viewed Turkey's policy of serving the cause of justice without covering up the scandal or launching an anti-Saudi offensive as mounting pressure on Riyadh. On Nov. 16, NBC said that Turkey, under Erdogan's leadership, was turning up the heat on Saudi Arabia.

The Trump administration, the same story claimed, had sided with the Saudis in an attempt to alleviate Turkish pressure. One of the trump cards at America's disposal, accordingly, was the pending extradition of Fetullah Gulen. Yet U.S. officials rejected the claim and stated that the two processes were independent of each other.

Claiming that Turkey was mounting pressure on the United States by exploiting the Khashoggi case, NBC noted that the country was one step closer to get what it wants.[5]

On Oct. 10, *The Washington Post*, which published Khashoggi's columns, ran a piece on the Trump administration's approach to the murder., which posited that the White House faced criticism for treating some authoritarian governments, such as Saudi Arabia and Israel, unlike others, including Iran, Venezuela and Cuba.[6]

In an Oct. 27, Bethan McKernan, *The Guardian's* correspondent in Istanbul, wrote that Erdogan mounted pressure on Riyadh by urging the Saudis to identify Jamal Khashoggi's killers. The Saudi foreign ministry, she said, viewed the Khashoggi murder as

---

4   Burhanettin Duran, "Kaşıkçı skandalında Ankara'nın dört seçeneği" [The four options available to Ankara in the Khashoggi scandal], Sabah, 20 October 2018.

5   Carol E. Lee, Julia Ainsley and Courtney Kube, "To Ease Turkish Pressure On Saudis Over Killing, The White House Weighs Expelling Erdogan Foe," NBC News, 15 November 2018.

6   Carol E. Lee, Julia Ainsley and Courtney Kube, "To Ease Turkish Pressure On Saudis Over Killing, The White House Weighs Expelling Erdogan Foe," NBC News, 15 November 2018.

the most serious political crisis since the 9/11 terror attacks.[7]

According to Hall Gardner, a professor at the American University of Paris and author of World War Trump, added that Turkey played its cards right and compelled Riyadh to respond. Speaking to Deutsche Welle, the international relations expert recalled that the Turks revealed Saudi lies after each statement from Riyadh, and attempted to repair its strained relations with the United States by captivating the international media and investigating the murder. Gardner also stressed that Fetullah Gulen, the mastermind behind the July 2016 coup attempt in Turkey, resided in the United States and argued that Turkey was using the Khashoggi murder to secure the coup leader's extradition. In recent weeks, various U.S. media outlets reported that the Trump administration was taking steps to extradite Gulen in order to ease the Turkish pressure on Saudi Arabia.

David Hearst, the editor-in-chief of the London-based news website Middle East Eye, said that there were two sides fighting in the United States and the Khashoggi murder emerged as a new front in the information war between the Central Intelligence Agency and the Trump Administration. According to Hearst, the Khashoggi case won't be closed for a long time. Predicting that the CIA will leak the evidence at its disposal going forward, the journalist claimed that the agency hoped to discredit Trump's calculus and refute the information at his disposal.

Hearst added that Turkey's leaks and official statements, along with mounting pressure in Washington, forced Saudi Arabia to change its position constantly, and warned that the Trump Administration was no different – in the sense that its position was subject to change. According to the MEE editor, Turkey's steps indirectly influenced ongoing clashes among U.S. institutions and noted that the Turkish leadership's target audience was always Washington.[8]

---

7   Bethan McKernan, "Saudi Arabia Says It Is A Beacon Of Light Fighting 'Dark' Iran", *The Guardian*, 27 October 2018.

8   Çağrı Özdemir, "ABD'deki güç çekişmeleri ve Türkiye" [The Tug-Of-War In The U.s. And Turkey], *Deutsche Welle Turkish*, 23 November 2018.

ANKARA'S 'VALUABLE PLURALITY'

To say that Turkey's target audience was Washington would be to miss the 'big picture'. Quite the contrary, Turkey's target audience was, first and foremost, humanity's civilized, moral and conscientious values. At a critical time in history, the Turks promoted humanitarian values in the United States, Europe, the Middle East, the Gulf, Russia and China over an incident that could have sparked conventional wars. They worked hard to accomplish that goal. In the end, Turkey wasn't sentenced to 'precious loneliness' – as the popular phrase goes.

Although Turkey was left alone in its fight against terrorist organizations PKK and FETO, that wasn't the case with regard to the Khashoggi murder. The fourth column, starting with U.S. media outlets, supported the Turkish view regarding what happened.

Even after the Saudis admitted to the Khashoggi murder, international media outlets, briefed by mysterious Turkish officials, did not stop reporting on the incident.

For example, CNN International aired CCTV footage of the body double, whom the Saudis had intended to use to blame the murder on Turkey. The Tiger Team had failed their mission spectacularly. Although the Saudis tried to save their operatives, they could not cover up the truth.

Speaking of PKK and FETO, Turkey is in a position to defeat those organizations by tapping into its vast experience in the area of counter-terrorism. Yet international cooperation is key to neutralizing those threats permanently and with greater speed.

And speaking of terrorism, the Khashoggi murder must be considered an act of terrorism that a dangerous yet powerful clique has carried out – not a secret service operation. Such dangerous attacks could have taken place elsewhere, had Turkey not blown the covers of Jamal Khashoggi's killers.

How do we know that? There were sleeper cells affiliated with the Tiger Team, which we discussed at length in the previous chapter.

How were those sleeper cells organized in Turkey and how did the authorities do to track their activities?

Let us wrap up this chapter with those critical questions and focus on the 'why'.

CHAPTER V

Why?

1

THE TIGER TEAM'S SLEEPER CELLS

The 30-Strong Reconnaissance Team

Ahmad Abdullah Al-Muzaini, the Saudi intelligence agency's station chief in Istanbul, was in charge of the Tiger Team's ten cells and 30 operatives on the ground. He was pleased to have successfully moved his thirtieth agent into a safe house. The Saudi rented or purchased seven apartments, which they promptly turned into safe houses, around the city. Al-Muzaini himself lived in a residence inside a gated community in the Maslak district.

A group of intelligence operatives, who were in contact with Al-Muzaini, mistakenly thought that they could work in Istanbul easily – that was obviously before the Khashoggi murder. The Turkish city that linked Europe and Asia wasn't just a preferred destination for Saudi dissidents. The Tiger Team's sleeper cells, too, thought they could conduct covert operations, just as the Iranian regime hunted down its critics in the 1980s.

It was no secret that Tehran eliminated dissidents, who sought refuge in Turkey, back in the day. Likewise, the country set the stage for a series of Russian assassinations of Chechen rebels in 2008-2015. Such attacks stopped since 2015, as the terrorist organization led by Fetullah Gülen, FETÖ, gradually lost control of the state apparatus.

In the wake of Mohammed bin Salman's 2017 appointment as crown prince, the Kingdom, too, decided to eliminate Saudi dissidents in Turkey. What they refused to acknowledge, however, was that Turkey had changed. Nor did they attempt to conduct those operations in line with the unofficial rules of espionage. Sooner or later, the Saudis were going to get caught red-handed – which is exactly what happened after the murder of Jamal Khashoggi.

More important, all the Tiger Team's undercover operatives in Turkey, whose covers were blown before they could take action, ended up having to flee the country.

The Turks did not have advanced technology, like the machine in Steven Spielberg's Minority Report, at their disposal. Instead, they relied on extended physical surveillance and hard work to evaluate all available information. As mentioned above, the Saudi sleepers left Istanbul as soon as they understood that the Turkish intelligence had blown their covers.

Officers from the National Intelligence Organization were watching Al-Muzaini, when he drove to the Belgrade Forest on Oct. 1 – the day before the Khashoggi murder. As a matter of fact, the station chief was there for a so-called detrap meeting with a Tiger Team cell. The secret meeting lasted 15 minutes and possibly involved an exchange of instructions. It would be Al-Muzaini's final meeting in Turkey. The following day, the Saudi station chief left Istanbul and never came back.

THE SAUDI SAFE HOUSES

In the wake of the Khashoggi murder, the Turkish intelligence analyzed cell phone signals, GSM base station logs and some 20,000 data packets, including GPRS traffic and texts, to establish what Al-Muzaini and his sleeper cells had been doing. That analysis revealed that the Saudi station chief's spy network had surrounded Saudi dissidents in Istanbul.

The Tiger Team's sleeper cells were gathering information about Crown Prince Mohammed bin Salman's opponents –

wealthy individuals who fled the Kingdom and relocated to Turkey. They were part of a covert operation that Riyadh bankrolled enthusiastically. Al-Muzaini would collect information from the cells and report it back to the center.

The Saudi operatives typically identified where Mohammed bin Salman's critics lived and rented –and, as a last resort, bought— apartments from the same or opposite buildings. Once there, they used video cameras and other equipment to monitor their targets.

To assist the Tiger Team's reconnaissance operatives, who worked independently of Khashoggi's killers, Al-Muzaini hired Turkish-speaking Arabs and even two Arabic-speaking Turkish citizens. Those two individuals were from the southeastern Turkish city of Mardin and their office was located on the top floor of the Saudi consulate in Istanbul.

Hence the Saudi effort to muddy the waters after Jamal Khashoggi's slaying by spreading disinformation about 'local collaborators'. By claiming that a Turkish citizen was responsible for disposing of the slain journalist's remains, Riyadh attempted to manipulate the public opinion.

Saudi Arabia's consulate in Istanbul paid for all reconnaissance activities immediately upon receiving related bills. In other words, it all seemed like a good deal for Saudi informants. What they failed to take into account, however, was that the Saudis were prepared to sell out a handful of Turkish citizens, whom they recruited in exchange for money – as their effort to blame 'local collaborators' clearly showed.

The Saudi attorney general's office announced on Nov. 13 that it had obtained a photograph of the local collaborator, who took Khashoggi's body from the assassins, and the individual who turned off the consulate's security cameras.[1] Yet Riyadh has been unable to identify the local collaborator to Turkish investigators until today. In the same statement, the Saudis confessed to the murder by saying that the journalist died after a brawl and due to an overdose of sedatives.[2]

---

1   "Kaşıkçı cinayetinde ölüm emrini veren isim açıklandı" [The Name Of The Khashoggi Murder's Instigator Released], CNN Türk, 15 November 2018.

2   "Kaşıkçı soruşturmasında flaş gelişme: 5 zanlı için idam" [Breaking News On

For the record, the two individuals from Mardin had nothing to do with the Khashoggi murder. Yet they did help the Tiger Team's sleeper cells in Istanbul, whose primary purpose was to carry out reconnaissance missions on the ground. According to our sources, the Turkish authorities questioned those individuals, yet concluded that they weren't involved in the Washington Post columnist's slaying.

CONFESSIONS OF AN ANONYMOUS SOURCE

A top secret source, whom the authors of this book interview, provided critical information about the Saudi station chief Al-Muzaini, his two deputies, the consul-general Al-Otaiba and the two employees from Mardin that assisted reconnaissance cells in Istanbul.

Our source, whom we can only compare to Deep Throat who leaked classified information to the *Washington Post*'s Bob Woodward and Carl Bernstein on the Watergate scandal, said they felt that they needed to come forward because they were unsettled by the Khashoggi murder.

The source reached out to the authors of this book through an intermediary and requested complete anonymity over personal security concerns before agreeing to a face-to-face meeting. They spoke with us before even sharing information with the Turkish investigators.

Given the Saudi death squad's recklessness in the Khashoggi murder, they weren't exactly exaggerating the threat. According to our source, the reconnaissance cells in Istanbul had nothing to do with the *Washington Post* columnist's death. The assassins, they said, received their orders directly from Riyadh.

Al-Muzaini, however, was responsible for managing the sleeper cells and guiding Khashoggi's executioners. The anonymous source told us that the Saudi station chief wielded extraordinary power during his time in Turkey and Al-Otaiba, the

---

The Khashoggi Investigation: Prosecution Asks For Death Penalty For 5 Suspects], *Sabah*, 15 November 2018.

consul general, could not override Al-Muzaini in many cases – including the Khashoggi murder. The source added that Al-Otaiba was significantly weaker than his predecessor. "The previous consul general may have not turned a blind eye to the way that Khashoggi was murdered," they said. "Yet Otaiba was quite passive and he attempted to make up for that by hunting. Muzaini instructed him to get ready, and he did what he was told. Otaiba's family in Saudi Arabia is quite powerful. The regime may have granted him immunity at the request of his family and his sheikh when he was recalled from Istanbul."

"EVEN THE AUTOPSY EXPERT WALKED FREE"

The same source claims that Salah Mohammad Al-Tubaigy, the president of the Saudi Institute of Forensic Medicine who dismembered Jamal Khashoggi's body within 30 minutes, was resettled in Jeddah along with his family. Crown Prince Mohammed bin Salman allegedly instructed Tubaigy to keep a low profile in Jeddah – away from the Saudi capital.

Tubaigy, our source alleges, lives is a luxury villa, which has a swimming pool among other amenities, in Jeddah. In other words, Saudi Arabia does not appear to have taken any actual legal action against the five murder suspects that it claims to have arrested. Quite the contrary, it would seem that the Saudi death squad's members are kept under surveillance in remote parts of the country. The most senior assassins, Mutreb, Tubaigy and Al-Harby, are not detained at all – not in the true sense of the word.

Let us now concentrate on the Tiger Team's activities on Turkish soil. The Saudi intelligence cells, which monitored Mohammed bin Salman's critics in Turkey and filmed or photographed them to the best of their technical ability, were particularly interest in individuals who could influence their native country's domestic politics through their tribal and other connections.

The Saudi intelligence found out what dissidents did in Turkey and reported their findings back to Riyadh. The Kingdom allegedly shared that information with the United Arab Emirates, whose crown prince, Mohammad bin Zayed, is best friends with Mohammed bin Salman.

Most Saudi dissidents, who were under surveillance by ten cells and 30 operatives linked to the Tiger Team, preferred to live in Istanbul, a metropolis whose influence hardly anyone could escape, rather than the capital Ankara – whose best part, a renowned Turkish poet once said, was the return trip to Istanbul.

Al-Muzaini and two additional members of the Saudi death squad, Saad Muid Al-Qarni and Muflis Shaya Al-Muslih, lived in the same gated community in Maslak. The Saudi station chief and some members of the local cells were photographed together at an event that the Saudi consulate hosted at the S Hotel in the Besiktas district to mark the 88th anniversary of the Kingdom's independence.

Until here, we have explained why the Saudis activated the Tiger Team and then put it back to sleep. The remainder of Chapter V will be devoted to the reasons why the Saudis killed Jamal Khashoggi. However, let us first go over past assassinations on Turkish soil by various intelligence agencies and explain why they came to a screeching halt.

Had the Turkish authorities failed to shed light on the Khashoggi murder, the Saudis would have activated the Tiger Team's local cells to conduct reconnaissance missions across the city and carry out attacks based on that information.

In the end, they had to retreat because their covers were blown. Like the Islamic State group's sleeper cells, which the Turkish security forces identified and destroyed in recent years, the Tiger Team's local operatives had no choice but to terminate themselves.

Even though Turkey's National Intelligence Organization was monitoring the Saudi cells, it refrained from cracking down on them in the absence of criminal activities such as assassinations and abductions – that is, until the Khashoggi murder.

The Turkish intelligence kept close tabs on the Saudis to see if they would break any laws – just as it followed two Russian assassins who came to Turkey in April 2016, months after the last successful assassination attempt against a Chechen community leader.

2

TARGETED ASSASSINATIONS BY FOREIGN INTELLIGENCE AGENCIES IN TURKEY

A Gentleman's Agreement With Russia

When the Saudis formed the Tiger Team, they followed in the footsteps of Mossad – a not too powerful intelligence agency that made a name for itself by conducting aggressive operations. Of course, the Kingdom also analyzed the Russian secret service SVR's international operations before planning missions to kidnap or eliminate Saudi dissidents abroad.

As we mentioned in Chapter I, the Russians carried out a series of thinly veiled assassinations in various Western countries, including the United Kingdom, where they targeted the former military intelligence agent Sergei Skripal.

Moscow conducted similar operations on Turkish soil in 2008-2015. Yet targeted assassinations ended suddenly and permanently in 2015. The main reason behind that development was the personal friendship between Turkish President Recep Tayyip Erdogan and his Russian counterpart, Vladimir Putin, which facilitated closer cooperation in the Syrian theater since 2016 as well as a gentleman's agreement between the Turkish and Russian intelligence services. That agreement was concluded after the Turks caught and interrogated two Russian operatives in 2016 – when the Russians established that they could no longer conduct missions potentially embarrassing to Turkey.

Another important factor was Turkey's crackdown on Fetullah Gulen's shadow state, officially known as FETÖ, which was gradually excluded from the country's law enforcement and intelligence communities, after the group covered up the Chechen murders.

On April 8, 2016, the Turkish intelligence apprehended two Russian agents who were involved in the murder of Vahid Edelgiriev – the eighth targeted assassination against Chechen leaders in Turkey since 2008. Their names were Alexander Smirnov and Yury Anisimov.

Turkey's National Intelligence Organization concluded that the men entered the country on November 1, 2015 to kill Chechen dissident Edelgiriev. On April 4, 2016, the suspects came back to Turkey to eliminate their next target. They rented a car and drove from Istanbul to Yalova. The Turkish intelligence was closely monitoring their activities at the time and detained the Russians upon their return to Istanbul.

The two intelligence agents who were involved in the Edelgiriev assassination were caught as part of a counter-intelligence operation that the Turks named kama after the Japanese blade. It was noteworthy that the Turkish intelligence would refer to their secret operation to repatriate Yusuf Nazik, the Reyhanli bomber, from Latakia after another deadly weapon – the dagger. Here's why they picked that name:

On November 1, 2015, when the Russian assassin attempted to kill Edelgiriev in Istanbul's Basaksehir district, his weapon got jammed and the Chechen leader was merely wounded. In the end, they had to finish the job using a kama. Therefore, the Turkish security forces made a reference to the murder weapon when they moved in to apprehend the suspects.

That operation did not prevent the rapprochement between Turkey and the Russian Federation at the time. Quite the contrary, it was quite beneficial. It wouldn't be wrong to suggest that the Turkish and Russian intelligence agencies drew their red lines in light of that incident.

THE SECRETS BEHIND OPERATION KAMA

Prior to the Edelgiriev assassination, as early as 2012, the Russian intelligence spread disinformation by leaking false information to the country's media outlets. One of those stories appeared on Channel One Russia, the country's largest national broadcaster, on February 26, 2012. It related to a supposed confession by would-be assassins, who were interrogated in the Ukrainian city of Odessa, that they were preparing to attack Russian President Vladimir Putin. Even though Turkish news outlets, which translated the story from Russian, did not mention Edelgiriev by name, the Russian media had identified the Chechen leader as a member of the imaginary death squad. As a matter of fact, Edelgiriev was with a suicide bomber in Ukraine, they claimed, when he detonated his vest prematurely.

A Russian news website in 2011 had claimed that three Chechens, who were assassinated on September 16, 2011, were responsible for a bomb attack against the Domodedovo International Airport in Moscow.

Alexander Smirnov and Yury Anisimov flew to Istanbul to eliminate Edelgiriev, whose name was mentioned in the fake news story. It was a certainty that they were employees of the Russian secret service. The two men appeared before a Turkish court, which ordered their arrest. In line with the most basic rule of espionage, they refused to share information with the Turks. One of the agents did not speak at all. The other talked, but made misleading and contradictory statements.

In accordance with another unwritten law of espionage, the Russian intelligence agency, SVR, did not admit that the two detainees worked for them. Instead, they attempted to obtain information through the Interpol's Moscow bureau, since their agents carried Interpol IDs. That was an indirect way of claiming their men.

The two captives were employees of Sluzhba Vneshney Razvedki, or the Russian external intelligence agency. They entered Turkey with fake passports and false Interpol IDs. The Turkish authorities found photographs of senior Russian officials, USB flash drives, five cell phones and a significant amount of U.S. dollars on them. The flash drives contained photographs that the Russians took during the reconnaissance mission as well as information about their target. Other material included a cache of images from an earlier mission in another European country.

The Russian agents could not explain why those images were on their phones and USB flash drives. Judging by the photographs, they captured images of security cameras and relatively remote parts of luxury hotels. One of the men told the Turkish authorities that he worked with a charity. Yet he could not account for the Interpol ID that he carried at the time of his arrest. According to sources, the Russians expressed concern that they could be poisoned when the Turks served them food behind bars.

It is necessary to analyze that significant counter-intelligence operation within the broader context of diplomatic and inter-agency talks to put the Turkish-Russian relations back on track. Taking all factors into account, the arrest of the two Russian operatives did not hurt those negotiations. If anything, it helped them. Here's why: the Turkish operation conveyed the message that Turkey was becoming more independent of Russia – as it was of the United States. As such, the Turks made it clear that they would not ignore a covert operation within their borders. Other countries in Europe and the rest of the world had not responded to Russian operations in this manner.

HOW THE CHECHEN ASSASSINATIONS ENDED

The first targeted assassination against high-profile Chechen targets in Turkey took place on September 6, 2008, when Gazi Edilsultanov, a former Chechen military commander, was shot dead in Istanbul's Basaksehir district after the killers put two bullets in the victim's head. Assailants carried out assassinations against Chechen leaders in places like Basaksehir, which they could access with relative ease.

The Turkish authorities established that Edilsultanov went to Basaksehir with two women who honeytrapped him. That method was quite popular among Russian intelligence operatives. At the time, however, the popular view was that Gazi Edilsultanov's death was related to an internal strife within the Chechen community – even though the Russians were probably involved. In other words, the Russian intelligence took advantage of tensions among Chechen leaders to eliminate the Kremlin's adversaries.

The Turks assessed that the Russian intelligence found it difficult to find logistical support in assassinations in which they were directly involved. To carry out the Edelgiriev assassination, for example, they had to buy an old pistol from a group of thieves.

By contrast, the Russians refrained from assassination attempts targeting Chechens living in gated communities. Yet Chechen leaders, who ignored warnings from the Turkish police and intelligence, found themselves at the business end of assassins' weapons.

Let us continue: Islam Dzhanibekov, who fought in the Chechen war, was killed with three bullets to the back of his head, as he returned from a personal visit with his wife and children on December 9, 2008. He was responsible for collecting donations that the Chechens sent back home. The reason behind the attack was unclear, but the authorities believed that Dzhanibekov, too, was killed in an internal power struggle.

On February 27, 2009, Ali Osaev, the Caucasus Emirate's deputy head of foreign relations, was killed in Istanbul's Zeytinburnu district by a group of gunmen that stepped out of a BMW.

Medet Onlu, the honorary consul of the Chechen Republic of Ichkeria and a businessman who assisted Chechens upon arrival in Turkey, lost his life in an armed attack in his place of business in Ankara on May 22, 2013. The Russian intelligence was behind that attack as well. Yet Moscow outsourced the hit to local hitmen with a criminal record.

The assassinations, which the Russians carried out themselves, came to be known in Turkey as 'the Zeytinburnu murders'. On September 16, 2011, Berg-Haj Musaev, who replaced Osaev after his death, along with Rustam Altemirov and Zaurbek Amriev, were murdered in Istanbul's Zeytinburnu district after performing the Friday prayer. The two Russian spies, whom the Turks caught five years later, were in contact with the assailants.

Targeted assassinations against Chechen leaders, like attacks against Iranian dissidents in the 1980s and the Khashoggi murder, conveyed the message that Turkey was an unsafe destination for dissidents.

The assassination of Russian Ambassador Andrei Karlov, which Fetullah Gulen's organization planned and carried out, was likewise intended to make Turkey look like a dangerous place and drive a wedge between Ankara and Moscow.

2

DECONSTRUCTING THE
CRIME SCENE

Why Choose Turkey?

The second most popular question about the Khashoggi murder –second only to the question why the Saudis killed Jamal Khashoggi in the first place— was why the assassins executed the *Washington Post* columnist in Turkey. Some answered that question by saying that Khashoggi was due to marry a Turkish citizen who resided in her native country, and therefore needed to obtain an official proof of his marital status from the Saudi consulate in Istanbul.

That answer, however, prevents the world from seeing the full picture. First of all, Jamal Khashoggi did not have to obtain that piece of paper from a Saudi diplomatic mission in Turkey. Legally speaking, he could have visited a Saudi embassy or consulate anywhere in the world.

Up until the moment when the Turks leaked CCTV footage of Mustafa Mohammad Al-Madani, also known as the body double, to the press, the claim that the Khashoggi murder was a deliberate and carefully planned plot to discredit Turkey reflected reasonable doubt, yet no concrete evidence. When the Istanbul police department found out which member of the Saudi death squad did what, where, when and how, the answer to the question why became clearer.

By having the body double of Jamal Khashoggi, whose murder and dismemberment inside the Saudi consulate in Istanbul had been planned all along, the killers hoped to spread fake news about the *Washington Post's* supposed disappearance and let Turkey take the fall when he went 'missing'.

A SENIOR TURKISH OFFICIAL'S ACCOUNT

We asked a senior Turkish official why the Saudis killed Jamal Khashoggi in Istanbul and left traces of the crime all around. Here's their response:

If you looked back at the incident after everything was over and the case was cracked, you'd rightfully ask that question. Had the operation succeeded, you would not have asked that question. Everyone would have known that the Saudi government –specifically, Mohammed bin Salman— was responsible for what happened, but we'd have no proof. And Saudi dissidents, who would have known that MBS was behind the murder, would be in fear.

Have you even considered to what the Khashoggi murder would have led if we did not have the audio recordings? Let me tell you: even if we'd gathered all the criminal evidence, we would have found no evidence linking [the Saudis] to the murder.

This gruesome murder, which is unprecedented in the history of espionage, would have gone down in history as a professionally-accomplished mission. Having conducted that covert operation, the Saudis would have intimidated their enemies. The murder would have served as a message to the regime's critics: "We will eliminate you in the country that you trust the most. You seek refuge in Turkey, but Turkey is unsafe."

Instead, we have audio files that amount to concrete proof. In other words, [the Saudi] fingerprint on the incident has been identified. They have been caught red-handed. The Khashoggi murder was an 'unsuccessful' operation.

The operation to repatriate Yusuf Nazik, by contrast, was a job that took 3.5 years of preparation, which was finished in secret. Turkey voluntarily took credit for the operation without revealing its methods. In other words, Turkey managed the process from start to finish. The Saudis lost the upper hand when it became clear that we had the audio files.

As such, here's the correct answer: They underestimated Turkey's intelligence capabilities. Their biggest mistake was to take us for a low-profile country and, by extension, not to adopt a solid strategy. They are now paying the price for that mistake.

That was arguably the most direct answer to the question why the assassins went after Khashoggi on Turkish soil.

It took a detailed analysis of everything that happened since the murder to arrive at that conclusion. Just as Turkey is compelled to combat terrorism and, if necessary, neutralize threats in Syria by launching cross-border operations with conventional military methods, so too must its intelligence and law enforcement agencies succeed in such situations. The Khashoggi case made that perfectly clear.

We repeatedly noted that the Khashoggi murder was unprecedented in world history for various reasons. The *Washington Post* columnist died inside his native country's consulate – which, we hope, won't set a precedent for others. At the same time, this was the first time that a government was forced to admit that its agents committed murder on 'their' sovereign soil and to grant permission, under legal and diplomatic pressure, to local investigators to search the premises.

That investigation shed light on all aspects of what happened – except the whereabouts of Jamal Khashoggi's remains. At least we know who the assassins were and who ordered the hit on the slain journalist. Obviously, it was curious that Khashoggi was murdered inside the Saudi consulate and, more broadly, within Turkey's borders. In a Nov. 2 op-ed essay for the *Washington Post*, Turkish President Recep Tayyip Erdogan himself highlighted the significance of the death squad's choice of location.

Four days later, *Hürriyet* columnist Abdülkadir Selvi attempted to answer the same question:

> Another point, which has not been stressed adequately, was that Khashoggi died in Turkey. Jamal Khashoggi, a journalist who resided in the United States and travelled frequently, could have been taken out anywhere. Why did [the killers] choose Istanbul and, as if they could not be more obvious, committed the murder inside the consulate? I do not believe that they would pick the consulate as the scene of their crime again, if they could go back in time, but it was significant that they chose Turkey. After all, Arab intellectuals have been gathering in Turkey for some time. The Khashoggi murder was a message to them: "You trust Turkey, but Turkey isn't safe for you. We will come to Istanbul and eliminate you."

> So long as the Crown Prince, who was caught red-handed, remains in power, the regime's opponents won't be safe. Having gotten away with the Khashoggi murder, the Crown Prince will keep ordering new political murders.[1]

THE BOOMERANG

Yasin Aktay, an advisor to the Justice and Development Party's chairman and the first person to hear about the Khashoggi murder after the slain journalist's fiancée, provided another answer to the question why the Saudis killed the *Washington Post* columnist in Turkey. In his view, the Khashoggi murder's primary purpose was to tell the world that Turkey was an unsafe country. In an interview with *Sabah's* Damla Kaya, Aktay elaborated on that argument:

---

1   Abdülkadir Selvi, "Kaşıkçı cinayetinde oynanan oyunlar" [The Games Played Over The Khashoggi Murder], *Hürriyet*, 6 November 2018.

What we know about the incident suggests that something much bigger was at play. It is crystal clear that [the Khashoggi murder] wasn't just about revenge, but a means to an attempted attack on Turkey.

Turkey was the target. If they made Khashoggi disappear without a trace, we could have argued that he was the target. That the body double visited the Blue Mosque and changed his clothes in a public restroom to leave a false trail indicates that the whole thing was planned in advance. The technical and detailed preparations took 3-4 days, but they started making plans earlier. Clearly, the Saudis did not want to miss their opportunity. Yet they could not anticipate that [their actions] would be uncovered.

In terms of its outcome, that plot could have resulted in a coup attempt with international dimensions. Had the Saudi operation succeeded, perhaps Saudi Arabia would have asked us to explain what happened. [Khashoggi's] murderers would have told the world's leading newspapers that he was a respected man that they loved and valued, and asked us for information about his fate. Perhaps they would have made an official decision to evacuate their citizens from Turkey. They may have gone beyond that and thought about the possibility of having the United States impose certain sanctions [on Turkey].[2]

The main reason why the Saudis opted to kill Jamal Khashoggi in Turkey was to disseminate false information about Turkey being unsafe for dissidents. For the Turks, it was crucial to challenge that claim – which they did by stopping several assassination attempts against Chechen leaders since 2015 and shedding light on the Khashoggi murder and sharing their findings with the world. In other words, Turkey turned the murder, which the Saudis saw as a means to discredit it, into a boomerang.

To be clear, that was exactly what the Turks were supposed to

[2]   Damla Kaya's interview with Yasin Aktay for this book.

do. After all, their country is a safe haven for millions of people from Syria and elsewhere, who sought refuge there because their livelihoods back home were at risk. Hence the Khashoggi murder's potential damage to Turkey's image. Luckily, the Saudis did not get their way.

WHY JAMAL KHASHOGGI?

When one asks why the Khashoggi murder took place at all, a number of interesting answers immediately come to mind. Yasin Aktay, one of the slain journalist's close friends, claims that "his words frustrated certain people, as people with archaic mindsets cannot stomach the slightest critique." In the end, those individuals decided to take revenge.

Obviously, that brief answer is nowhere near enough. Let us now turn our attention to an Oct. 10 story that appeared in the *Washington Post*, Jamal Khashoggi's final professional home. According to the outlet, Saudi officials close to Crown Prince Mohammed bin Salman had been trying to persuade Khashoggi to return to the Kingdom and offering him prestigious jobs. Yet the *Washington Post* columnist was skeptical of such offers and maintain that MBS would not keep his promises in the end:

[The *Washington Post*] claimed, citing U.S. intelligence intercepts, that Saudi Arabia's crown prince, Mohammed bin Salman, ordered an operation to lure the *Washington Post* columnist Jamal Khashoggi back to Saudi Arabia and then detain him.

Some of Khashoggi's friends said that Saudi officials close to Prince Mohammed had been calling him for four months, offering him protection and even high-level government jobs. His friends stated that Khashoggi was skeptical of those offers and told one of his friends that the Saudi government would never keep its promise not to harm him.[3]

3   "Veliaht Prens'in Kaşıkçı'nın vaatlerle Suudi Arabistan'a çekilip tutuklanmasını

Keeping in mind that Jamal Khashoggi once served as an adviser to Prince Turki bin Faisal, who oversaw the Saudi intelligence agency, that MBS offered the victim a job is not entirely impossible. For the record, Khashoggi's former boss ended up making the case that the Central Intelligence Agency was not trustworthy when Langley concluded that the Saudi crown prince had ordered the hit on the slain journalist. Recalling the CIA's 2003 conclusion that Iraq had weapons of mass destruction, which led to the U.S. invasion of that country, Prince Turki urged the U.S. justice system to hold the agency accountable.[4] That statement meant that Khashoggi's former boss had cozied up to Mohammed bin Salman to survive and was willing to stomach his former adviser's dismemberment in return.

Khashoggi, who turned down the Saudi crown prince's job offer, did many other things to 'anger' Mohammed bin Salman. Provided that he was involved in various projects, including the Army of Bees, which we discuss in greater detail in Chapter VI, it was clear why the Saudi regime targeted the slain journalist. Upon hearing Omar Abdulaziz, the Canada-based social media expert whom Khashoggi contacted regularly, one immediately reaches that conclusion.

In an interview with the authors of this book, Abdulaziz explained why he thought Jamal Khashoggi was murdered:

The Saudi government was unhappy because we launched certain projects. They did not want Jamal to work on those projects. They were unhappy with his pieces in the Washington Post. Therefore, they thought that Jamal was dangerous and needed to be silenced. There is something that the Turks, in particular, must know. In his final days, Jamal made the case that "Saudi Arabia must be Turkey's ally, not its enemy." He called on MBS to work with the Turks if he wanted to solve the Middle East's problems and help the

emrettiği iddia ediliyor" [The Crown Prince Allegedly Ordered Officials To Lure Khashoggi To Saudi Arabia With Promises To Place Him Under Arrest], *Bloomberg HT*, 11 October 2018.

4   "Suudi Prens: CIA'e güvenmiyoruz" [Saudi Prince: We Do Not Trust The Cia], Deutsche Welle Turkish, 24 November 2018.

Syrian people.

Jamal added: "We have Iran on one side and Turkey on the other. Please do not go and form a new alliance with Egypt, Bahrain or the UAE. Do not be enemies with Turkey. That won't help [your] regime." That was the solution on Jamal's mind. The solution was to cooperate with Turkey. Yet they did not listen to him. They did not wish to hear his voice, so they had to silence him. That's why they killed him.

Omar Abdulaziz notes that Khashoggi wanted Turkey and Saudi Arabia to improve their bilateral relations. Indeed, the *Washington Post* columnist wanted Ankara and Riyadh to get along and, more important, saw Turkey as a model for Saudi Arabia and the rest of the Islamic world. That view was part of the reason why the Saudis targeted him – and, possibly, why they killed him in Turkey.

Another noteworthy response to the same question appeared in the *Washington Post*. On Oct. 16, David B. Ottaway, a Middle East fellow at the Wilson Center, talked about a popular claim that lacked proof:

> I believe the main reason the crown prince feared Khashoggi so much was that he was launching a project to establish a foundation dedicated to promoting democracy in the Arab world, particularly in Saudi Arabia. He told me about the project during one of our lunches here in Washington last spring. He said he already had the money for it. He did not disclose his financial backer(s) for the project but hinted its headquarters would be located here.[5]

In other words, MBS wanted to get rid of Khashoggi because the journalist was an obstacle before the crown prince's political agenda. That claim is certainly plausible, yet, as the author himself stated, there is no concrete evidence to support it.

5   https://www.washingtonpost.com/opinions/saudia-arabias-crown-prince-went-a-ghastly-step-too-far/2018/10/16/50d60f76-d16a-11e8-83d6-291fcead2ab1_story.html?utm_term=.2874a5e092da

The same newspaper published another article on Oct. 8 purporting to reveal Mohammed bin Salman's hidden political agenda. Charles Lane argued in that piece that the Saudi crown prince had no intention of promoting individual freedoms in his country. Instead, he wrote, MBS wanted to modernize the monarchy in an attempt to strengthen its grip on power:

> The crown prince wants Saudi Arabia's economy to be less dependent on oil, and its military and intelligence forces more capable of battling Iran. ... Both reform and repression are aspects of the centralization of power.[6]

Recalling that the Khashoggi murder showed the Saudi regime's true face, Lane, citing Samuel Huntington, concludes that the process of pressure and reform will lead to a bloody revolution. Although there are possibly underlying tensions in Saudi Arabia, to think that the country could end up in such a situation, especially in the absence of a foreign intervention, would be a stretch. After all, it is no secret that bloody revolutions tend to follow international meddling.

Another response to the question why the Saudis killed Jamal Khashoggi came from Washington Post columnist David Ignatius, who maintained that Riyadh's motive was quite straightforward on Oct. 25:

> Khashoggi was seen as dangerous for the simple reason that he couldn't be intimidated or controlled. He was an uncensored mind. He didn't observe the kingdom's "red lines." He was an insistent, defiant journalist. ... Those who truly want a modern and prosperous Saudi Arabia could start by building on Khashoggi's legacy.[7]

---

6   https://www.washingtonpost.com/opinions/in-saudi-arabia-you-cant-separate-reform-from-repression/2018/10/08/6365ddf0-cb12-11e8-a3e6-44daa3d35ede_story.html?utm_term=.1121bc7fe839
7   https://www.washingtonpost.com/opinions/global-opinions/let-jamal-khashoggi-be-a-beacon-of-light-even-in-death/2018/10/25/94249cce-d896-11e8-aeb7-ddcad4a0a54e_story.html?utm_term=.fb1871b56e0a

According to Mark Perry, who provided a detailed account of the reasons behind Jamal Khashoggi's slaying in his Oct. 22 piece for the American Conservative, the *Washington Post* columnist was killed because he was a vocal critics of the Saudi regime:

> "Bin Salman, they said, was a leader who promised to create "a more modern, more entrepreneurial, less-hidebound and more youth-oriented society. That promise, it seems, has now been drowned out by the screams of a reporter who dared tell the truth."[8]

In an August 2018 piece, which Perry cited in his article, Khashoggi had noted that the United States hated the Muslim Brotherhood and Washington's problems with the group was at the root of a regionwide problem.

Eliminating the Muslim Brotherhood, he warned, would result in the elimination of democracy and ensure that Arabs continued to live under authoritarian and corrupt regime in the future. Khashoggi argued that the United States was on the wrong side and with wrong friends:

> During the Obama presidency, the U.S. administration was wary of the Muslim Brotherhood, which had come to power in Egypt after the country's first-ever free elections. Despite his declared support for democracy and change in the Arab world in the wake of the Arab Spring, then-President Barack Obama did not take a strong position and reject the coup against President-elect Mohamed Morsi. The coup, as we know, led to the military's return to power in the largest Arab country — along with tyranny, repression, corruption and mismanagement.
>
> …

> The United States's aversion to the Muslim Brotherhood, which is more apparent in the current Trump administration,

---

8   https://www.theamericanconservative.com/articles/why-jamal-khashoggi-was-killed/

is the root of a predicament across the entire Arab world. The eradication of the Muslim Brotherhood is nothing less than an abolition of democracy and a guarantee that Arabs will continue living under authoritarian and corrupt regimes. In turn, this will mean the continuation of the causes behind revolution, extremism and refugees — all of which have affected the security of Europe and the rest of the world. Terrorism and the refugee crisis have changed the political mood in the West and brought the extreme right to prominence there.

There can be no political reform and democracy in any Arab country without accepting that political Islam is a part of it. A significant number of citizens in any given Arab country will give their vote to Islamic political parties if some form of democracy is allowed. It seems clear then that the only way to prevent political Islam from playing a role in Arab politics is to abolish democracy, which essentially deprives citizens of their basic right to choose their political representatives.

...

There are efforts here in Washington, encouraged by some Arab states that do not support freedom and democracy, to persuade Congress to designate the Muslim Brotherhood as a terrorist organization. If they succeed, the designation will weaken the fragile steps toward democracy and political reform that have already been curbed in the Arab world. It will also push backward the Arab countries that have made progress in creating a tolerant environment and allowing political participation by various components of society, including the Islamists.

Islamists today participate in the parliaments of various Arab countries such as Kuwait, Jordan, Bahrain, Tunisia and Morocco. This has led to the emergence of Islamic democracy, such as the Ennahda movement in Tunisia, and the maturing of democratic transformation in the other countries.

The coup in Egypt led to the loss of a precious opportunity for Egypt and the entire Arab world. If the democratic process had continued there, the Muslim Brotherhood's political practices could have matured and become more inclusive, and the unimaginable peaceful rotation of power could have become a reality and a precedent to be followed.

The Trump administration always says it wants to correct Obama's mistakes. It should add his mishandling of Arab democracy to its list. Obama erred when he wasted the precious opportunity that could have changed the history of the Arab world, and when he caved to pressure from Saudi Arabia and the United Arab Emirates, as well as from members of his own administration. They all missed the big picture and were governed by their intolerant hatred for any form of political Islam, a hatred that has destroyed Arabs' choice for democracy and good governance.[9]

THE MUSLIM BROTHERHOOD CONNECTION

Jamal Khashoggi, whose above-quoted piece was possibly one of the reasons behind his eventual murder, saw himself largely aligned with the Muslim Brotherhood yet did not refrain from openly criticizing the group.

Turan Kışlakçı, a friend of the slain journalist who manages the Turkish-Arab Media Association, argues that Khashoggi was critical of the Muslim Brotherhood, even though many consider him a staunch supporter of that organization:

During his stay in the United States, Jamal Khashoggi attended certain events along with other Saudi dissidents and criticized Saudi Arabia's war in Yemen, the country's diplomatic spat with Canada, and the arrest of women's rights activists in his *Washington Post* column. There were major

9   https://www.washingtonpost.com/news/global-opinions/wp/2018/08/28/the-u-s-is-wrong-about-the-muslim-brotherhood-and-the-arab-world-is-suffering-for-it/?utm_term=.f496ab8401e9

problems between Khashoggi and the Saudi government – especially over Yemen.[10]

According to Kışlakçı, the slain journalist had turned down a job offer from Mohammed bin Salman, the chief suspect in his murder investigation.[11]

The Muslim Brotherhood was an Islamic movement established in Egypt in 1928 to resist Western colonialism.[12] It promoted civilian and democratic methods at the expense of armed struggle. The movement's founder, Hassan Al-Banna, was assassinated in Cairo, Egypt on 12 February 1949.

The Brotherhood's rise to power in Egypt, its birthplace, in 2011 was a source of hope for the group's supporters across the Arab world.

The Freedom and Justice Party in Egypt and the Ennahda Party in Tunisia came to power. The Justice and Development Party, the Islamic Action Front and the Islamic Constitutional Movement contested elections successfully in Morocco, Jordan and Kuwait, respectively. At the same time, the Muslim Brotherhood played a central role within social movements in Libya, Yemen and Syria. That the organization emerged as a source of hope unsettled Gulf monarchies, including the Saudi royal family.[13]

THE MEXICAN WAVE STOPS IN THE GULF

That sociopolitical movement, which moved from the Maghreb to the Gulf like a Mexican wave, stopped in Egypt, its literal and figurative birthplace, as a result of Gen. El-Sisi's coup d'état in 2013. The coup's primary sponsors included Saudi Arabia and the United Arab Emirates. At the same time, it was the political brainchild of the United States and Israel. It was a com-

10   Turan Kışlakçı's remarks on 5 October 2018 to the author Ferhat Ünlü on his TV show.
11   Ibid.
12   Abdullah Muradoglu, "İhvan-ı Müslimin'in ibret verici kısa tarihi" [A Brief History Of The Muslim Brotherhood], *Yeni Safak*, 1 July 2012.
13   Onur Erem, "Suudi gazeteci Cemal Kaşıkçı kimdir?" [Who Is Saudi Journalist Jamal Khashoggi?], BBC Turkish, 23 October 2018.

bination of Washington and Tel Aviv's 'think' and the Egyptian general's 'tank'. And the Gulf paid for that tank's fuel.

A similar coup attempt took place in Turkey, which is all too familiar with terror attacks and attempted coups, in the form of a false flag operation bearing the fingerprints of the Turkish Armed Forces. On 15 July 2016, a group of military officers, who were previously unidentified members of FETÖ, the organization led by Fetullah Gulen, tried to overthrow the country's elected government and, luckily, failed. The Turkish people, led by their president, crushed Washington's 'think' and Gulen's 'tank'.

That Turkey opposed the military coup in Egypt was frustrating for Saudi Arabia and the United Arab Emirates. Saudi journalist Jamal Khashoggi, who had been urging tolerance for non-violent political movements, sided with the Turks in that debate. As a matter of fact, he interviewed Erdogan after the July 15 coup attempt. The Saudis and the Emiratis, by contrast, had hoped that the failed coup would succeed.

Saudi Arabia and the UAE were also unhappy with Qatar, a Gulf state with excellent relations with Turkey, for supporting the Muslim Brotherhood. In 2014, Doha came under criticism over a series of interviews by *Al Jazeera* with MB leaders. Three years later, the country faced isolation, a politically-motivated blockade and military threats from Egypt, Israel, Saudi Arabia and the UAE. At that moment, Turkey helped the Qataris break the blockade by offering military assistance to Doha and setting up a military base there.

MBS GOES OUT OF LINE

Having nurtured a close personal relationship with Jared Kushner, U.S. President Donald Trump's son-in-law, Saudi Crown Prince Mohammed bin Salman strengthened his grip on his country before turning his attention to Turkey and Qatar. He referred to the Muslim Brotherhood as a hotbed of terrorism that must be destroyed, and described Turkey, Iran and Qatar as the axis of evil.

MBS did not stop there. He agreed to serve as Washington's

proxy in Syria and began to provide financial assistance to the terrorist organization PYD in the east of the Euphrates river. Against that backdrop, Jamal Khashoggi, who had supported the Muslim Brotherhood since the Egyptian coup and hailed Turkey as a model for the Islamic world, became the Saudi crown prince's enemy.

Around the same time, the *Washington Post* columnist started receiving phone calls from Saudis, who urged him to return to his native country. Among them was Khaled bin Salman, Riyadh's ambassador to the United States and Mohammed bin Salman's younger brother. The Saudi ambassador reportedly met Khashoggi four times in three months to convey the message that he was not in trouble and he needed to go to Riyadh.[14]

Working closely with UAE Crown Prince Mohammad bin Zayed, MBS accused Qatar of supporting Iran-linked groups in his country's Qatif governorate as well as Bahrain and Yemen. Meanwhile, some media outlets claimed that the Emir of Qatar, Tamim bin Hamad Al-Thani, said in an address to military cadets that there was no point in being hostile toward Iran. Isolation and a blockade against the country followed.

Fully aware of the growing polarization among the Gulf states, U.S. President Donald Trump visited Saudi Arabia in May 2017 and concluded a $350 million arms deal with his hosts. In Riyadh, he called for the creation of a 40,000-strong military coalition against Iran – some kind of Arab NATO. To be clear, the U.S. president could not care less about the security of Gulf states. He was just playing nice to do business.

According to media reports, Prince Turki bin Faisal, Khashoggi's former boss, was among the Saudi officials tasked with luring the *Washington Post* columnist back to his native country. He assured Khashoggi that his life was not in danger and told him to visit the Saudi consulate.[15]

---

14   Ibid.
15   Ibid.

3

THREE COMPONENTS OF THE KHASHOGGI MURDER

Access to Hidden Files

In light of the above, it is necessary to keep three components in mind when answering the question why Jamal Khashoggi was murdered: the slain journalist's sympathy for the Muslim Brotherhood, his knowledge of covert operations from his time with former Saudi intelligence chief Prince Turki bin Faisal, and his public criticism of Saudi Crown Prince Mohammed bin Salman.

Moreover, Khashoggi was critical of Washington's tacit support for the Qatar blockade due to the Trump administration's alliance with Crown Prince Mohammed bin Salman. The close personal relationship between the U.S. president and the heir to the Saudi throne, the slain journalist maintained, was ultimately dangerous to the Kingdom.

On Oct. 14, the Washington Post published a story in an attempt to clarify why the Trump administration was desperately trying to save Mohammed bin Salman, and concluded that Jared Kushner, Trump's son-in-law, had been "dangerously naïve to trust Mohammed."[1] Recalling that the Saudi crown prince resorted to ruthless and manipulative actions to strengthen his grip on power, reporters Philip Rucker, Carol Leonnig and Anne Gear-

---

1   https://www.washingtonpost.com/politics/two-princes-kushner-now-faces-a-reckoning-for-trumps-bet-on-the-saudi-heir/2018/10/14/6eaeaafc-ce46-11e8-a3e6-44daa3d35ede_story.html

an wrote that the U.S. intelligence community was concerned about Kushner's contacts with the Saudi royal family. According to the Post, CIA officials were worried that Trump's son-in-law could exploit the administration's relations with foreign governments, including the Kingdom and the United Arab Emirates, for his personal financial and political gain – at the expense of U.S. interests.

When an alleged meeting between Emir Tamim bin Hamad Al-Thani of Qatar and Jamal Khashoggi, who supported Qatar against Saudi Arabia and the UAE, leaked to the press, the Saudis labeled the *Washington Post* columnist as the Muslim Brotherhood's man in the Kingdom and a representative of Qatari interests.

That Khashoggi criticized the mass arrests in Saudi Arabia in his columns and raised that issue in interviews further angered Mohammed bin Salman.

MBS responded to the critics of his regime's wave of arrest by claiming that Riyadh's actions had nothing to do with repressing political opponents or restricting the freedom of expression. In an interview with Bloomberg, the crown prince conceded that he had approximately 1,500 critics arrested, yet denied that he was going after this rivals and dissidents.[2]

The Saudi crown prince's totalitarian leadership style was backed up by national security concerns. It is important to note that unelected political leaders in places like the Kingdom tend to prioritize their personal interests over the interests and safety of their country. To make matters worse, Saudi Arabia and others, unlike countries like Turkey, do not think about national security with reference to the state or its citizens. They are driven by the royalty's relentless efforts to keep their seats.

THE VICTIM'S FINAL STATEMENT

Crown Prince Mohammed bin Salman's survival instinct did

2   https://www.bloomberg.com/news/articles/2018-10-05/saudi-crown-prince-discusses-trump-aramco-arrests-transcript

not stop Jamal Khashoggi from speaking up. In the weeks leading up to his untimely death, the *Washington Post* columnist had become a more vocal critic of the Saudi regime. In an interview with the British public broadcaster BBC, which was recorded on Sep. 30 –just two days before the murder—, Khashoggi took another jab at the Kingdom's *de facto* ruler. BBC did not air that interview until it became clear that the 60-year-old journalist had gone missing inside the Saudi consulate in Istanbul. In his final television interview, Khashoggi stuck to his guns:

BBC: When do you think that you'll be able to go back home again?

Khashoggi: I don't think I will be able to go home. I heard of the arrest of a friend who did nothing worth [getting] arrested. … Maybe he [said] something critical at a dinner party. That's what we are becoming in Saudi Arabia. We never experienced [that].

BBC: Are people spying on each other there?

Khashoggi: Yes. People now question why so-and-so got arrested. Recently, a columnist and an economist, who was close to the royal court, got arrested. That scared many people because we are talking about someone who was close to the government. I don't want to use the term "dissident" – they are not dissidents. They just have an independent mind. Until now, I [never] called myself an [opponent]. I always say that I am just a writer and I want a free environment to write and speak my mind. That's what I do in the Washington Post. They gave me a platform to write freely. I wish I had that platform in my home.

BBC: Would Saudi Arabia be a better country if there was freedom of expression?

Khashoggi: Very. We are going through a period of transformation that is going to involve [all Saudis]. As one of England's [past] kings says: "What affects the people must be discussed by the people." [But] this serious transformation isn't discussed. The prince surprises us every couple of weeks or months with a huge, multi-billion-dollar project that wasn't discussed in the Parliament or the newspapers. The people will just clap: "Great! We want to have more!" Things don't work that way.[3]

Another reason behind the Khashoggi murder was the *Washington Post* columnist's vocal criticism of Mohammed bin Salman's devastating proxy war in Yemen. Three weeks before his death, Khashoggi wrote that the Kingdom had to confront the legacy of its war and called on the crown prince to end violence immediately:

Saudi Arabia must face the damage from the past three-plus years of war in Yemen. The conflict has soured the kingdom's relations with the international community, affected regional security dynamics and harmed its reputation in the Islamic world. Saudi Arabia is in a unique position to simultaneously keep Iran out of Yemen and end the war on favorable terms if it change its role from warmaker to peacemaker. Saudi Arabia could use its clout and leverage within Western circles and empower international institutions and mechanisms to resolve the conflict. However, the window for achieving a resolution to the conflict is rapidly closing.

The-U.N. sponsored Geneva peace talks that were scheduled to open last Thursday have practically collapsed, in part because Houthis rebels who control the capitol (and most of western Yemen) were afraid their return would be halted due to Saudi Arabia's control of Yemen's airspace. The Saudis could provide their enemy and the U.N. officials with travel support — or perhaps they could even offer them a Saudi plane. Even better, Saudi Arabia could announce a cease-fire and offer peace talks in the Saudi Arabian city of Taif, where previous peace talks with Yemenis have taken place.
Saudi Arabia's actions in Yemen were driven by national security concerns due to Iranian involvement in the country. However, Saudi Arabia's war efforts have not provided an

---

extra layer of security but have rather increased the likelihood of domestic casualties and damage. Saudi defense systems rely on the U.S.-made Patriot missile system. Saudi Arabia has been successful in preventing Houthi missiles from causing substantial damage. Yet, the inability of Saudi authorities in preventing Houthi missiles from being fired in the first place serves as an embarrassing reminder that the kingdom's leadership is unable to restrain their Iranian-backed opponent.

Each missile fired by Houthi forces poses both a political and financial burden on the kingdom. The cost of an Iranian missile supplied to the Houthis is uncertain, but one can speculate that each missile does not compare to the cost of a $3 million Patriot missile.

Unexpected costs associated with the conflict in Yemen means Saudi Arabia has increasingly been borrowing funds in international markets without clearly saying what the funds are for. The kingdom has reportedly raised $11 billion in a loan from international banks.

...

Saudi Arabia does not deserve to be compared to Syria, whose leader seemingly did not hesitate to use chemical weapons against his people. But further continuation of the war in Yemen will validate voices saying that Saudi Arabia is doing in Yemen what Syrian President Bashar al-Assad, the Russians and Iranians are doing in Syria. Even the south of Yemen that has been "liberated," protesters are currently staging a civil disobedience campaign, chanting slogans against the Saudi-led coalition, which is seen as the actual power on the ground, rather than Yemen's exiled government.

Peace talks will provide Saudi Arabia with a golden opportunity. Riyadh will almost certainly find international support if it enters into a cease-fire as negotiations take place. It must utilize its global clout and incorporate international institutions and allies to financially pressure Tehran to stand down in Yemen. The Saudi Arabian crown prince must also accept that the Houthis, the Islah (Sunni Islamists) and the southern separatists should play a future role in the governance of Yemen. Obviously, Riyadh will not get all of what it wants and would leave Yemenis to sort out their differences with their fellow Houthis in a National Congress — instead of on bloody battlefields.

…

The longer this cruel war lasts in Yemen, the more permanent the damage will be. The people of Yemen will be busy fighting poverty, cholera and water scarcity and rebuilding their country. The crown prince must bring an end to the violence and restore the dignity of the birthplace of Islam.[4]

In November 2017, Khashoggi had charged Crown Prince Mohammed with acting like Russian President Vladimir Putin.[5] That the Russian leader high-fived MBS at the G20 summit in Argentina just two months after the journalist's slaying indicated that Khashoggi may have been right all along.

SAUDI SISTERS ON THE BANKS OF HUDSON RIVER

In her Nov. 5 column for the Guardian, Nesrine Malik compared Khashoggi's fate to the assassination of Saddam Hussein's sons and claimed that the people behind the journalist's murder and the deaths of two Saudi sisters, whose bodies washed up on the bank of the Hudson River in New York, may have been the same.

Recalling that millions of people died in Yemen yet could

---

4   https://www.washingtonpost.com/news/global-opinions/wp/2018/09/11/
saudi-arabias-crown-prince-must-restore-dignity-to-his-country-by-ending-yemens-cruel-war/?utm_term=.d448a7f313eb
5   https://www.washingtonpost.com/news/global-opinions/wp/2017/11/05/
saudi-arabias-crown-prince-is-acting-like-putin/

not have the world's attention because they weren't journalists or western researchers, the author made an indirect reference to Joseph Stalin's famous words: *"A single death is a tragedy. The death of a million people is a statistic."*[6]

On Oct. 29, the British newspaper Sunday Express reported that the Government Communications Headquarters, or GCHQ, had advance knowledge of the Saudi plot:

Murdered journalist Jamal Khashoggi was about to disclose details of Saudi Arabia's use of chemical weapons in Yemen, sources close to him said last night. The revelations come as separate intelligence sources disclosed that Britain had first been made aware of a plot a full three weeks before he walked into the Saudi consulate in Istanbul.

Crucially, the highly-placed source confirms that MI6 had warned his Saudi Arabian counterparts to cancel the mission - though this request as ignored.

"On October 1 we became aware of the movement of a group, which included members of Ri'āsat Al-Istikhbārāt Al-'Āmah (GID) to Istanbul, and it was pretty clear what their aim was.

"Through channels we warned that this was not a good idea. Subsequent events show that our warning was ignored."

...

"We know the orders came from a member of the royal circle but have no direct information to link them to Crown Prince Mohammad bin Salman."[7]

---

6   https://www.theguardian.com/commentisfree/2018/nov/05/jamal-khashog-gi-coverage-victim-saudi
7   https://www.express.co.uk/news/world/1037378/Khashoggi-mur-der-news-saudi-arabia-chemical-weapons-use

Although the Western media was captivated by the Khashoggi murder, news outlets from Qatar, along with Turkey and the United States, kept the momentum going. Al Jazeera, among others, repeatedly interviewed the authors of this book. In the weeks after the murder, reporters from the United States, the United Kingdom and Germany visited the offices of *Sabah's* Special Intelligence Unit. Even the Japanese media covered the story and interviewed us.

Chinese news outlets, too, followed the Khashoggi murder closely. Having managed to distract global attention from the sudden disappearance and reported arrest of Meng Hongwei, the former president of Interpol, on Oct. 5, Beijing was quick to blame the West over double standards.[8] By contrast, the Chinese authorities were quick to charge the high-profile detainee with bribery and prevented his arrest from turning into a global issue.

Needless to say, China enjoyed a distinct advantage in this case. It was the world's second largest economy after the United States – whereas Saudi Arabia, which boasts the world's 19th largest economy, carried out a targeted assassination in Turkey, which was in 18th place.

The Saudi crown prince, who was politically responsible for Jamal Khashoggi's death, managed to survive the first round by capitalizing on his relationship with U.S. President Donald Trump and even Russian President Vladimir Putin, who high-fived him at the G20 summit. If he stays in power despite extraordinary global pressure thanks to the eagerness of two superpowers to look the other way, what did not kill Mohammed bin Salman could make him stronger.

THE MOST EXPENSIVE MURDER ON RECORD

The Khashoggi murder had diplomatic, intelligence, criminal and economic repercussions. The *Washington Post* journalist's death arguably came with the highest price tag in history. When news of Khashoggi's disappearance hit the wires, the Saudi stock

---

8   http://www.globaltimes.cn/content/1123266.shtml

exchange closed at a six-month low.

Even though the Tadawul recovered in the end, MBS, who runs Saudi Arabia like a reckless playboy (unlike Trump, who runs the U.S. like a chief executive officer), fears that the Kingdom's economy will suffer.

The Trump administration has no intention of scrapping the $350 million arms deal that it signed with the Saudis over the Khashoggi murder. Ironically, the U.S. president would arguably do MBS a favor by cancelling Riyadh's orders under the circumstances. After all, the Saudi regime has to pay for all the equipment.

The global backlash over the killing of journalist Jamal Khashoggi, along with the financial toll of new arms deals and Riyadh's geostrategic responsibility to contain Iran's regional influence, placed a heavy burden on the Kingdom's shoulders.

Then there is the Aramco controversy. The Saudi Arabian petroleum company was co-founded by Americans and Saudis in 1933. Specifically, King Abdulaziz of Saudi Arabia and U.S. President Franklin D. Roosevelt launched that project. Valued at $34 billion, or one eighth of the Kingdom's annual budget, will be the subject of an initial public offering. Yet the move has been repeatedly postponed, largely because MBS claims the company to be worth $2 trillion. In recent months, Aramco signalled that it seeks to increase its market value by launching joint projects. If it succeeds, the company will pick up the check for Crown Prince Mohammed's Vision 2030.

In 2011, the Kingdom of Saudi Arabia –which boasts the world's 19th largest economy after Turkey— spent a sixth of its annual budget to prevent the Arab Spring from taking root within its borders. Jamal Khashoggi shared that information in an interview with the German magazine Der Spiegel. The slain journalist knew perfectly well that Riyadh, whose entire national security strategy was shaped by money (specifically, throwing cash at problems), could not survive for a very long time:

> That method does not work. You could not make everyone happy if you were to distribute $100 trillion to the people

tomorrow. What will happen when the oil runs out? Everyone wants to be modern, but they are unwilling to cope with the side effects of modernity. Some day, this nation, like all others, will implement reforms. We, too, need freedom, transparency, the rule of law, an elected prime minister and a real parliament. What will happen if Tunisia and Egypt succeed in their struggle for democracy? We cannot risk political isolation. Time flies and it cannot be stopped.[9]

Khashoggi had a point. Time was irreversible and unstoppable. Yet the United States, where he moved after leaving the Kingdom, had installed the two crown princes, Mohammed bin Salman and Mohammad bin Zayed, as its Trojan horses in the Middle East. They had one job: to stop history.

KHASHOGGI'S FINAL COLUMN

On Oct. 3, the day after Jamal Khashoggi disappeared into the Saudi consulate in Istanbul, his assistant/translator emailed the *Washington Post* columnist's final piece to *Global Opinions* editor Karen Attiah.

The Post did not publish that column for two weeks, hoping that Khashoggi would come back. In the end, when the Saudi journalist's editors gave up their hope, Khashoggi's final piece appeared in the *Washington Post* on Oct. 18:

I was recently online looking at the 2018 "Freedom in the World" report published by Freedom House and came to a grave realization. There is only one country in the Arab world that has been classified as "free." That nation is Tunisia. Jordan, Morocco and Kuwait come second, with a classification of "partly free." The rest of the countries in the Arab world are classified as "not free."

As a result, Arabs living in these countries are either un-

9   Ibid.

informed or misinformed. They are unable to adequately address, much less publicly discuss, matters that affect the region and their day-to-day lives. A state-run narrative dominates the public psyche, and while many do not believe it, a large majority of the population falls victim to this false narrative. Sadly, this situation is unlikely to change.

The Arab world was ripe with hope during the spring of 2011. Journalists, academics and the general population were brimming with expectations of a bright and free Arab society within their respective countries. They expected to be emancipated from the hegemony of their governments and the consistent interventions and censorship of information. These expectations were quickly shattered; these societies either fell back to the old status quo or faced even harsher conditions than before.

My dear friend, the prominent Saudi writer Saleh al-Shehi, wrote one of the most famous columns ever published in the Saudi press. He unfortunately is now serving an unwarranted five-year prison sentence for supposed comments contrary to the Saudi establishment. The Egyptian government's seizure of the entire print run of a newspaper, al-Masry al Youm, did not enrage or provoke a reaction from colleagues. These actions no longer carry the consequence of a backlash from the international community. Instead, these actions may trigger condemnation quickly followed by silence.

As a result, Arab governments have been given free rein to continue silencing the media at an increasing rate. There was a time when journalists believed the Internet would liberate information from the censorship and control associated with print media. But these governments, whose very existence relies on the control of information, have aggressively blocked the Internet. They have also arrested local reporters and pressured advertisers to harm the revenue of specific publications.

There are a few oases that continue to embody the spirit of the Arab Spring. Qatar's government continues to support international news coverage, in contrast to its neighbors' efforts to uphold the control of information to support the "old Arab order." Even in Tunisia and Kuwait, where the press is considered at least "partly free," the media focuses on domestic issues but not issues faced by the greater Arab world. They are hesitant to provide a platform for journalists from Saudi Arabia, Egypt and Yemen. Even Lebanon, the Arab world's crown jewel when it comes to press freedom, has fallen victim to the polarization and influence of pro-Iran Hezbollah.

The Arab world is facing its own version of an Iron Curtain, imposed not by external actors but through domestic forces vying for power. During the Cold War, Radio Free Europe, which grew over the years into a critical institution, played an important role in fostering and sustaining the hope of freedom. Arabs need something similar. In 1967, *The New York Times* and *The Post* took joint ownership of the *International Herald Tribune* newspaper, which went on to become a platform for voices from around the world.

My publication, *The Post*, has taken the initiative to translate many of my pieces and publish them in Arabic. For that, I am grateful. Arabs need to read in their own language so they can understand and discuss the various aspects and complications of democracy in the United States and the West. If an Egyptian reads an article exposing the actual cost of a construction project in Washington, then he or she would be able to better understand the implications of similar projects in his or her community.

The Arab world needs a modern version of the old transnational media so citizens can be informed about global events. More important, we need to provide a platform for Arab voices. We suffer from poverty, mismanagement and poor education. Through the creation of an independent international forum, isolated from the influence of nationalist governments spreading hate through propaganda, ordinary people in the Arab world would be able to address the structural problems their societies face.[10]

WHAT WE STILL DO NOT KNOW

Obviously, what got Jamal Khashoggi killed was everything he said and wrote before the above column. Still, that the slain journalist devoted his last column to restrictions on press freedom and freedom of expression in the Arab world was ironic. When Khashoggi complained about his Saudi colleague's five-year prison sentence, he clearly could not imagine what the Kingdom's assassins were going to do to him.

What could have caused the Saudis to murder Jamal Khashoggi in such a barbaric manner? In this chapter, we discussed why the Washington Post columnist, whom the Tiger Team was following closely, was killed. Even though we found many answers, none of those reasons justify Khashoggi's fate and what the Saudis did to his remains.

Every question that we pose about the Khashoggi murder seems to take us back to square one. Launching a social media project called the Army of Bees, criticizing the Kingdom's war in Yemen, sympathizing with the Muslim Brotherhood, having served as an adviser to the Saudi intelligence agency's former head, finding oneself amid a power struggle within the Saudi royal family, identifying Turkey as a role model for the Islamic world, and being accused of working for Qatar...

Those 'reasons' provide us with a limited understanding of the reasons behind Jamal Khashoggi's slaying, but fail to account for

---

10   https://www.washingtonpost.com/opinions/global-opinions/jamal-khashoggi-what-the-arab-world-needs-most-is-free-expression/2018/10/17/adfc8c44-d21d-11e8-8c22-fa2ef74bd6d6_story.html?utm_term=.b2adff7bfd7d

the way in which the killers treated their victim. To be perfectly honest, nothing could account for what happened. Even someone who knows the darkest secret in the world and hints that they could use that information to do something bad wouldn't deserve to be treated like Jamal Khashoggi.

Until now, the world has been unable to grant Jamal Khashoggi's final wish: to be buried in his hometown of Medina. Nor does the slain journalist have a tomb, where his friends and family can recite prayers.

Who would deserve such an end?

CHAPTER VI

Who?

1

JAMAL KHASHOGGI'S SECRET PROJECT

The 'Army of Bees' That Stung the Crown Prince

Jamal Khashoggi was born sixty years ago in Madina, Saudi Arabia, where Prophet Mohammed died and his remains are still today. Khashoggi's last will was to be buried in his place of birth. Unless Saudi Arabia decides to cooperate with the Turkish authorities, it is unlikely that the slain journalist's final wish will ever come true.

Born on 13 Oct. 1958, Jamal Khashoggi was a patriotic journalist. Circumstances, however, compelled him to live in exile – albeit voluntary— and, to paraphrase Adorno's words, the act of writing became home for the *Washington Post* columnist who no longer had a home.

The above quote from Adorno possibly described Khashoggi's situation than the experiences of anyone else.

Having always found a place to publish his writings over the course of his thirty-odd-year journalism career, Khashoggi's final home was the prestigious Washington Post.

The authors of this book read many stories and commentaries that appeared in various media outlets since Jamal Khashoggi's death. Our conclusion is as follows:One of the most significant stories about the Khashoggi murder appeared in the *Washington Post* on Oct. 17 with the bylines of Loveday Morris and Fareed Zakaria. It was an important piece, as it contained some critical information about the secret project, on which Khashoggi worked until his death.

The project was called 'Army of Bees'. We learned more about this Twitter army that was going to counter-balance the troll army that Saudi Crown Prince Mohammed bin Salman's Goebbels-like propagandist, Saud Al-Qahtani, had launched under orders from the Kingdom's de facto ruler, by speaking with the Canada-based activist Omar Abdulaziz. We will also provide insights into the cyber war between MBS and the Saudi regime's exiled critics.

However, let us first turn our attention to the *Washington Post* story, which included valuable information about the 27-year-old activist's private contacts with two messengers from the Saudi crown prince,[1] one of the most important characters in Khashoggi's final months.

According to the same story, the two men made Abdulaziz, whom they met at a café, an offer: to accompany them to Saudi Arabia, where he would rejoin his family, or to face imprisonment. Abdulaziz's brothers was with them.

Abdulaziz, who enjoyed political asylum in Canada, told what appeared to be two Saudi intelligence operatives about some projects that may have led MBS to flag him as a problem, and informed them that Khashoggi, too, was working on those projects. The project was the Army of Bees. Khashoggi had reportedly wired $5,000 to Abdulaziz in return.

Judging by the *Washington Post* story, it would appear that the Army of Bees was intended to challenge the Saudi troll army, which Al-Qahtani had built for MBS. In other words, Saudi dissident wanted to launched their army of bees to combat the crown prince's troll army – which they called the army of flies.[2]

---

1   According to CNN International, those individuals identified themselves as Malek and Abdullah. They told Abdulaziz that they were visiting on Salman's orders and circumvented the usual channels to offer him a job.

2   Dissidents referred to those trolls as "electronic flies."

THE CYBER WAR BEHIND THE MURDER

Jamal Khashoggi made it clear that the project had to be kept secret. The obvious question, of course, is why and for whom the slain journalist wanted to build a troll army.

The *Washington Post* story does not answer that question, even though it claims that the project was the brainchild of Abdulaziz and adds that Khashoggi supported that idea.

Whether Khashoggi knew that the project, if successful, would go beyond the limits of journalism and venture into the realm of espionage is unclear. Moreover, another significant question is whether Khashoggi used his own financial resources to pay $5,000 to Abdulaziz or received funds from another source.

According to the Post, Khashoggi told Abdulaziz on June 21 that he would try to find the money: *"We must do something. You know that I am affected by the attacks on occasion."* In other words, the slain journalist was unable to rely on his own financial means to make the payment and searched for funding.

Abdulaziz told the *Washington Post* that the Saudi troll army insulted Jamal Khashoggi frequently and claimed that Khashoggi was targeted because he was an important voice in the Western media.

That information demonstrated that Qahtani took aim at Khashoggi under orders from the Saudi crown prince. Abdulaziz also disclosed that he was targeted by Saudi spyware and the Saudi authorities were able to monitor all communications between the two men.

The Washington Post story indicates that Abdulaziz assumed the two Saudi men to be on Qahtani's payroll by the way they talked. Although Qahtani himself did not work for the Saudi intelligence, he was privy to all of the crown prince's dirty business, including covert operations and assassinations. Perhaps more important, Qahtani was the commander in chief of the Saudi troll army, who, Khashoggi alleged, contacted him prior to his death.

Omar Abdulaziz met Jamal Khashoggi in Washington, DC in the summer of 2017:

"THEY CALLED ME ERDOGAN'S SPY"

Omar Abdulaziz, a key figure on whom *The Washington Post* and CNN International reported, made exclusive statements to the authors of this book. He answered our questions sincerely. We hereby publish an unedited version of that interview:

How did you end up in exile after criticizing the Saudi regime? Could you tell us your story and talk about your life in Canada?
I became a political refugee in Canada in 2014. Before that, I was critical of the Saudi Arabian regime. I felt that my life was in danger. I requested asylum from Canada and they accepted. I continued to criticize the regime. Yet some people were unhappy. I kept working on my video projects and my Twitter and YouTube channels. The Saudi troll army, whom we call the Saudi flies, called me a Muslim Brotherhood agent and Erdogan's spy. They spread the false rumor that Erdogan and Qatar paid me off. In truth, everything was alright until MBS arrived. When he came to power, he began to control everything. Sure, I criticized King Abdullah and the old regime as well, but they did no harm to myself or my family.

In 2017, McKinsey published a report. They handed it to MBS. They did not talk about it openly, but described me as an opponent of [the crown prince] and the regime and a ruthless critic. It wasn't just me. There were two others mentioned in the same report. They were outspoken critics as well. Most of the hashtags mentioned in the report were mine. I was unaware of it until *The New York Times* reported on it. In 2018, MBS sent me two messengers. They came to Montreal, Canada to meet me and have a chat. They told me that MBS wanted me to come back. "Return to your country," they said. "You can help us change Saudi Arabia." They told me those things to convince me to return. I did not believe them. I thought that it was a trap. I felt that something bad was going to happen to me. One of my siblings was with them. Still, I rejected their proposals. On 23 June 2018, they hacked my phone. They monitored my phone calls and text messages – including those involving Jamal [Khashoggi].

In early August 2018, I learned that two of my siblings, including the one who arrived with the messengers, and a group of my friends were taken into custody. That was Saudi Arabia's way of telling me to keep silent. I did not comply. I did not and I won't keep silent. I have a right to keep criticizing them. At the time, I was unaware that my phone was hacked. I received a call from Citizen Lab and they told me that my phone had been hacked. They informed me that the hackers knew about everything that was on my phone. During that period, i.e. in the months of June, July and August, I was working on different, important projects to control social media with Jamal Khashoggi. These were projects against the troll army. On Aug. 18, I told Jamal that my phone had been hacked. I said that they were aware of what we had been doing. Jamal said that was a big problem. They knew that we worked on a range of projects together. Jamal was like a teacher to me.

How did you meet Jamal Khashoggi?
I met Jamal Khashoggi in Saudi Arabia. Yet we weren't good friends back then. We had certain disagreements. I was a little child at the time. Jamal, in turn, was a public figure. Everyone knew him. Moreover, he was a supporter of the government back then. Our friendship kicked off in 2017, when he left Saudi Arabia. We started to work together. In mid-September 2018, Jamal wired me $5,000. He told me to complete the project and he would get more money. He believed in that project. I took the money. I do not wish to lie to the world about it. Yes, I took the money.

And did Khashoggi use his own financial resources or find money from elsewhere?
No, he sent his own money. He said that he was going to send more. "I will see if there are businessmen who wish to support the project," he said. "I have many friends. They can help you." He said that there were many issues that he wanted to discuss with me and he would come to Canada to meet. His visa was approved. He was going to come here, had he not been killed. His actual plan was to visit Canada before going to Turkey. This is very important. He said that he was going to get his passport back in two weeks, but could not wait that long. So he said he was going to fly to Turkey and back. That plan never worked out.

What kept you from going to the Saudi Embassy upon receiving the invitation? Was there something you knew?
To be honest, I wasn't 100 percent sure. Had I gone, they could have killed me or kissed me! I can't give you a clear answer. Jamal was one of my friends who warned me not to go there by myself. He told me to always meet MBS's messengers in crowded places.

You were working on the Army of Bees project with Khashoggi. What was the main idea behind it and its purpose. And whose idea was it?
We launched the project to combat the army of flies that the Saudi Arabian regime funded. In other words, we wanted to work with the opposition in Saudi Arabia and other Muslim countries to stop the hate that [the flies] spread. Saudi Arabia's troll army targeted and insulted Khashoggi. They threatened him. Same goes for me. They told me that they were going to kill me. They said: *"You are Erdogan's slave, Sheikh Tamim's slave. You are the Muslim Brotherhood's slave. We know you, you are liars."*

I am 27 years old and I could stand it, but Jamal was sixty. That some children were talking about him in that way offended him. They told Khashoggi that he wasn't Saudi but Turkish – that he wasn't one of them. They said he was more interested in supporting his ethnic kinsmen than his own country and called him a traitor.

I shared my idea with Jamal: "We must form our own army. Yet we need money for it," I said. "We have to stop those people. If they have an army, we must have an army too. He responded that he was going to give me $5,000. He was going to give me more [money] later. However, he did not mention a specific businessman. He said we would talk a great deal more when he visited Canada. I said "OK" and began to wait.

At what stage was the project when he died?
We were in the preliminary stages. We were working on the background but certain that we would keep working on the project. We were going to tell people what was really happening in our country. That was our duty. Now it is my duty. I will keep working even if I do not get paid. To be clear, we will need money, because I will fight not just Saudi trolls but also Egyptian and Emirati trolls. They work together to steal our people's freedom. They spent billions of dollars on a man like [Egyptian President Abdel Fattah] Sisi. In 2013, they gave him more than $100 billion to destroy the revolution and prevent the Muslim Brotherhood from ruling the country – because they were allies with Turkey and Qatar. If Erdogan were opposed to our nation's sovereignty, I'd tell him that he was wrong. But Erdogan supported the Arab League.

Everything is related to freedom. Egypt has almost the same resources as Turkey, but just look at where the two countries are. They are in very different positions. Look at the unemployment rate, the poverty rate and the number of incarcerated people in Egypt. Look at their quality of life.

Why? Because they do not have democracy. They do not have good people running their country. That's the difference. I'm not saying that Erdogan and the AK Party are perfect. Nothing is perfect. But there is a democratic system in Turkey. We have seen the elections. Erdogan won 51 percent of the vote – not 99 percent. That is democracy.

I hope that Turkey will be a better place in the future. But we also want our country to be like Turkey. Why can't we build institutions like Turkey? We have the same resources as Turkey. But we do not have honest people. Some might disagree. We do not have educated and talented administrators. It's as simple as that. Look at Sisi. He used to be a soldier. Now he's destroying [Egypt].

In terms of development, countries like Egypt must be Turkey's equals. Only then can we challenge the world. That's the way to build better Muslim countries. That's the way to have more opportunities than others. Syria, Iraq, Egypt, Yemen, Saudi Arabia, Qatar, Libya and Algeria – we can do many things together. We could accomplish a great deal if only we had honest and talented leaders that think about the people rather than their own pockets.

I am not a Turkish or Qatari agent. But I want my countrymen to live as well –actually better— than people in Turkey. Look at Yemen and Syria and Egypt. Why do people in those countries suffer? What is really happening there? We have the same resources. Egypt possibly has more resources than Turkey. But corruption in Egypt drains the country's resources. Egypt is disturbed. The military controls everything. That's why Sisi came to power. They do not want democracy.

You said you promised Khashoggi that you'd finish the project. What will be your next step in that regard?
Going forward, we will continue to work with volunteers. If

a good businessman wants to help us, we will receive assistance from them. But we do not want anyone to tell us what to write and what not to write. The financiers must believe in our cause. Obviously, we do not know if such a sponsor will emerge. But I promise you, as I promised Jamal.

Won't potential financiers be intimidated by the Khashoggi murder?

I do not know. But I can speak for myself: Alhamdulillah, I am stronger than ever. I am more motivated and enthusiastic than ever. I am only concerned about my family. I am concerned for my family, my friends and my people. I do not worry about my own life. I am just a man. Of course they could kill me. But I am sure that I did not kill or cheat or lie to anyone. I am worried for my people but I am not afraid. I am only concerned about the way things are going. Will we be like Syria, Qaddafi or Saddam in the end? Will we make the same mistakes because of MBS? Will we make the same mistakes just because his father was the king and he does not know how to rule a country? He isn't smart, competent, experienced or persuasive. He has no good plans. He has nothing. Would you trust that kind of person with your own country?

Why is Turkey investigating the Khashoggi murder? Because it's not about Saudi Arabia but MBS. Turkey sees MBS as a national security threat. That man will try as hard as he must to bring down Turkey and Qatar. That's why Erdogan turned down their money. He said he won't stop talking about the Jamal Khashoggi case. MBS is a problem not just for Saudis but also Qatar, Yemen, Egypt and Syria. He is a headache for the Middle East. At the same time, he is bad for his own country. The most recent developments left foreign investors scared. [The Saudis] also intimidated investors by being hostile toward Canada.

The Khashoggi murder scared away tourists. People will

think: "If they could do those things to Jamal Khashoggi outside the country, what could happen to me there?" The consulate is obviously Saudi soil, but they used Turkish hotels, restaurants and airports to commit the crime. That's a big problem.

People will think what the situation is like in [Saudi Arabia] if all those things could happen abroad. All of MBS's plans are going down. He couldn't finish the Aramco deal, because people don't find it realistic that the company is worth so much money. Now he's manipulating the oil prices to stay in power. How? By increasing the supply of oil to the world market. Some countries will benefit from that. But MBS is ruining the economy. Now Aramco's value will diminish. Therefore, his Vision 2030 will fail as well.

You said that Jamal Khashoggi was planning to visit Canada. Was that your final conversation? If it were, was there anything that he mentioned specifically?
In his final days, Jamal had given up on MBS. He used to say that MBS was a threat and turned into a man who devoured everything. He'd tell me that MBS would arrest whomever he wanted. "MBS is a monster," he said. "A monster large enough to consume anyone that opposes him." After killing Jamal, however, MBS said that he respected Turkey and he had an excellent relationship with Erdogan – because he is afraid of Turkey. Still, MBS's troll army continues to mock Turkey and the Turkish people on social media. They insult Erdogan and other officials. They spread insulting rumors. What they do isn't in line with what they say.

Shortly before his death, Jamal Khashoggi tweeted about the bees coming. What do you have to say about that?
Jamal believed in this project. He thought that the Army of Bees could stop the troll army. Saudi Arabia isn't powerful. All they have is their power on Twitter and social media. They cannot tolerate opposition channels. To destroy the

troll army is our only mission. That's why the Army of Bees is coming.

You said they threatened your family. Are you able to communicate with your family members in Saudi Arabia?
No. I haven't spoken to my mother in four months. My two siblings and friends are in custody. Why? Because I criticize the government. They criticize Erdogan because people, who participated in the July 2016 coup attempt, are behind bars. Isn't it ironic? I am not making any secret plans. I haven't called for regime change either. I only criticized it. Imagine what would happen if I wanted regime change?[3]

WHO IS THIS QAHTANI?

The commander-in-chief of what Omar Abdulaziz described as the army of flies was Saud Al-Qahtani – the keeper of Mohammed bin Salman's darkest secrets. According to BBC, Qahtani also led the Tiger Team, whose members were responsible for Jamal Khashoggi's death. Another member of the Qahtani family, Gen. Ali Al-Qahtani, was killed by the team directed by Saud Al Qahtani because he knew too much.[4]

Saud Al-Qahtani, for whose arrest the Turkish authorities issued a warrant on Dec. 4, is among the individuals that the Saudi attorney general's office has been trying to protect. The arrest warrant, which the Turkish prosecution requested and a Turkish court approved, mentions Qahtani alongside Ahmad Al-Assiri, the deputy head of the Saudi intelligence agency. Like Qahtani, Assiri was sacked by the Saudi government over his involvement in the Khashoggi murder.

The chief prosecutor in Riyadh claimed in a statement that Qahtani's role in the murder was limited to meeting the assassins in the Saudi capital. Qahtani, the statement said, was banned from

---

3   Transcript of Omar Abdulaziz's statements to the authors on 3 December 2018.
4   "Cemal Kaşıkçı'yı Kaplan Takımı öldürdü iddiası" [The Tiger Team Allegedly Killed Jamal Khashoggi], CNN Türk, 7 November 2018.

leaving Saudi Arabia and questioned. As always, the Saudi authorities refrained from disclosing when Qahtani was interrogated and
which questions he was expected to answer.

Qahtani allegedly oversaw the Tiger Team, which the Saudis
used to eliminate the regime's critics, and spoke with the assassins
in Istanbul on the day of the Khashoggi murder via Skype. He
reportedly told the killers to "bring me the head of that dog." Two
Saudi officials made that claim in statements to the British media.
It is no secret that Qahtani follows the Saudi crown prince's orders
to the letter in all his dealings.[5]

On Nov. 4, *The New York Times* published an interesting story
about Saud Al-Qahtani.[6] The story, which appeared with the bylines of Michael Forsythe, Mark Mazzetti, Ben Hubbard and Walt
Bogdanich, claimed that Mohammed bin Salman had signed an
agreement with Booz Allen Hamilton, a U.S. consultancy, during
his trip to the Silicon Valley to train the Kingdom's growing cyber
army.

In a statement, Qahtani said that the agreement would develop
the skills of Saudi cybersecurity experts and broaden their hori-
zons. Here's the relevant excerpt from the NYT story:

While Mr. Khashoggi's death prompted investors from
around the globe to distance themselves from the Saudi
government, Booz Allen and its competitors McKinsey &
Company and Boston Consulting Group have stayed close
after playing critical roles in Prince Mohammed's drive to
consolidate power.

In addition to standard consulting work like doling out economic advice and helping burnish Prince Mohammed's image, they have taken on more unconventional assignments.
Booz Allen trains the Saudi Navy as it runs a blockade in
the war in Yemen, a disaster that has threatened millions

5   "Prensi kurtarma hamlesi" [The move to save the prince], *Yeni Şafak*, 16 November 2018.
6   *Qahtani* is a common last name in Saudi Arabia. There are four men with the
same name mentioned in this book: A member of the Saudi death squad, Mohammed bin
Salman's propaganda adviser, the intelligence general who was supposedly investigating
the Khashoggi murder, and the general who was allegedly murdered.

with starvation. McKinsey produced a report that may have aided Mr. Qahtani's crackdown on dissidents. BCG advises Prince Mohammed's foundation.

Its report singling out the kingdom's prominent on-line critics drew widespread condemnation when The Times revealed it last month. The dissidents — including Khalid al-Alkami, a writer critical of Saudi policies, and Omar Abdulaziz, a Saudi now living in Canada — were described in detail, alongside photos of them.[7]

An Oct. 20 story by the same newspaper quoted Maggie Mitchell Salem, who had been friends with Khashoggi for more than 15 years, as saying that the slain journalist was under attack by the Saudi troll army:

Mr. Khashoggi's online attackers were part of a broad ef-fort dictated by Crown Prince Mohammed bin Salman and his close advisers to silence critics both inside Saudi Arabia and abroad. Hundreds of people work at a so-called troll farm in Riyadh to smother the voices of dissidents like Mr. Khashoggi.[8]

CIA'S KHASHOGGI BRIEFING SHAKES UP U.S. SENATE

While the Saudi attempted to respond to the devastating back-lash of the Khashoggi murder with the help of social media trolls, Turkey shared information about the incident with various coun-tries through diplomatic channels and in a responsible manner.

A classified briefing by CIA Director Gina Haspel, to whom the Turks had made available the audio recording of Jamal Khashoggi's final moments, to U.S. Senators was one of the most significant developments around that time.

On Dec. 4, a small number of senators, who attended the

---

7   https://www.nytimes.com/2018/11/04/world/middleeast/mckinsey-bcg-booz-allen-saudi-khashoggi.html

8   https://www.nytimes.com/2018/10/20/us/politics/saudi-image-cam-paign-twitter.html

briefing, told reporters afterwards that Saudi Crown Prince Mohammed bin Salman was complicit in the *Washington Post* columnist's slaying. In other words, they confirmed earlier reports that the CIA possessed evidence that MBS had ordered the hit on Jamal Khashoggi.

The senators' remarks indicated that Haspel either directly told her audience that the crown prince was politically responsible or shared information with them that led the senators to conclude that MBS was guilty. *The Washington Post* reported on Dec. 4 that the senators in question viewed the links between MBS and the Khashoggi murder as follows:

> Senators emerged from an unusual closed-door briefing with the CIA director on Tuesday and accused the Saudi crown prince of complicity in the killing of journalist Jamal Khashoggi.
>
> In some of their strongest statements to date, lawmakers said evidence presented by the U.S. spy agency overwhelmingly pointed to Crown Prince Mohammed bin Salman's involvement in the assassination.
>
> *"There's not a smoking gun — there's a smoking saw,"* said Sen. Lindsey O. Graham (R-S.C.), referring to the bone saw that investigators believe was used to dismember Khashoggi after he was killed Oct. 2 by a team of Saudi agents inside the country's consulate in Istanbul.

Armed with classified details provided by President Trump's handpicked CIA director, Gina Haspel, senators shredded the arguments put forward by senior administration officials who had earlier insisted that the evidence of Mohammed's alleged role was inconclusive.

The gulf that has emerged between Republican lawmakers and the president over how to respond to the journalist's killing appeared to widen after Tuesday's briefing, with Graham, one of Trump's closest Senate allies, announcing that he was no longer willing to work with the crown prince, whom the White House regards as one of its most important allies in the Middle East.

In recent days, Secretary of State Mike Pompeo and Defense Secretary Jim Mattis have said that no single piece of evidence irrefutably links Mohammed to the killing. But the senators, in effect, said that did not matter, because the evidence they heard convinced them beyond the shadow of a doubt.

"If the crown prince went in front of a jury, he would be convicted in 30 minutes," said Sen. Bob Corker (R-Tenn.), the chairman of the Senate Foreign Relations Committee.

Haspel, who had declined to appear alongside Mattis and Pompeo at a briefing on U.S.-Saudi policy for the full Senate last week, was joined by agency personnel and gave what lawmakers described as a compelling and decisive presentation of the evidence that the CIA has analyzed since Khashoggi, a Washington Post contributing columnist, was killed.

"We heard the clearest testimony I've heard from intelligence this morning," Corker said later during a confirmation hearing for Trump administration nominees. "I've been here 12 years," he said. "I've never heard, ever, a presentation like was made today."

Graham declined to say what the CIA officials had said, but in a brief interview with The Post he said, "You can be assured it was thorough and the evidence is overwhelming."

Graham leveled sharp criticism at Pompeo and Mattis, saying he thought they were "following the lead of the president." He called them "good soldiers." But, Graham added, one would "have to be willfully blind not to come to the conclusion" that Mohammed was "intricately involved in the demise of Mr. Khashoggi."

Graham made clear that the crown prince's culpability had caused a breach in the U.S.-Saudi relationship and said the United States should come down on the government in Riyadh like "a ton of bricks." He said he could no longer support arms sales to the Saudis as long as Mohammed was in charge.

"Saudi Arabia's a strategic ally and the relationship is worth saving — but not at all costs," Graham said.

Sen. Richard J. Durbin (D-Ill.) said that senators had asked

Haspel to return later and provide the same briefing to all members of the chamber.[9]

Another story, which *The Post* published the same day, noted that the content of Haspel's briefing was "completely contrary to the narrative that has been put forward by President Trump and his secretary of state, Mike Pompeo."[10]

MIT HOSTS A CURIOUS WORKSHOP

A series of unofficial meetings between Hakan Fidan, the head of Turkey's National Intelligence Organization, and members of the U.S. Congress around the same time attracted as much attention in Washington as Gina Haspel's briefing. Serdar Turgut, the Washington correspondent for Habertürk, broke that story:

U.S. sources told [*Habertürk*] that MIT Undersecretary Hakan Fidan was at the U.S. Congress and held a series of meetings behind closed doors, during which he shared information about the Khashoggi murder with members of Congress.

Our sources did not clearly answer the question whether Fidan was visiting on his own accord and invited. Nor could it be established whether he, if invited, was invited by the CIA Director or the Select Committee on Intelligence.

It is a matter of public record that CIA Director Gina Haspel took an overnight flight to Turkey and saw the evidence, which MIT officials and the senior leadership agreed to show her. It is possible that Hakan Fidan's current visit is a response to Haspel's earlier visit.

---

9   https://www.washingtonpost.com/world/national-security/cia-director-briefs-senators-on-saudi-role-in-khashoggi-killing/2018/12/04/e6d6498c-f7d5-11e8-8d64-4e79db33382f_story.html?utm_term=.587acdeb747b
10   https://www.washingtonpost.com/politics/2018/12/04/gop-senators-come-out-say-it-trump-administration-is-covering-up-khashoggis-killing/?utm_term=.60283d89fa09

U.S. officials find it interesting that the MIT chief will share information with the Senate at a time when the Khashoggi murder fuels tensions between the Senate and the White House, and the Senate takes a stand against Mohammed bin Salman. Those sources believe that the White House could react against that development.[11]

Before we go into the details of that unusual briefing, let us quote another story about the same issue. The following story, which Reuters shared with its subscribers, appeared in the New York Times:

Turkey's head of intelligence has traveled to Washington to meet with U.S. lawmakers and intelligence officials, sources said.

Hakan Fidan, a close confidant of Turkey's President Tayyip Erdogan, has met with senators to discuss NATO issues and was expected to meet with U.S. intelligence officials later on Friday.

But it was not a central subject in discussions with senators and the Turkish side has refrained from making it the focus of their meetings, the sources added.

Top U.S. senators have said they want to punish Saudi Arabia for the killing, despite President Donald Trump's decision to stand by the long-time ally.

While the two countries have collaborated on the Khashoggi investigation, U.S.-Turkey ties have been strained by disagreements over a number of issues from Syria to Turkey's desire to buy Russian defense systems.

Relations between Ankara and Washington began to im-

11   Serdar Turgut, "MİT Başkanı Hakan Fidan ABD Kongresi'nde" [MIT President Hakan Fidan at the U.S. Congress], *Habertürk*, 6 December 2018.

prove after U.S. pastor Andrew Brunson, who was on trial over terrorism-related charges in Turkey, was released in October.

But the NATO allies remain divided on other issues, including U.S. policy in Syria, Ankara's ambition to purchase Russian missile defense systems and Turkey's request for the United States to extradite Fethullah Gulen, a cleric Ankara blames for organizing an abortive 2016 putsch. Gulen denies involvement.

Fidan was expected to discuss the murder of Khashoggi, a Washington post columnist and critic of the Saudi Arabia's Crown Prince Mohammed bin Salman, in his meeting with U.S. intelligence officials, sources said. It was not immediately clear if Fidan was to meet with Gina Haspel, director of the CIA.

The CIA has assessed with medium to high confidence that the crown price, the kingdom's de facto ruler, ordered the killing of Khashoggi when he visited the consulate on Oct. 2. Saudi Arabia has said the prince had no prior knowledge. Trump cast doubt on the CIA assessment, saying the agency had not formed a definitive conclusion. U.S. Secretary of State Mike Pompeo has said there was no direct evidence linking the prince to the killing.[12]

THE TURKISH SPY CHIEF'S SECRET TRIP TO CANADA

It was true that Hakan Fidan, the powerful head of Turkey's intelligence agency, shared some information with certain members of the U.S. Congress about the Khashoggi murder. When asked whether Serdar Turgut's claim, which cited congressional sources, MIT officials said they could neither confirm nor deny.

---

12   https://www.reuters.com/article/us-usa-turkey/turkeys-top-spy-in-us-to-meet-senators-intelligence-officials-sources-idUSKBN1O62AB

Provided that "neither confirm nor deny" usually means that intelligence sources do not wish to confirm a true allegation, we approached other sources and received confirmation. As a matter of fact, we learned more than what we knew in the first place:

Apparently, the Turkish intelligence chief did not only visit the U.S. Congress. He also held talks with CIA Director Gina Haspel in Langley, Virginia and attended some kind of workshop at Harvard University to share information about the incident.

Moreover, Hakan Fidan, upon returning from Argentina, held a series of secret meetings with Canadian officials known to have distanced themselves from Mohammed bin Salman's de facto rule in Saudi Arabia.

With Erdogan's approval, Fidan took a private jet registered to the Turkish intelligence after the G20 summit in Argentina to visit Canada. In the Canadian capital Ottawa, the Turkish spy chief met Prime Minister Justin Trudeau's special representative and his Canadian counterpart. Later, he flew to Washington, where he attended a roundtable meeting with U.S. congressmen. Fidan also held talks with President Trump's national security adviser. Upon meeting the Turkish intelligence chief, the Canadians became more convinced that Mohammed bin Salman was responsible for the Khashoggi murder.

Obviously, Fidan took all of those meetings with Turkish President Recep Tayyip Erdogan's approval. The roundtable on the Hill, which was not in line with intelligence or diplomatic conventions, was also an unofficial meeting in the form of a workshop. Our assessment is that some congressmen were dissatisfied with Gina Haspel's confidential briefing and wanted to receive information from the Turkish spy chief directly.

Although where U.S. President Donald Trump stood on that meeting remains unclear, we could presume that the CIA Director knew about the congressional roundtable in advance and possibly welcomed that briefing. That Fidan met Haspel after the event supports that view.

It is possible to view that meeting as a manifestation of Turkey's growing political power in the diplomatic arena. As late as the early 2000s, CIA officials visiting Turkey often neglected to notify the National Intelligence Agency in a break with protocol and met senior officials from the Military Chief of Staff directly. Many such cases took place in the past. Today, it would be unimaginable for the CIA Director to visit Turkey and by-pass the Turkish intelligence to take meetings in Ankara.

That change reflects Turkey's strong political leadership, which centralized power in the hands of the Presidency thanks to Erdogan's determination and the country's new system of government.

In addition to creating various political results, Ankara's successful diplomatic efforts after the Khashoggi murder was influential on a decision by Time Magazine to designate the slain journalist as its Man of the Year for 2018.[13]

THE ARREST WARRANT

Turkey's strong political leadership made it possible for the judiciary to take bold steps after the Khashoggi murder. Having issued warrants for the arrest of the 15 assassins and three others, who planned the assault, the Chief Prosecutor's Office in Istanbul proceeded to request arrest warrants for Ahmad bin Mohammed Al-Assiri, the deputy head of the Saudi intelligence agency, and Saud Al-Qahtani, the Saudi crown prince's adviser, because it suspected that the two men were among the planners of the Khashoggi murder. Within hours, a Turkish court issued the order.

An official document, signed by Acting Chief Prosecutor Hasan Yilmaz and addressed to the Criminal Court on Duty, outlined the prosecution's findings and called on the court to issue an arrest warrant for two additional individuals – Assiri and Qahtani. The prosecution stated that both men were charged with "premeditated murder with monstrous emotions or through torture." Here's what the document said:

The Chief Prosecutor's Office launched an investigation

---

13   "Time dergisi Cemal Kaşıkçı'yı yılın kişisi seçti" [Time magazine names Jamal Khashoggi person of the year], CNN Türk, 11 December 2018.

into the claim that Jamal Khashoggi, a citizen of the Kingdom of Saudi Arabia, visited the KSA consulate in Istanbul
on Oct. 2, 2018 for marriage formalities, never came out
and went missing. With the investigation still underway, the
KSA authorities formally announced that Khashoggi was
murdered. Our investigation led to the conclusion that 15
suspects came to Istanbul from the Kingdom of Saudi Arabia on commercial flights and aboard private jets on Oct.
1, 2018, went to the KSA consulate, where Khashoggi was
killed, and the consular residence on Oct. 2, 2018, and returned to Saudi Arabia on the same day aboard private jets
and on commercial flights.

It has been established that the 15 suspects, who came to
Istanbul from the Kingdom of Saudi Arabia, were Badr Lafi
Al-Otaiba (born 1990, passport number S077451), Walid
Abdullah Al-Shahry (born 1980, passport number R120404),
Mustafa Mohammed Al-Madani (born 1961, passport num-
ber P797794), Abdulaziz Mohammed Al-Hossawi (born
1987, passport number W188493), Khaled Aiz Al-Taby
(born 1988, passport number P39681), Mohammed Saad
Al-Zahrani (born 1988, passport number T233763), Naif
Hassan Al-Arifi (born 1986, passport number S077455),
Mashal Saad Al-Bostani (born 1987, passport number
R339037), Fahd Shabib Al-Balawi (born 1985, passport
number N163990), Sair Ghaleb Al-Harby (born 1979,
passport number P723557), Turki Musharraf Al-Shahry
(born 1982, passport number R910638), Salah Mohammed
Al-Tubaigy (born 1971, passport number S052512), Sayf
Saad Al-Qahtani (born 1972, passport number U051094),
Mansour Othman Aba Hussein (born 1972, passport number
D122725) and Maher Abdulazez Mutreb (born 1971, pass-
port number D088677).

It has also been established that three employees of the
KSA consulate, Ahmad Abdullah Al-Muzaini (born 1970,
passport number D093511), Muflis Shaya Al-Musleh (born

1987, passport number D120719) and Saad Muid Al-Qarni (born 1980, passport number D121398), who are also suspects, returned to the Kingdom of Saudi Arabia alongside the 15 aforementioned suspects.

We have learned that the judicial authorities of the Kingdom of Saudi Arabia are investigating Ahmad bin Mohammad Al-Assiri and Saud Al-Qahtani, along with the 18 aforementioned suspects, noting that Al-Assiri and Al-Qahtani were among the planners of Jamal Khashoggi's slaying.

A warrant for the arrest of 18 suspects, who are strongly suspected of having killed with premeditation, monstrous emotions or through torture Jamal Khashoggi, who visited the KSA consulate in Istanbul on Oct. 2, 2018 for marriage formalities.

In light of the information revealed by the investigation by the judicial authorities of the Kingdom of Saudi Arabia, we strongly suspect that Al-Assiri and Al-Qahtani were among the planners of the murder that the 18 suspects carried out. As such, there is strong suspicion that Al-Assiri and Al-Qahtani, along with the 15 suspects that came to our country from the Kingdom of Saudi Arabia and the three employees of the KSA consulate in Istanbul, murdered Jamal Khashoggi, who visited the KSA consulate in Istanbul on Oct. 2, 2018 for marriage formalities, with premeditation and monstrous emotions or through torture. The investigation into other individuals, who were complicit in the crime, continues.

In light of the above: On behalf of the people, we request that a warrant for the arrest of the suspects, whose personal information is listed below, under Article 100 of the Penal Procedure Code.

Suspect: Ahmad bin Mohammed Al-Assiri (born 1950 – Asr, Saudi Arabia)
Charge: Murder with premeditation and monstrous emo-

tions or through torture
Under: Articles 81 and 82/a and /b of the Turkish Penal
Code No. 5237
Date of Crime: 2 October 2018
Place of Crime: Besiktas, Istanbul

Suspect: Saud Al-Qahtani (born 7 June 1980 – Riyadh, Sau-
di Arabia)
Charge: Murder with premeditation and monstrous emo-
tions or through torture
Under: Articles 81 and 82/a and /b of the Turkish Penal
Code No. 5237
Date of Crime: 2 October 2018
Place of Crime: Besiktas, Istanbul[14]

Before this book went to print, an important development
took place. Having just taken over as term president of the G20
for 2020, Saudi Arabia rejected the Turkish request for the extradition of the two suspects. According to news reports, the Saudi
reasoning was as follows:

Saudi Arabia turned down Turkey's request for the extradition of Saudi citizens who were mentioned in the investigation into the murder of Jamal Khashoggi.

In response to a question asked during a press conference
after the Gulf Cooperation Council summit on Sunday, Saudi Foreign Minister Adel Al-Jubeir said "we cannot extradite our citizens."

Earlier this week, Turkey issued an arrest warrant for the former deputy head of the Saudi intelligence, Ahmad Al-Assiri, and the Crown Prince's former adviser Saud Al-Qahtani.
In his speech, Jubeir accused Ankara of failing to cooperate
adequately with Riyadh. Jubeir said that Turkey "has not

been as open as we thought it should have been" and added that "the information they shared with us was the same as what was leaked to newspapers."

Jubeir also said that they expected evidence from Turkey that would be admissible in the court of law:
"We requested from our friends in Turkey evidence that we can use in the court of law. We did not receive them as we should have."

Referring to the Khashoggi murder as a tragedy, Jubeir claimed that Saudi officials had been trying to discover who committed crime, and how, since the very beginning.

In the immediate aftermath of the Khashoggi murder, Saudi Arabia claimed that the Saudi journalist had walked out of the building.

The Chief Prosecutor's Office in Istanbul, which oversees the Khashoggi investigation, requested a warrant for the arrests of Ahmad Al-Assiri, the former deputy head of the Saudi intelligence, and Saud Al-Qahtani, a former adviser of the Crown Prince, on charge of murder with premeditation and monstrous emotions or through torture.

The Criminal Court on Duty, which processed the request, issued the arrest warrant. Ahmad Al-Assiri and Saud Al-Qahtani are among the five officials who have been dismissed in the wake of the Khashoggi murder.

Earlier, Saudi Arabia had turned down a Turkish request for an international investigation into what happened.
In response to Turkish Foreign Minister Mevlut Cavusoglu, who noted that "we believe now that an international investigation is necessary," Jubeir said that Saudi Arabia was conducting its own investigation and an international investigation was not needed.

Shalan Al-Shalan, deputy attorney general and a spokesman for the attorney general's office, announced that 11 suspects would be put on trial and the prosecution would ask for the death penalty for five individuals.[15]

MBS'S FAVORITE PILOT

Riyadh's response to the Turkish warrant for the arrests of Ahmad Al-Assiri, the former deputy head of the Saudi intelligence, and MBS adviser Saud Al-Qahtani established yet again that the Saudis were going to do everything in their power to cover up the Khashoggi murder.

Ahmad Al-Assiri, whose extradition the Turks requested, is no less important than Al-Qahtani. He is believed to be one of the closest confidants of Saudi Crown Prince Mohammed bin Salman.

The 66-year-old Assiri, who was born in a small village in the Kingdom's southwest, rose through the ranks upon joining the Saudi military. He served in the Air Force for more than three decades and eventually became a Major General. Assiri was trained at some of the world's most prestigious military schools, including the Royal Military Academy Sandhurst in the United Kingdom, West Point in the United States and Saint-Cyr in France.

A native Arabic speaker, Assiri was fluent in English and French. He became a prominent figure in Saudi Arabia after the country began to crack down on Houthi rebels in neighboring Yemen in March 2015. Assiri served as a spokesman for the international coalition that conducted the military operation in Yemen and became a member of the Saudi crown prince's inner circle. As a matter of fact, many senior officials who were involved in the Yemen campaign proceeded to assume prominent roles in the Saudi government. After all, the Saudi operation in Yemen was an important part of MBS's military strategy.

Assiri caught the world's attention by responding aggressively to allegations that Saudi Arabia was carrying out airstrikes in

15   "Suudi Arabistan, Türkiye'nin 2 şüpheliyle ilgili iade talebini reddetti" [Saudi Arabia Rejects Turkish Request For The Extradition Of Two Suspects], *Habertürk*, 10 October 2018.

Yemen without making a distinction between military and civilian targets.

Known as a calm man who was prepared to answer all types of questions, Assiri lost his nerve during a visit to London in March 2017, where protesters threw eggs at him to protest the Yemen war. Video footage from the protest shows that Assiri, hit by an egg, flipped the crowd in response. He took over as deputy head of the Saudi intelligence shortly afterwards.[16]

THE OTHER KEEPER OF SAUDI SECRETS

It was Turkey's legal diplomacy strategy that compelled Saudi Arabia to dispatch its attorney general, Saud Al-Mujeb, to Istanbul in order to find out what evidence the Turks had against the suspects. The arrest warrants for Qahtani and Assiri was part of the same gameplan.

Other than to confirm that the killer always returns to the scene of the crime, the Saudi attorney general's visit to Istanbul meant little. Still, Turkey was able to mount pressure on Riyadh in the legal arena – as it had in the realm of intelligence.

The official delegation that traveled to Turkey alongside the attorney general included a general from the Saudi intelligence, whose identity and mission remained a secret until this book's publication. That individual had the same last name as Saud Al-Qahtani, the crown prince's adviser, right-hand man and confidant. That man, Abdullah Al-Qahtani, officially joined the Saudi delegation as head of the crisis desk. In other words, he was responsible for keeping tabs on all the other officials. Having arrived the day before the Saudi attorney general, Qahtani had no problem exploring Istanbul's vibrant nightlife after a hard day's work – with all his recklessness, despite his background in espionage.

Three men with the Qahtani last name, which is quite common in Saudi Arabia, were linked to the Khashoggi murder. Saud Al-Qahtani, also known as the lord of the flies after the troll army

---

16   "Suudi Arabistan'dan Kaşıkçı açıklaması: Bir daha asla..." [Statement By Saudi Arabia On Khashoggi: Never Again], *Akşam*, 26 October 2018.

he commanded, discredited Jamal Khashoggi as a traitor. There is a warrant for his arrest on the charge of premeditated murder with murderous emotions or through torture.

Sayf Saad Al-Qahtani, who was a member of the Saudi death squad that executed and dismembered the slain journalist in Istanbul, played a prominent role in the implementation of the assassination plan. Finally, Abdullah Al-Qahtani visited Turkey for the purpose of covering up the Khashoggi murder and had to return home after unsuccessful meetings with officials from the Chief Prosecutor's Office in Istanbul and the National Intelligence Organization.

All three individuals were directly responsible for Jamal Khashoggi's death or attempts to cover up the incident in retrospect. Without answering the question who Jamal Khashoggi, the man targeted by the Saudi political leadership that brought together those men, it would be impossible to understand the whole story.

2

JAMAL KHASHOGGI

The Victim's Journalism Career

Jamal Khashoggi's extended journalism career comprised years of deep relationships, censorship, restrictions and exhaustion. There were milestones along the way that led the slain journalist, whose relationship with King Salman bin Abdulaziz's son was strained at best, to his eventual death. In retrospect, perhaps the single most significant development was Khashoggi's decision to launch the Army of Bees, which possibly encouraged the Saudi crown prince to sign the Washington Post columnist's death warrant.

In truth, Khashoggi encountered censorship and pressure at all stages of his journalism career. For example, Prince Mohammad bin Nayef, who preceded Mohammed bin Salman as crown prince, shut down a large number of news organizations that the slain journalist managed. MBS, in turn, ordered the hit on Jamal Khashoggi, making Mohammad bin Nayef the lesser evil among potential candidates to replace King Salman after his death.

Mohammad bin Nayef, like MBS, wasn't a pet project of U.S. President Donald Trump but also the Anglosaxon deep state. It was no coincidence that John Brennan, the former director of the Central Intelligence Agency, came out in support of Mohammad bin Nayef by saying that the number of arrests declined under his tenure as cabinet minister and crown prince, and went back up in the wake of Mohammed bin Salman's rise to crown prince. Nor was it random that the former crown prince received training at the Federal Bureau of Investigation and, later, the Scotland Yard.

Like Mohammad bin Nayef, Jamal Khashoggi completed his education in the United States. Born in Medina, Saudi Arabia on October 13, 1958, he finished middle and high school in his native country before relocating to the United States for college. During his time as an undergraduate student at Indiana State University, he familiarized himself to Islamic movements.[1]

Khashoggi enrolled in graduate school immediately after receiving his undergraduate degree in 1982 and became a master of business administration the following year – at the age of 25. He returned to Saudi Arabia and served as regional manager at Tihama Bookstores in 1983-84, before going into journalism.

Between 1985 and 1987, Khashoggi was an assistant manager at the Saudi newspaper Okaz. Later, he was based in Afghanistan as a war correspondent for Arab News, a Riyadh-based English-language publication. He traveled to Afghanistan in 1988 and made contact with Arab fighters that arrived at the conflict zone from Saudi Arabia and other countries. In May 1988, during his time with Arab News, Khashoggi published a series of news stories about Afghanistan. In addition to reporting for Arab News, he worked with Al Sharq Al Awsat, a Jeddah-based Arabic-language newspaper.

Against the backdrop of the Soviet-Afghan War, during which the United States supported Osama bin Laden, Khashoggi repeatedly interviewed the future Al Qaeda leader in Afghanistan and Sudan. At the time, he published stories in the Al-Hayat newspaper about the Afghan jihad. Jamal Khashoggi, who gained vast field experience, was one of the world's leading experts on Afghanistan and possibly the most knowledgeable journalist on armed groups in the area.

During the same time period, Khashoggi strengthened his personal relationship with Prince Turki bin Faisal, the head of Saudi Arabia's General Intelligence Directorate and son of King Faisal.

---

1   https://www.middleeasteye.net/opinion/jamal-khashoggi-different-sort-saudi

Obviously, the Kingdom was involved in the Soviet-Afghan War along with the United States. The Saudi involvement in the conflict amounted to a proxy war.

As an senior intelligence officer, Prince Turki benefited primarily from Jamal Khashoggi's expertise on the Afghan jihad. Some sources claim that the slain journalist was involved in an effort to make peace between Osama bin Laden and the Saudi royal family in the early 1990s.

At the time, Prince Turki was an intelligence operative with close ties to the Central Intelligence Agency. The relationship was so close that the Saudi spy chief allegedly handled Osama bin Laden to manage Langley's covert operations in Afghanistan as early as December 1979. Khashoggi's ally in the Saudi intelligence stepped down in August 2001 – just two weeks before 9/11.

Prince Turki oversaw the Saudi intelligence for 27 years, more than half the amount of time that J. Edgar Hoover led the Federal Bureau of Intelligence. He was appointed as the Saudi ambassador to London in 2003 and Washington, DC two years later, and hired Khashoggi as his adviser. *The Washington Post* columnist worked with Prince Turki until 2007.

Turan Kışlakçı, one of Jamal Khashoggi's closest friends, told the authors of this book that the slain journalist described his professional relationship with Prince Turki as follows:

> I told [Khashoggi] that he was a journalist working in intelligence and asked him why he advised Turki bin Faisal. He responded that "there is only one wing within the Saudi regime and that wing has a tendency to exclude religious people and conservatives on occasion. That is why I played a role, and I am pleased to have served that role. After all, the [Saudi] government's support for Palestinian groups was all because of me."[2]

Having worked with various periodicals, including Al Sharq Al Awsat, Al Majalla and Al Muslimoon, in the Arab media,

---

2   Turan Kışlakçı's statements to the authors.

Khashoggi served as managing editor and acting editor-in-chief for Al Madina in 1991-1999. During that time period, he reported on Afghanistan, Algeria, Kuwait, Sudan and the Middle East for international publications. Khashoggi's Afghanistan-related pieces appeared in the English-language daily newspaper *Saudi Gazette* among others.

During his tenure at Al Madina, Khashoggi closely followed political developments in Turkey. In 1996, he traveled to the country to report on parliamentary elections, in which the Welfare Party won the highest share of the vote.

In 1999-2003, Khashoggi moved back to the *Arab News*, where he worked as deputy editor-in-chief, before accepting a position at Al Watan, a prominent reformist outlet, as managing editor. There, his stint lasted just 52 days, as the newspaper's management sacked him for publishing a piece that criticized Saudi Arabia's religious structures. The Saudi regime, unhappy with the severity of Al Watan's critique, compelled Jamal Khashoggi to go on self-imposed exile in London. It wasn't until April 2007 that he was reinstated as managing editor of Al Watan – where he remained until May 2010, when he was forced to resign for publishing critical pieces.

Surprisingly enough, Khashoggi's 52-day stint at Al Watan wasn't his quickest departure from a news organization. At some point, the slain journalist served as editor-in-chief of Al Arab, a Bahrain-based television channel that the authorities shut down after eleven short hours. The Saudi billionaire Al-Waleed bin Talal had landed him that job. Khashoggi also appeared on various international television channels, including MBC, BBC, Al Jazeera and Dubai TV, as a commentator.

Sources claim that the former Saudi crown prince, Mohammad bin Nayef, was involved in the decision to shut down Al Arab – which is why Khashoggi was allegedly not in good terms with him. It should go without saying that the two men's strained relationship was hardly as consequential as the deeply troubled, structurally problematic relationship between Khashoggi and MBS. Although the MBS regime was obviously unhappy with the *Washington Post* columnist, even under the current crown prince's *de facto* rule was Khashoggi not put on trial in his native country. There was no warrant for Khashoggi's arrest in the Interpol database. That did not stop the MBS regime from targeting and eventually murdering him.

Jamal Khashoggi was a pro-Turkey journalist. He believed that Turkey could serve as a model for many Arab countries, including his native Saudi Arabia. Although Khashoggi criticized the Turkish government occasionally, he nonetheless viewed Turkey as a positive example for the Islamic world. Especially in the wake of the July 2016 coup attempt in Turkey, Khashoggi called on the world to support Turkish President Recep Tayyip Erdogan. At the same time, the slain journalist was a vocal critic of Mohammed bin Salman's anti-Turkish foreign policy.

In December 2016, the prestigious British newspaper The Independent claimed that Jamal Khashoggi was no longer allowed to appear on television for criticizing U.S. President Donald Trump. The following year, when MBS became the Kingdom's *de facto* ruler, Khashoggi went on self-imposed exile once again and moved to the United States. There, he began to write a column for *The Washington Post*.[3]

Khashoggi felt that MBS could come for him soon when he received news of wealthy Saudi princes, including Al-Waleed bin Talal who launched Al Arab several years prior, were detained as part of a supposed anti-corruption campaign and kept in a luxury hotel. That was his reason for leaving Saudi Arabia.

Having moved to Washington, DC in 2017, Khashoggi met Hatice Cengiz at an event in Istanbul in May 2018. Within months, he had decided to marry her. The rest, as they say, is history.

KHASHOGGI'S WORLD VIEW

It is no easy task to describe any person's worldview – even if they publicize their opinions in newspaper columns and on television shows. Especially today, when circumstances often require

---

3   Çağıl Kasapoğlu, "Cemal Kaşıkçı neden Suudi Arabistan'ın hedefiydi?" [Why Did Saudi Arabia Target Jamal Khashoggi?], BBC Turkish, 23 October 2018.

asymmetrical alliances and relationships, one finds it particularly difficult to make such clear-cut definitions.

It is no secret that Khashoggi was a 'radical' in the 1980s and possibly the 1990s who believed that the only way to remove corrupt governments from power in Arab countries was to infiltrate the political system and seize control – or to overthrow them through political violence.

Time, however, gradually changed Jamal Khashoggi like everyone else. In his final years, the Washington Post columnist emerged as a master of letters who did not subscribe to any single ideology, opposed Wahhabism and Salafism, and believed that his identity as a Muslim did not have to remain within the limits imposed on it by the MBS administration and the Saudi regime's past rulers.

In public statements and interviews, Khashoggi called for a reform of religious education in Saudi Arabia to prevent the spread of false beliefs in the country. He believed (and openly stated) that the Saudis must not pay too much respect to the words of Ibn Taymiyyah, an Islamic scholar who laid the groundwork for Salafism. During tenure at Al Watan, Khashoggi faced backlash from Saudi religious scholars for running articles and cartoons criticizing the Salafi ideology. As a matter of fact, some sheikhs even issued fatwas stipulating that purchasing Khashoggi's newspaper would amount to a sin.

Like many authors, Jamal Khashoggi was interested in books, music and the arts. Obviously, he was not a liberal in the western sense of the word. Yet he cared for freedom of expression. In an Oct. 7 column, The Washington Post's David Ignatius likened Khashoggi to George Orwell, the celebrated author of the dystopian novel 1984:

George Orwell titled a regular column he wrote for a British newspaper in the mid-1940s *"As I Please."* Meaning that he would write exactly what he believed. My Saudi colleague Jamal Khashoggi has always had that same insistent passion for telling the truth about his country, no matter what.[4]

4   https://www.washingtonpost.com/opinions/global-opinions/jamal-khashog-

Khashoggi embraced Turkey's political atmosphere and want-ed the same for Saudi Arabia. A staunch supporter of the Turkish military presence in Syria, the slain journalist once claimed on a television show that Turkey presented a huge opportunity to Syr-ians: "Turkey proved that it was the best partner for the Syrian people. Afrin was a spectacular success. It wasn't just how [the military plans] were implemented, but also because it was a very clean war. There was no destruction whatsoever."[5]

Moreover, Khashoggi told an Egyptian broadcaster that Saudi Arabia desperately needed the kind of freedom that existed in Tur-key. In the same interview, the *Washington Post* journalist said the following about Turkey:

The Libyan revolution had to take place, because there are two kinds of regimes in Arab countries. The first type can be reformed. The latter cannot. Muammar al-Gaddafi's regime could not have been reformed. Again, the Bashar [al-Assad] regime could not be reformed.

Therefore, a revolution had to take place that would facili-tate regime change altogether. That's what happened in Lib-ya. The Libyan revolution, which caused a lot of pain, had to succeed. It had all the resources necessary for success.

A small population, oil-based wealth and an educated peo-ple... The expectation was that it would succeed. Yet it could not find any Arab brothers or European friends.

Unfortunately, the vast majority abandoned the Libyan peo-ple and distances themselves from them. Again, it is painful that the Libyan people responded to their solitude. In the end, the Libyan revolution failed and ended up where it is today.

---

gi-chose-to-tell-the-truth-its-part-of-the-reason-hes-beloved/2018/10/07/4847f1d6-
ca70-11e8-a3e6-44daa3d35ede_story.html?utm_term=.5655d3a0f2ce
5   "Gazeteci Cemal Kaşıkçı'nın röportajı ortaya çıktı" [An Interview With Journalist Jamal Khashoggi Surfaces], *Timetürk*, 20 October 2018.

I wrote many pieces about King Salman's administration. One of them was called: "There is a ruler and a foreign policy for every time period."

Politics, whose content was stuck in past, was doomed to fail. One way or another, we had to change it. I believe that I wanted to say the following to the state: You must change your policy of opposing the Arab Spring.

Let us look at the Turkish case. You and I have stayed up all night. If we were to go to any mosque in Istanbul at 6 a.m. to perform the morning prayer, young people will be there praying. I have seen it with my own eyes. If you look closely, you'd see that there is no institution here in Istanbul that beats people up for not performing the prayers. Those young people go to the mosque on this cold morning out of their own free will. That is the beauty of religion.

The country desperately needs freedom. Freedom would greatly help Prince Mohammed bin Salman. After all, only then can the people's voices reach him.

…

The Prophet himself identified the limits of Saudi Arabia's strategy. He said: *"God, bless our Damascus and our Yemen."* Damascus and Yemen mark the limits of Mecca. We must interpret the Iranian threat against Mecca with reference to Damascus and Yemen. That Iran strengthened its influence in recent years was Saudi Arabia's fault. Where is the Saudi-Turkish solidarity? It is in crumbles.

Some say that "Turkey is our enemy because it treats us unjustly and it will station troops on Sawakin Island." First of all, that information is false. Even Sudan announced that there was no military agreement on Sawakin.

Their goal is to revive that historic place. Historically, it is close to Jeddah. Indeed, Saudi Arabia could have assumed that role itself. After all, the buildings in Jeddah closely resemble those in Sawakin. And even if there were a military agreement on Sawakin, then what?

Are the Turks our enemies? The Turks protected the Red Sea and the Holy Mosques for more than three hundred years. Who protected the Holy Mosque from the Portuguese? In the seventeenth century, the Portuguese attempted to set foot on Medina. Sultan Selim formed a navy and built ports along the Red Sea. The Turks are one of us. They are part of the ahl al-sunna and the [Islamic] community. Our fate and theirs are one and the same. So why all this hostility against the Turks?

We used to dream of Turkey's return to the Arab domain. Now that it did, are we suddenly unhappy with it? That makes no sense. Erdogan once said that those who gave up on Jerusalem have given up on the Holy Mosques. I believe that statement is accurate. After all, Jerusalem complements the Holy Mosques. None must be angered by that statement. It is indeed accurate. Emir Mohammed must say that we see Jerusalem as we see the Holy Mosques. He must say that he is a son of the servant of the Holy Mosques and that, for him, Jerusalem cannot be separated from the Holy Mosques. He must say that his legitimacy won't be complete without Jerusalem.

Since King Faisal's death, we have been printing a picture of Jerusalem on the 50 riyal bill. We say that Jerusalem is the last will of King Faisal. Why are we disturbed by that statement now? It is an accurate statement! What are we worth in Damascus or Jakarta without Jerusalem? How could we see Jerusalem as a different entity? Yes, truly, we have lost it militarily. Yet we must protect it.

...

Turkey has certain responsibilities toward Qatar. Both countries are politically independent and they have signed treaties among themselves. Why should we see that as an act of hostility against Saudi Arabia?

Despite all the negative coverage in the Saudi media, Turkey works hard to maintain cordial relations with Saudi Arabia. We must support close relations between Saudi Arabia and Turkey. We must not let some men bomb the relationship between the two remaining leading nations of the Islamic ummah.

We must preserve that relationship to the best of our ability. I appreciate the Turkish position. Obviously, I am always accused of being pro-Turkey. Indeed, I see those, who sit in dark rooms and no longer consider me their friend, as my friends. They attack me because I call for solidarity. Turkey is a successful country and it deserves respect. Turkey and Saudi Arabia could work together to oppose two or three things: Iran's regional expansionism, the regionwide chaos, and the failure to get back on our feet.[6]

THE KHASHOGGI FAMILY'S ROOTS

Jamal Ahmad Khashoggi was the grandson of Mohammad Khashoggi of Kayseri, Turkey, who served Abdulaziz bin Saud, Saudi Arabia's founder, as his doctor. In other words, Khashoggi was linked to Turkey through his grandfather.

The Khashoggi family relocated to Medina in the nineteenth century, long before the Ottoman Empire disintegrated. The family, which hailed from Germir-Kayseri, came to be known as the Khashoggi family in the Arabian peninsula. The Khashoggis, or *spoon makers*, saw themselves as a family from Medina – rather than a Saudi family. As such, Jamal Khashoggi cared deeply about

---

6   Transcript of the TV show Yaz Boz.

his native city and often complained about unplanned construction in Medina and the rest of the country.

Soheir Khashoggi, the daughter of Mohammad Khaled Khashoggi, was the mother of Dodi Fayed, who was in a relationship with Diana, Princess of Wales, before the couple's death in a car accident in Paris.

One of Mohammad Khashoggi's sons, Adnan, made a fortune as an oil trader and arms dealer. Adnan's brother, or Jamal's father, was Ahmad Khashoggi. In an Oct. 15 column, historian Murat Bardakci provided the following information about the Khashoggi family:

Much has been written [in Turkey] about Jamal Khashoggi's family over the years, yet most of those pieces were related to the personal life of Adnan Khashoggi, Jamal's uncle and once one of the world's richest men.

Having seen that Turkey has completely forgotten about the Khashoggi family and Adnan Khashoggi, I wanted to share a few reminders.

Hailing from Medina, the Khashoggi family's history has been the subject of a heated debate. According to the popular view in Turkey, the Khashoggis were originally from the village of Germir near Kayseri. Some of the men from that family traveled to Arabia some three centuries ago to perform the hajj and settled in Medina. Over time their Turkish name was Arabized as Khashoggi. In the early 1900s, they joined the Committee of Union and Progress and served as tax collectors in Medina. Mohammad Khaled Khashoggi, who fathered Adnan Khashoggi and studied medicine in Europe, became the private doctor of King Abdulaziz – the founder of Saudi Arabia.

Jamal Khashoggi, who walked into the Saudi consulate in Istanbul and never came out, was the son of Ahmad Khashoggi – another one of Mohammad Khaled's sons.

Adnan was Jamal's uncle and Dodi Fayed, who died in a car accident in 1997 alongside Princess Diana, was his cousin. For years, the Khashoggi family has been rumored to be originally Turkish. As a matter of fact, there are some documents in the Ottoman archives pertaining to a Khashoggi, who served as a tax collector in Medina, and some of his family members. Yet there is no record of the family's history.

According to some European studies, the Khashoggis were Circassian rather Turks. They hailed from Kashghan to the north of the Black Sea, where Muslims have been living since the time of Genghis Khan. Rumor has it that the family left their native lands under pressure from the Russian tzars, went to Medina and settled there.

...

Until Jamal Khashoggi's disappearance, Adnan Khashoggi would the first person that came to mind thanks to his wealth and adventurous life as a prominent member of high society. There was a time when newspapers and magazines around the world wrote about Adnan's billions of dollars, mansions around the globe, private jet, giant yatch (which he proceeded to sell to Donald Trump), receptions, friends and lifestyle.

Adnan Khashoggi, who is rumored to have had many jobs including arms dealer and investor, entered Turkey's radar in the early 1980s thanks to Suha Ozgermi, another celebrity of the period.

Suha Ozgermi was known as the country's national playboy, since he was always surrounded by beautiful women. Yet not many people knew that this descendant of Ottoman aristocrats and the grandson of Faik Bey, who worked in Sultan Abdulhamid's personal office, owned textile factories and paid record amount of taxes up until the 1980s. ... His family included many prominent statesmen.

The late Suha, who was a dear friend, sold his factories in the early 1980s and his life, which was already fast since his youth, became even more colorful after his departure from the world of business. He traveled around the world, had a lot of fun, and started hosting beauty contests in various cities.

One of the celebrities that Suha Ozgermi met during his time in Europe was Adnan Khashoggi. Around that time, Khashoggi made an attempt to do business in Turkey with the help of Juan Carlos, the King of Spain, yet he had no success, as Turkish President Kenan Evren did not like him.

Although Adnan Khashoggi could not enter Turkey as a businessman, he appeared before us as an excellent tabloid figure thanks to Suha Ozgermi! Not just himself but also his daughter Nabila, after whom he named his world renowned yatch, became famous at the time. Nabila Khashoggi served as a member of the jury in beauty contests hosted by Suha Ozgermi.

...

At the time, Suha Ozgermi brought Adnan Khashoggi to Turkey repeatedly and made a lot of effort to do business with him here. Even though other entrepreneurs made similar efforts later, it never worked out. Suha Ozgermi's money ran out years later and he passed away in 2013. Over time, Khashoggi's fortune reversed itself, as he even ended up in a Swiss prison. His wealth, too, faded away and he died in a British hospital last year without a dollar in his name.[7]

There are many urban legends surrounding the Khashoggi family's origins. One of the more interesting (yet baseless) allegations is that the Khashoggi family ran into trouble with the Ottoman Empire, because they owned the Spoonmaker's Diamond, and relocated to Medina.

Others believe that the Khashoggis served as muezzins in Kay-

7   Murat Bardakçı, "The Khashoggi, Or Haşukci, Family", *Habertürk*, 15 October 2018.

seri and, later, Medina – and even served in the Masjid an-Naba-
wi. Jamal Khashoggi would tell his friend, Turan Kışlakçı, about
his relative, Adnan, before his death: "He is in a different area and
I am in a different area. We have no connection!"

Adnan Khashoggi, the only famous member of his family until Jamal's death, was an arms dealer in the 1970s and the 1980s.
Around the same time as the Watergate scandal in the United
States, Khashoggi reportedly accumulated over $4 billion thanks
to his close relations with the U.S. administration.

Although Jamal Khashoggi distanced himself from his rela-
tives, he nonetheless cared for them. He had six sisters and two
brothers – along with two sons, Abdullah (34) and Salah (36), and
two daughters, Nuha (28) and Rezan (26).

Mustafa Ozcan, a journalist and writer, shared the following
information about the interesting story of Khashoggi's self-exile
from Saudi Arabia in a column that appeared in the Fikriyat news
website:

> The Saudi regime attempted to convince him to return to
> his country, which he left in a problematic and complicated
> manner, in order to keep him under control. They detained
> his wife and did not let her leave the country with him.
> Quite the contrary, they compelled him to divorce his wife
> and forced them to separate. In other words, they did not let
> him take his wife with him. At the time, he was married to
> the daughter of Abdullah Omar Nasseef, a general secretary
> of the World Muslim Congress. In the end, the Saudi ad-
> ministration invoked the Umayyad method – which calls for
> the annulment of one's marriage for breaking one's bayah.
> Consequently, Jamal Khashoggi had been living as a bach-
> elor in Washington for more than one year.[8]

Another claim about Jamal Khashoggi's personal life was that
he concluded a religious marriage with an Egyptian woman. H.
Atr told *The Washington Post*, fifty days after the murder, that she
got married to Khashoggi and shared her personal correspondence

---

8   Mustafa Özcan, Karakutu [The Black Box], *Fikriyat*, 11 October 2018.

and photographs from their wedding ceremony with the newspaper.[9] The Egyptian woman's allegations appeared to be part of an attempt to discredit the slain *Washington Post* columnist in the public eye.

9   "Kaşıkçı'nın dini nikahlı eşi ortaya çıktı" [Khashoggi's Religiously-Wed Spouse Surfaces], *Yeni Şafak*, 18 November 2018.

3

THE DEATH SQUAD'S DOG TAGS

All members of the death squad, which traveled to Turkey to execute Jamal Khashoggi, were professionals in the employ of various Saudi government agencies. Maher Abdulaziz Mutreb was arguably the most senior member and leader of the group.

According to the Turkish National Police, Mutreb (born 1971, passport number D088677) was a brigadier general in the Saudi intelligence and part of the so-called special intervention team.

Mutreb's name appeared on a 2007 list of diplomatic officials published by the British government. Accordingly, he served as first secretary at the Saudi Embassy in London. Photographs from March 2017 establish that Mutreb accompanied Saudi Crown Prince Mohammed bin Salman on at least three foreign trips over the course of several months. One of those photographs was taken during MBS's visit to the Massachusetts Institute of Technology.

After Mutreb's photograph appeared in *Sabah*, CNN International, citing sources, established that the Saudi operative was a colonel in the Saudi intelligence. It appeared that Mutreb had risen through the ranks since his London days.

THE FORENSIC SCIENTIST

The second most senior member of the Saudi death squad was Salah Mohammed Al-Tubaigy (born 1971, passport number S052512), a forensic scientist that dismembered Jamal Khashoggi's body. In addition to chairing the Saudi interior ministry's Forensic Medicine Institution, he was a lieutenant colonel in the military.

Tubaigy completed his postgraduate education in 2004 at Glasgow University, where he specialized on cadavers. The following year, he spent two months at the Victorian Institute of Forensic Medicine in Australia. Tubaigy's Twitter account described him as the head of Saudi Arabia's forensic science institution and featured a link to the Saudi interior ministry's website.

In 2014, the London-based Arabic newspaper Al Sharq Al Awsat described Tubaigy as a lieutenant colonel in the Interior Ministry's Public Safety Department – which was also true.

A professor of criminal investigation at the Naif Arab University, Tubaigy lectured Saudi security and intelligence operatives on forensic medicine. In 2014, he launched a mobile autopsy laboratory thanks to a $2.4 million investment from the Saudi government. There is no other mobile autopsy lab in the world.

Ertugrul Ozkok, a columnist for the Turkish daily newspaper *Hürriyet*, shared the following information on Tubaigy on Oct. 18:

[Tubaigy] is the author of a book on dissection and mobile autopsy. … There are more interesting details. He taught a graduate-level course on DNA tests on bones. His other area of expertise is the use of formaldehyde to preserve cadavers. In 2014, he persuaded his employer to invest $2.5 million into a mobile autopsy truck. That mobile laboratory was used specifically for pilgrims. It reportedly could detect contagious diseases within seven minutes. In other words, it was a system designed to get quick results.

Just the thing they needed in Istanbul, where [the assassins] raced against the clock. They formed the perfect team to commit the perfect murder. Here's my conclusion: Nobody would even entertain the idea that the Saudi crown prince did not know about the murder in advance. And here's the question stuck in my mind: What happened to the victim's body? What kind of procedure did the DNA expert perform [on the body] with a bone saw?[1]

MBS'S FAVORITE LIEUTENANT

Sair Ghaleb Al-Harby (born 1979) helped the killers choke Khashoggi to death and helped Tubaigy to dismember the victim's body. He was an intelligence officer from the agency's protection division. Harby carried a Saudi passport with the number P723557 during his stay in Turkey. In October 2017, he was promoted to lieutenant for his courage during the defense of the crown prince's palace in Jeddah as part of the Saudi Royal Guard. At the time, an armed assailant shot dead two royal guards and injured another three before being neutralized.

Abdulaziz Mohammad Al-Hossawi, another member of the Saudi death squad, was born in 1987. He carried the passport with the number W288493 during his trip to Turkey. *The New York Times* reported, citing an anonymous French source, that Hossawi was a member of Mohammed bin Salman's personal guard that travelled with him. Indeed, the Arabic caller identification application MenoM3ay describes the man as a member of the Saudi Royal Guard.

Mohammad Saad Al-Zahrani (born 1988, passport number T233763) was an intelligence operative and part of the Saudi death squad. According to MenoM3ay, he was a member of the Saudi Royal Guard. According to the human rights activist Iyad Al-Baghdadi, Zahrani was filmed and photographed at an event in 2007, which MBS also attended, where he wore a badge bearing his name.

Khaled Aiz Al-Taby (born 1988, passport number P139681) was a lieutenant colonel in the Riyadh Administration. MenoM3ay

1   Ertuğrul Özkök, "Kadavra uzmanlığından kemik testereli cinayete" [From Cadaver Specialization To A Bone-Saw Murder], *Hürriyet*, 18 October 2018.

refers to him as a member of the Saudi Royal Guard. According to the Washington Post, a man carrying the same passport entered the United States three times – around the same time as members of the Saudi royal family.

Another intelligence operative who was part of the Saudi death squad was Naif Hassan Al-Arifi. Born in 1986, he was a lieutenant colonel. According to the Washington-based translator Qutaibi Idlbi, there was a Facebook account under the same name, where users could see photographs of Al-Arifi wearing the Saudi Special Forces uniform. Moreover, MenoM3ay lists him as an employee of the crown prince's office.

Mustafa Mohammad Al-Madani (born 1961, passport number P797794), who was flown to Istanbul as a body double, was just three years younger than Jamal Khashoggi. He was listed as a brigadier general in the Riyadh Administration. MenoM3ay refers to him as an intelligence operative.

Saad Mashal Al-Bostani (born 1987, passport number R339037) was an intelligence officer specialized in aerial security. On Facebook, a user with the same name is listed as an Air Force lieutenant. According to MenoM3ay, however, he was a member of the Saudi Royal Guard. Al-Bostani died in a suspicious traffic accident shortly after the Khashoggi murder.

Waleed Abdullah Al-Shahry (born 1980, passport number R120404) was another member of the assassination team. He was an intelligence officer with the Protection Department that is responsible for the Saudi king's personal safety. According to Saudi media outlets, he was a member of the Air Force – which the crown prince promoted to fleet commander last year.

Mansour Othman Aba Hussein (born 1972, passport number D122725) was a major general and therefore the highest ranking member of the death squad. Syrian translator Qutaibi Idlbi states that an individual with the same name was listed as a Saudi intelligence officer on MenoM3ay. Again, someone with the same name was described by a Saudi outlet as a colonel at the Civil Protection Department in 2014.

Fahd Shabib Al-Balawi (born 1985, passport number N163990) was listed on MenoM3ay as a member of the Saudi Royal Guard.

Badr Lafi Al-Otaiba (born 1973, passport number U051094) was listed on MenoM3ay as an intelligence colonel.

Sayf Saad Al-Qahtani (born 1973, passport number U051094) could be seen in CCTV footage next to the body double. According to *The Washington Post*, he was listed as an employee of Crown Prince Mohammed bin Salman on MenoM3ay.

Finally Turki Musharraf Al-Shahry (born 1982, passport number R910638) was an intelligence officer specialized in strategy, planning and combat.

4

WHO IS
MOHAMMED BIN SALMAN

The Crown Prince's Unstoppable Rise

It would not be wrong to describe Mohammed bin Salman, who –even U.S. President Donald Trump, one of his staunchest supporters, had to admit— was the political decisionmaker behind the Khashoggi murder, as the most powerful man in the Kingdom today. MBS accumulated that power when King Salman, his father, relieved the former crown prince, Mohammad bin Nayef, of his duties and designated Prince Mohammed as the heir to the Saudi throne in 2017.

Today, MBS serves as King Salman's right-hand man. At the same time, he presides over royal councils on economic and development affairs as well as political and security affairs, and is a member of the council of ministers. The youngest man ever to hold those powers, Prince Mohammed could be reasonably viewed as the true owner of King Salman's throne. The claim that his father suffers from Alzheimer's Disease supports that claim.

The Saudi crown prince was the mastermind behind recent efforts to curb the power of religious institutions and lift a ban on female drivers. Among those showpiece reforms were the admission of women into stadiums, lifting the ban on female singers and permitting women to participate in the workforce.

Mohammed bin Salman's most prominent project is called

Vision 2030. It represents an effort to invest in non-oil-related sectors, such as technology and tourism, in order to diversify and strengthen the Saudi economy. The ill-fated initial public offering of Aramco, the country's petroleum and natural gas company, was part of the same program.

Yet Prince Mohammed's celebrated efforts to facilitate Saudi Arabia's social and economic liberalization could not salvage his poor political reputation, which has been plagued by arbitrary arrests, torture and murder. It is no secret that the Saudi crown prince's proxy war in Yemen forced some 13 million civilians to face starvation. To make matters worse, observers blame the escalation of a diplomatic crisis with Qatar, the mass arrest of Saudi royals in November 2017 and the Khashoggi murder, among other things, on MBS.

Upon graduating from King Saud University, Prince Mohammed worked in the private sector for several years. He proceeded to become a consultant to Saudi Arabia's royal cabinet. In December 2009, at the age of twenty four, the future crown prince started his political career by serving as governor of the state of Riyadh and as special counsel to his father. At the same time, he wore many hats: general secretary of the Competition Authority, adviser to the chairman of the executive board of the King Abdulaziz Center for Research and Archives, and a member of the Al Bir Society's board of trustees.

When Prince Sultan bin Abdulaziz died in October 2011, MBS was appointed Second Deputy Prime Minister. In January 2015, Salman bin Abdulaziz ascended to the Saudi throne after King Abdullah's death and appointed his son as Defense Minister. At the same time, Prince Mohammed was elected general secretary of the Royal Court and began to serve as a state minister.

THE ARCHITECT OF THE WAR IN YEMEN

The escalation of political tensions in Yemen from 2011 onwards evolved into a problem, in which Prince Mohammed, as minister of defense, became directly involved. By 2014, the Houthi rebels gained control over Northern Yemen. In response, MBS started launching airstrikes against the Houthis in early 2015. His goal was to form a GCC-wide coalition in the wake of a series of suicide attacks in Sanaa and to impose a naval blockade on the Houthi rebels.

In March 2015, Saudi Arabia became the leader of an international anti-Houthi coalition. The royal princes in Riyadh agreed that they had to resort to military power to stop the Houthi rebels, who seized control of Yemen's capital and forced that country's government into exile. In the end, MBS launched a military campaign without ensuring coordination among the various parts of the Saudi Armed Forces. At the expense of vast civilian casualties, the Saudi crown prince managed to push back against the Houthi rebels and reinstate Abdrabbuh Mansur Hadi as president of Yemen. Ironically, those developments only served to further complicate the situation in Yemen.

In April 2015, King Salman issued a decree to designate his nephew, Mohammad bin Nayef, as crown prince and his son, Prince Mohammed, as deputy crown prince. By the end of that year, MBS met U.S. President Barack Obama and emerged as a more prominent figure in the Saudi royal family. As a matter of fact, Prince Mohammed became Washington's favorite around the same time. Under the Trump administration, the White House followed in Obama's footsteps and supported, like the terrorist group PYD in Syria, Mohammed bin Salman in the Kingdom.

On Jan. 4, 2016, *The Economist* published an interview with Prince Mohammed, in which he was described as the architect of the war in Yemen. The crown prince claimed in that interview Saudi Arabia's military intervention in the conflict zone was based on a consensus among all relevant decision-makers. He added that the Houthi rebels usurped legitimate political power in the capital Sanaa before his appointment as defense minister.

Upon Washington's request, MBS launched in December 2015 the Islamic Military Counter Terrorism Coalition against the Islamic State group. The Coalition's first meeting took place in Riyadh, Saudi Arabia in November 2017 with the participation of defense ministers and officials from 41 countries.

On June 21, 2017, Mohammed bin Salman replaced Mohammad bin Nayef as crown prince under his father's orders and became the heir to the Saudi throne. The German intelligence agency BND had reportedly predicted that change as early as December 2015.

U.S. President Donald Trump congratulated Mohammed bin Salman on his appointment as crown prince, as the two men agreed to strengthen their cooperation on security and economic affairs.

In April 2017, MBS told *The Washington Post*, one of whose columnists he was going to have killed in October 2018, that Saudi Arabia would have looked like North Korea, had it not been for Washington's cultural influence on his country. In doing so, he effectively declared that he intended to rule the Kingdom as a U.S. client.

Upon securing U.S. support, Mohammed bin Salman proceeded to lead Riyadh's effort to restructure the Saudi economy and unveiled Vision 2030, the country's strategy for the next fifteen years, in April 2016.

As part of Prince Mohammed's plan, the Kingdom introduced tax breaks, reduced subsidies and took steps to set up a $2 trillion wealth fund, whose seed money would come from the sale of Aramco shares. Yet the Saudi crown prince has been unable to accomplish that goal until now.

Vision 2030 represents an attempt to diversify the Saudi economy and privatize public companies in order to promote sustainable development through non-oil-related revenues. Given the Saudi economy's dependence on its own oil and the long shadow of Washington's military on the nation, Mohammed bin Salman's plan is unlikely to successfully transform the Kingdom.

MBS'S SHOWPIECE REFORMS

Before assuming *de facto* control of the Kingdom in June 2017, the Saudi crown prince had already launched a social reform movement in the country. He limited the power of religious institutions and came up with hardly original ideas, such as issuing green cards to non-Saudis.

In February 2017, MBS appointed the first female head of the Saudi Arabian Stock Exchange. Two months later, he unveiled an ambitious plan to build one of the world's largest entertainment, sports and culture cities in Southwestern Riyadh. In February 2018, the crown prince made it legal for Saudi women to launch businesses without male approval. The following month, Saudi mothers became eligible to maintain custody of their children after getting divorced, without having to file an additional lawsuit. In April 2018, the country's first public cinema reopened its doors after a 35-year ban.

For Mohammed bin Salman, arresting billionaire princes, whom he considered political rivals, and releasing them in return for hefty payments was another way of funding his ambitious projects. In May 2017, he pledged to punish anyone involved in corruption, even royal princes and cabinet ministers.

On November 4, 2017, the Saudi authorities announced that Prince Al-Waleed bin Talal was under arrest. Several senior officials, including the Minister of National Guard, Mutaib bin Abdullah, and Admiral Abdullah bin Sultan bin Mohammad Al-Sultan, who was Commander of the Royal Navy, were either dismissed or detained. Altogether, approximately two hundred princes and businessmen were picked up as part of what many saw as a coup by MBS against his political rivals and placed under house arrest at the luxurious Ritz Carlton Hotel – only to be released on 'bail'.

TRUMP'S TWITTER DIPLOMACY

Around the same time, U.S. President Donald Trump went on a Twitter diplomacy offensive and threw his support behind Mohammed bin Salman's decisions: "I have great confidence in King Salman and the Crown Prince of Saudi Arabia, they know exactly what they are doing..."[1]

To be clear, that was hardly surprising. After all, Mohammed bin Salman, along with Mohammed bin Zayed, his best friend and

---

1   https://twitter.com/realdonaldtrump/status/927672843504177152?lang=en

crown prince of the United Arab Emirates, had offered to give money to Donald Trump's election campaign. In August 2016, Trump received a messenger from MBS and MBZ. Joel Zamel, an Israeli social media expert, the Lebanese-American businessman George Nade and Erik Prince, the founder of the private security company Blackwater, were present at the meeting.

Mohammed bin Salman's net worth is an estimated $3 billion. In 2015, he paid the Russian vodka magnate Yuri Shefler $500 million for Serene, an Italian-made super yacht registered in the Bahamas. According to *The New York Times*, the Saudi crown prince also purchased Chateau Louis XIV in France for $300 million the same year.

In December 2017, Prince Mohammad allegedly paid $450 million for Leonardo Da Vinci's *Salvator Mundi* through the proxy of his close friend, Prince Badr bin Abdullah bin Mohammad Al-Farhan.

In June 2016, MBS visited the Silicon Valley and met leaders of the tech industry, including Facebook founder Mark Zuckerberg.

By early 2018, the Saudi crown prince was already making inroads with U.S. politicians and Hollywood stars. As part of his charm offensive, he met Donald Trump, Bill and Hillary Clinton, Henry Kissinger, Michael Bloomberg, George W. Bush, George H.W. Bush, Bill Gates, Jeff Bezos, Oprah Winfrey, Rupert Murdoch, Richard Branson, Eric Garcetti, Michael Douglas, Morgan Freeman and Dwayne Johnson.

In the wake of the Khashoggi murder, Mohammed bin Salman's critics called him *Mr. Bone Saw* – a wordplay on his three-letter abbreviation.

THE PRINCE'S POLIGAMY PARADOX

In this subsection, we concentrated on the professional life of Mohammed bin Salman, who was politically responsible for the Khashoggi murder. Some of the things, which we could have mentioned in the very beginning, have been kept from the reader until now.

The Saudi crown prince was born in Riyadh on August 31, 1985. His mother was Fahda bint Falan bin Sultan bin Hathleen – the third wife of Salman bin Abdulaziz, a.k.a. *The Polygamous King*. Mohammed bin Salman's mother was also the granddaughter of Rakan bin Hithalayn, the head of the Al-Ajman tribe.

MBS was his mother's first child. Hence his current position as crown prince. He has five brothers: Prince Turki, Prince Khaled, Prince Nayef, Prince Bandar and Prince Rakan. His brother, Khaled, continues to serve as the Kingdom's ambassador to Washington.

In 2008, MBS married Princess Sara bint Mashhoor and together they have four children. Whether the crown prince, like the polygamous kings of the past, will remarry remains unclear. That answer to that question is important, as it will influence future conflict over the Saudi throne.

MBS could refrain from polygamy, as it would contradict his showpiece reforms to promote women's rights in the Kingdom. In other words, he might have to give up on 'male privilege' that has been the rule within the Saudi royal family. At the very least, Prince Mohammed is unlikely to take such risks until the global backlash over the Khashoggi murder, which shook his throne before he could even assume it, is behind him. After all, the crown prince has far more significant paradoxes to deal with than the paradox of polygamy.

AFTERWORD

In our introduction to **Diplomatic Savagery**, we identified the purpose of this book as present a collection of information and documents that shed light on the dark secrets behind the Khashoggi murder and, more important, to make new findings available to the public.

We sincerely hope that this book, which is based on three months of research and the product of twenty days of writing, served its purpose by bringing into light the dark secrets behind the Khashoggi murder – one of the most interesting, if not the most interesting, crime in history.

We remain hopeful that the information we provided in this title, which was separated into six chapter named after the fundamental questions of journalism, will contribute to the public's understanding of the Khashoggi murder. We believe that the chapters on the what, the where, the how and the why will serve that purpose more effectively than the rest.

In Islam, death represents a moment of transition into the eternal life, in which we will be held accountable for our actions in this world. Without a doubt, it is foreordained for all. How one's death takes place, even if one were to die by murder, could be nothing but a mere detail within the big picture.

Yet Jamal Khashoggi's death could not possibly be viewed as an ordinary end. Our decision to write this book was motivated not just by our the unique nature of this diplomatic, intelligence and crime story, but also the inhumane treatment that the victim suffered after his death.

The Saudis, who treated one of their citizens, a fellow human being and a family man in this way, disrespected all human and religious values. Going forward, they have but a single responsibility: they could still get a confession out of the suspects and establish the whereabouts of Khashoggi's remains – which, in our view, is the most important question yet to be answered— in order to ease the victim's suffering to some degree. The Khashoggi family and the slain journalist's friends need to access whatever was left of the diplomatic savagery and bury it – a tomb where they can pray for his soul. After all, burial places are one's sole connection to their loved ones in the Islamic culture.

Even though we found the answers to many key questions about Khashoggi and his murder by reaching out to trusted sources, we are still unable to answer the most obvious question, whose answer should be easy to give. We apologize for failing to establish where the remains of our colleague, Jamal Khashoggi, are today.

That is the one answer that we cannot find without the help of the Saudi authorities. One way or another, the Saudis are compelled to answer that question. The whole world is waiting for an answer – at the very least.

FERHAT ÜNLÜ
ABDURRAHMAN ŞİMŞEK
NAZİF KARAMAN

CPSIA information can be obtained
at www.ICGtesting.com
Printed in the USA
BVHW072204040719
552614BV00006B/103/P

9 781945 959363